Voices
from the
Other Side

Living in the US during World War II (AND Korea, AND VietNam, AND Iraq AND Afghanistan) was/is safe and comfortable for most people. But war is ugly wherever it occurs, not only on the battlefield but also for the populations living in the countries or near the belligerents and their corresponding combat zones. They can be subjected to destructive aerial bombardment, displacement, vital life shortages, political intimidation, occupation by foreign troops, and all the fear and suffering that accompanies those wartime situations.

The German stories in this book are a sample of such conditions, as told by civilian "victims" as well as military personnel describing hardship and suffering unknown to American civilians. They also offered descriptions of their coming to America—the "Promised Land"—and their successes here.

These subjects were mostly from the Front Range of Colorado. The memoirs presented here are a fraction of what is out there waiting to be recorded; every American city and state could likely publish its own version from their immigrant residents.

Don't wait. Time is getting short as these valuable chroniclers age.

Cover: The swastika overshadows this peaceful, prewar scene of Eric Muetlein overlooking his parents' resort in a beautiful Alpine valley.

Voices from the Other Side

INSPIRING GERMAN WWII MEMOIRS

Jean Goodwin Messinger

White Pelican Press

Loveland, Colorado

OtherWorks

Pride, Politics, and Style: History of the 1903 El Paso County Courthouse

A Closer Look at Beaver Dam

Faith in High Places: Historic Country Churches of Colorado (co-author)

Where Thy Glory Dwells: Historic Churches of Colorado Springs (co-author)

Hannah: From Dachau to the Olympics and Beyond

In the Best of Families

Same War Different Battlefields

With Love from Grandma Jean

Brody's List

Copyright 2014 by White Pelican Press
All rights reserved
444 Logan Avenue
Loveland, CO 80537

ISBN: 978-0-615-95007-5

Dedication

This work is dedicated to the memory of every individual affected by the Nazi Regime and World War II.

with Best Wishes
Dean Messinger

Acknowledgements

The first kudos go to the wonderful contributors who made this project possible. They were cooperative, honest, congenial, and many friendships resulted from this enterprise. Getting to know such fine people in the process of making this endeavor a reality is the biggest reward for this author and a privilege highly regarded.

Thanks to Dr. Dale Greenawald for his support and for sharing his expertise in German history. In addition, and no less important, are the professional services rendered by Channing Meyer and his wife Mary Bahus-Meyer, who together did the layout, artistry, editing and marketing through their business, Full Circle Creative. Initial, informal editing and critiquing by members of Loveland Library's three book discussion clubs was also valuable and much appreciated. Thanks to their leader Janice Benedict. Equally important is Rick Arneson, always reliable and a joy to work with, at Pioneer Printing in Loveland. Having such a team to depend on makes the publication process a smooth and pleasant operation, which I have experienced with them on several previous occasions associated with other publications.

Thank you to everyone involved. I couldn't have done it without you.

Win Schendel celebrates becoming an American citizen in 1952, with his
mother Margarete, wife Joanne, and son Victor

◄ Table of Contents ►

⫷ Introduction ⫸

T
he seed for this project may have been planted in 1970 when I saw a German cemetery on a visit to the Normandy D-Day beachheads. My husband and I were driving a rented VW (how is that for political incorrectness?!), and on a stretch of highway somewhere along the route, there appeared on one side of the road an American military cemetery. Identical white crosses stretched as far as the eye could see. On the opposite side of the road was a German cemetery, with white crosses identical to the American crosses.

I wept for both. Shamefully, I had never before given that situation a thought. Because of the stigma of Nazism it was easy to ignore that each German cross, like its American equivalent, represents a son, husband, father, brother, neighbor, or friend doing what he understood as his patriotic duty to defend his country or at least fulfill a requirement to serve. Indeed, he may have been sincerely following his false god.

As for the placement of the cemeteries, what genius "strategy." Was it deliberate? I wonder what was the nationality of the individual or group who had such sensitivity to place those two cemeteries in close proximity to each other. How unfortunate more people can't be subjected to the impact of that forceful reminder of the tragedy simultaneous with the victory it represented—a reminder of the losses that occurred on both sides of such an immense conflict. Besides human loss and suffering, irreplaceable historic treasures and entire cities were destroyed, international relationships severed, and questions remain unanswered, like "Where was God during the Holocaust?"

Historians, psychologists, politicians, sociologists, and political analysts have devoted endless pages since the end of WWII trying to explain, even justify, the phenomenon of Nazi Germany. We are aware and probably in agreement that postwar WWI conditions in Germany provided a ripe climate for a charismatic leader who would promise to bring back prosperity, honor, and self-respect to a fallen and disgraced nation. The puzzle remains how its leaders were able to turn a society of law-abiding, hard-working, God-fearing, family-oriented people into instruments of destruction for the most horrific war in the history of mankind.

Perhaps the quest for understanding of those years will never be completely satisfied nor unified in conclusions. Ultimately, by understanding, the civilized world hopes to avoid a re-occurrence of such madness, which brought unimaginable destruction to Europe and shame to Germany in the name of the vilest ideology. And is it a warning that if it could happen in Germany it might happen somewhere else?

These same citizens had seen their forebears by the thousands come to America, and they made the U.S. a better place wherever they settled. Germans of 150 years ago and Germans today are still highly respected for their many admirable qualities: their work ethic, devotion to family and education, practicality, thrift, discipline, industriousness, and organizational ability. Many Americans proudly claim heritage from those immigrants, and many parts of America retain a distinctive German character. This author had a German grandmother and grew up in a German environment in southern Wisconsin, a state with pages of every telephone book filled with German names.

When my call went out for (non-Jewish) Germans residing in the U.S. to tell their stories, I accepted the perspectives of all who responded, and I expected and demanded honesty— criticism of America included. My purpose was to present American readers with personal, first-person recollections of prewar, wartime, and post-Nazi German life. Except for two Jewish contributors, I excluded Holocaust victims because I thought their stories are already well-documented and presented a specific perspective. Readers should also be aware that not every German— Jew or non-Jew— experienced the extreme suffering we have come to associate with the Holocaust era.

These published memoirs give contributors an opportunity to share their stories publicly. In one case, the younger generation of her family was not interested in hearing what happened to Mama and actually refused to listen. That valuable resource was eager for "listeners" and is grateful for the opportunity to share her story, although anonymously, in this presentation.

Unfortunately, this project comes too late to retrieve many stories. It also misses the generation that lived before the war as adults, when Nazism pervaded their society, initially with a more positive, acceptable complexion. My subjects are now mostly in their eighties, some in their nineties. They were mostly teenagers or younger during the conflict, and several served in the military. But they remember family issues like Father being whisked off in the middle of the night for expressing anti-Hitler sentiments, never to be heard from again— as well as wondering why Jewish classmates and neighbors suddenly disappeared.

An additional benefit of this collection of memoirs from narrators who were young during this era is their unique perspective. They describe the endless disruptions in their lives, instability that would tear the hair out of any child psychologist or parent in normal times. They describe separation from parents and family as well as friends. Their schools were destroyed or closed, reopened, closed again, sometimes re-located. They lost their dwelling place and possessions to fire and bombardments in addition to spending endless, fearful nights trying to sleep in a basement or crowded, noisy, public bomb shelter.

The final straw was to see their entire community blasted off the map. Surprisingly, there isn't a trace of bitterness or self-pity in any of these accounts. Of course, there is the healing effect of time and a present secure life in America, but several of these memoirs were recorded many years ago, with the result that details that might be forgotten during the intervening years have been preserved.

Although each story is different in details, readers will recognize common threads throughout the accounts. In addition to the horrors of life under Russian occupation, there are descriptions of German family life that parallel American counterparts: parents that expected responsible behavior from their children, a good work ethic, and performance in the classroom. (The severity of classroom discipline, however, is startling and disturbing.) Descriptions of military service involve common issues that probably occur regardless of the flag served. In the end, readers will also be impressed by the skill with which these contributors articulate in English.

My purpose is to remind readers of all ages and nationalities how war imposes hardship and heartbreak on all levels of the populations involved, as well as long-lasting psychological and/or physical damage to certain military participants. I hope affected families have preserved or will record their own memories from parents and grandparents. For some people it has taken many years and detachment to be willing to relive their horrors by sharing them. But catharsis can result from "opening up." Most importantly, it is vital that these stories be preserved. I hope readers and listeners will learn from and be inspired by these revelations from "ordinary" people, like people you may know— exploits of heroism, endurance, and courage, as well as adversity of unimaginable severity.

I'll conclude with a quote from the Introduction to an earlier work of mine— *Same War Different Battlefields* *, a similar collection of memoirs from multi-nationals of how WWII impacted them as civilians.

"There comes a time when a war is over. Combatants from both sides go home and become civilians again, even friends, dads and moms, sons and daughters, spouses, teachers, bricklayers, neighbors, and trading partners across the seas." Are they really so much different from us, whoever we are?

*Same War Different Battlefields
White Pelican Press, 2008, ISBN 978-60725-043-2

Voices from the Other Side

⊰FriedaRosinWuest⊱

A wartime story of the Rosin family is also recorded by brother Reinhard in my book SAME WAR DIFFERENT BATTLEFIELDS (referred to in the Introduction), with different details and naturally a bit different perspective to avoid duplication. The Rosin episode that appears in this volume is based on my interviews with Frieda and Mimi Wahlfeldt's biography of Frieda compiled in 2008.

I was born Frieda Rosin to German parents in 1925 in Kultschin, Poland, the eldest of ten surviving children—seven boys and three girls. We lived on a farm twenty kilometers from the Ukrainian border, among a community of Germans. The area had been German until World War One; consequently there were more Germans there than Poles. My father served in the Russian army during the First World War; his parents homesteaded there and lived in Siberia for a while. Our family was Lutheran and very religious. We said devotions together every day and sang a song before and after.

The house I was born in was no more than a one-room clay shack with a big oven. There was only one window and one door. Six more children were born in that modest dwelling. A year after I was born, my parents built a barn and granary and in 1929 a new house. Later, after the Germans took over Poland in 1939, our family was forced to leave and move to East Germany.

We went to a public school about three and a half miles from the farm, and we walked both ways, summer and winter. I didn't attend school until I was seven years old and finished the sixth grade in 1939, when I was fourteen. Then I was needed at home, and there wasn't money to send me on, and that would have been quite far from home. The principal of the school urged my parents to send me to high school; I had always had good grades and probably showed some promise. I loved history, arithmetic, reading, and writing. As a kid, most everything interested me. But my mother would have had to hire help to replace me. Polish public school ended after the sixth year; German schools went to the eighth grade, and attendance wasn't required.

The teachers were so strict. Obedience and authority were primary. I experienced a male teacher beating in class a boy my age. The teacher started hitting him right in front of us; I can see it now. We were all crying and too scared to say anything. He was bleeding from his nose and mouth. The next day he didn't come to school; he had died during the night. The reason for the beating was because we were supposed to bring five pennies to school so they could buy paper to make flags for a national holiday celebration. This boy didn't have the money; his dad said it wasn't necessary. I had to push this with my dad too. I told him I'd get a whipping if I don't bring it. Whenever I did get whacked by the teacher's oak rod, I got another whipping from my mother when I got home. One time the teacher hit me so hard on the palms of my hands that they swelled up terribly and hurt a lot.

The Rosin family, Frieda standing in the center

My mother worked out in the field, and being the

oldest, I stayed in the house and raised my siblings. My dad was an invalid from the First World War; one hand was shredded. And so, my childhood was centered around work. There were few toys, and play in any form, including sports, was considered nonsense. We kids would get together and pick up little pebbles and rocks, and find some sticks to make a fence, and things like that. The same discipline was expected of both girls and boys. My grandfather on my dad's side, Martin Rosin, lived with us, and he was the meanest person you could imagine. My mother told him it was all right for him to spank us. And he did!

I was fourteen in 1939 when the war started. During the summer before the invasion, relations between the Poles and resident Germans were uneasy. We felt threatened, because Polish soldiers would come to our farm looking for spies and German soldiers hiding.

When the war started, it took the Germans just ten days in September to conquer the country. In 1940 the Germans required the Germans where we lived to resettle in East Germany. Poles living in East Germany were forced to return to Poland. Returned Germans took over the expatriated Poles' property. German authorities searched our records for many months to be sure we weren't Jewish, because our name was Rosin. They finally accepted that we were not. We were put on a farm near a village called Mahlen. I was fifteen by this time, and my two youngest siblings were born while we lived there.

On January 20, 1945, the Russians were closing in on East Germany. I was nineteen by this time. We were directed by the authorities via the mayor, who came to our house, to evacuate immediately. Our parents were in town shopping, and so we started to pack what we could into a wagon, which couldn't hold much, but we took blankets because it was so cold. (The winter of '44-45 was the coldest in Europe in a hundred years.) There was laundry hanging outside, but it was frozen stiff, and we had to leave it behind. The only food we had to take along was twelve loaves of my mother's freshly-baked bread. There was no McDonald's or Safeway or even fields with leftover potatoes to glean. We only had an hour or two to get ready to leave, and it was dark when we left. It was so cold! The nearest town was twelve kilometers away, and we didn't know where we were going or where we would find refuge.

We travelled on foot beside a horse-drawn wagon, nonstop for three days. We only had our bread to eat and snow for drinking. Although we had very young children with us, we mostly had to walk. My grandfather was ill, and he rode on a neighbor's wagon. One of our hired men went with us for a week. The German Army led the way.

On the third day, it was snowing, and Grandfather died on that neighbor's wagon. We kept his body for three days; then an order came that said if we had dead bodies, wrap them up in whatever you can get hold of and leave them on the road-side. We just had barely enough to cover up ourselves. So we wrapped him in—I can't even tell you what—and put him by the roadside. I imagine the soldiers came and dug holes and put them in there. Many refugees lost family members during the flight; some were babies. They were forced to leave them by the side of the road. What else was there to do?

Many families got separated during this time. My mother's parents, Samuel and Julianne, also fled during this time but they weren't with us. While they were fleeing, Russian soldiers took all of Samuel's winter clothing. He became ill from being exposed to the cold weather and eventually died from pneumonia. *[Read Brother Reinhard's account in SAME WAR of toddler Irma, who got lost along the way but was found again.]*

Our flight lasted two months. It got easier after a few days. Since the German Army was present, occasionally we got a hot meal. Our feather beds that we brought from home were really vital, and they were often covered with snow. Sometimes, when we were lucky, we slept inside on straw on the floor of a school house. The Americans bombed the refugee caravans just like the Germans had bombed other "hostile" refugees.

While we lived in Mahlen earlier during the war, I frequently made trips into the neighboring town on my bike and experienced some terrifying attacks from an occasional enemy plane. German soldiers sometimes disguised themselves in women's clothing, and apparently knowing this, Allied bombers went after travelers like me, suspicious of my identity and purpose.

As we were a very religious family, we wondered "Where is God?" We prayed to be taken all together.

We arrived two months later in March in West Germany at Suderwitingen, near Hannover and Hamburg, where we lived for seven years, until we left for America in 1952. We lived on the property of an elderly couple and found work mostly on nearby farms. My older brothers, my mother, and I all worked to support our family. My dad died in 1949.

My brother Arnold had been taken into the army at age sixteen, and we had lost touch with him. We didn't find him until 1947, through the Red Cross. He was taken prisoner by the Americans and was put on a personal detail by an American general. After the war, the general released him because he was so young. When he returned to East Germany looking for his family, which was occupied by the Russians, he didn't fare so well. About the time he was notified that he was going to be sent to Siberia, a friend of the family recognized him, notified the family in West Germany; he escaped and was reunited with the family just before Christmas of 1948. Until that time we didn't know if he were dead or alive.

My dad used to say that if he ever had a chance, he would go to live in America. But he never had the chance. In 1952 President Eisenhower opened up immigration for us, and we saw a brochure circulated by the mayor. I told my mom, "I'm going to go to the United States. Dad talked about it, and I'm going to get away from here." We really weren't treated very well in Germany after we came back from Poland; we were always regarded as immigrants—taking jobs, food, lodging, etc.

My mother didn't want to go, and I would have come alone. However, we worked through the Lutheran World Federation of Churches so we could all come together. There was endless bureaucracy to deal with, physicals to take, papers to fill out. We had to provide birth certificates and prove our loyalty, that we weren't Nazis. The family agreed to make this move, then changed their minds part-way through the process, but I was determined to come alone if I had to. Then they gave in and we proceeded. Brother Arnold was married and had a small child and didn't come to the U.S. until 1955.

After we all assembled in Hamburg and were approved, we moved on to Bremerhaven to await orders. We were told not to pack anything in straw, in order to forestall bedbug infestation. However, there were some who ignored this ruling, and when they went through customs in New York, their cases were completely disassembled and belongings scattered.

A pastor met us at the boat in Bremerhaven, prayed for us, and told us, "You are going to the United States, where you will be free to speak up. You don't have to be afraid." We were unaccustomed to that! All our lives up until then, we were always under orders.

A few more hitches delayed our journey. A little boy who was scheduled to make the same voyage got sick, and we were all quarantined for a couple weeks.

The trip took ten days. The first thing I saw was the Statue of Liberty, and I still get choked up every time I think of that and what it meant to all of us.

We didn't know anyone in America and had no idea where we would end up. We had no money and didn't speak English. We were originally supposed to go to Massachusetts, but there were too many refugees already there. We stayed an additional ten days in Bremerhaven until we eventually found sponsors on a farm in Weld County, Colorado, near the community of Milliken north of Denver, where we could stay as a family. We arrived in May of 1952. My grandmother came in July, all alone, at the age of seventy-two.

When we left New York on the train for Colorado, we were each given $10—$100 for the entire family of ten. We were required to pay that back, plus the train fare to Colorado. Our commitment was for one year, and the sponsors were responsible for us for one year.

The sponsors met us at the train in LaSalle, near Greeley, and a minister was there too. They all spoke German. They needed two cars to pick everyone up! The accommodations on the farm where we settled were primitive to say the least, but we were accustomed to that. It was a two-room beet shack with no bathroom or plumbing. I slept on the couch at first but quickly discovered that bedding was covered with bedbugs, so I slept on the floor and

Frieda

7

insisted the owners spray the premises.

At the beginning, things were tough. We got free breakfast but had to pay for the rest of our meals. The Mexican workers on that farm were paid $1.00 an hour; we got 65 cents. There was no water provided for us while we were working in the fields, so we drank water from the irrigation ditches and naturally got sick. In the winter there was no work in the fields, and we still had to repay for several months of meals.

I found temporary work as a housekeeper in town, where I lived and had my own room. Then I worked as a housekeeper and caregiver at a senior residence facility in nearby Greeley.

After our year was up on the farm, we moved into Greeley into a house we purchased. I was able to learn English with the help of a supervisor and by studying an English Bible and German Bible simultaneously. The family prospered and is grateful to be here. My brother Ewald graduated valedictorian from Milliken High School, quite an accomplishment for a non-native speaker. One teacher said he had a remarkable command of the language—speaking, spelling, reading, and writing.

I married my husband Art when I was thirty-two years old, and we had two sons. We later moved to California for a few years but are back in Greeley, retired, and enjoying our grandchildren.

Frieda was grateful for her many blessings—her family, life in America, good health, and the life lessons her adversities taught her. She and Art have passed away since Frieda shared her story with me.

Frieda Rosin Wuest

⊰George Niedermayr⊱

George's story has an unusual twist in that he is an American-born citizen who served in the German military. He was made a POW at the end of the war and achieved a successful postwar life back in the U.S. His descriptions of school life in Germany provide a very different picture from what American children experience.

I am the first-born son of Agnes Steinhilber and George Niedermayr. They met in New York, and I was born in 1926 in Brooklyn, delivered at home by a midwife. My mother was originally from Moessingen Kreis, Tuebingen, in the state of Wuerttenberg, Germany. My dad's family was from Bavaria in south Germany.

My earliest recollection of life is the voyage in August 1931

August 1931. Trip to Germany with Aunt Amalia to see George's grandparents.

on board the ship *Hamburg* traveling to Hamburg, Germany, with my uncle John (Father's older brother) and his wife, Aunt Amalia. The reason for this trip was for me to meet my grandparents in Germany, but it turned out to be an extended visit of several years. My parents had emigrated independently after the First World War and had in mind to join me later and meet their respective families.

After visiting my father's parents and family in Fernhag, Bavaria, Uncle John and Aunt Amalia took me to stay with my mother's family, the Steinhilbers, in Moessingen later in August. Being the first grandchild on both sides of the family, I was catered to; you could say "spoiled." At the time, Germany, having lost WWI, was down and out. Unemployment was rampant, and those with jobs did not make a living wage. This in turn brought Hitler and his National Socialist Party to power.

Moessingen, where I lived with my maternal grandparents, was a poor town of four thousand peasants and textile workers. In 1933, the day after Hitler wrested the chancellorship from President Hindenberg, who was an old military man, there was a sort of riot in Moessingen. Men of all ages marched through the town, opposing Hitler's takeover. I was six years old, and my buddies and I walked alongside. When the police from nearby cities of Tuebingen and Reutlingen appeared, everyone scattered and hid from them; so did we youngsters. Many of the adults were arrested, some of our neighbors among them, and sent to detention camps (later called "concentration" camps) for their supposedly Communist leanings.

My buddies Hermann Neth and Willy Mayer and I were of kindergarten age. We sometimes took our snacks from home and went to the town dump and river to play instead of going to kindergarten.

Otherwise I had to go with my uncle Albert, Aunt Louise, and Aunt Klara to work alongside my grandparents in the fields to plant, weed, and harvest in order to nourish ourselves. We also had lots of trees and plants with cherries, plums, and berries, then pears and apples to harvest in the fall. They were stored in hay until late winter. All these were welcome as our main source of food besides bread.

In 1933, I started school (*volksschule*) in Moessingen. We were around sixty students in our class. Our first-grade teacher was Herr Mueller, who was strict with all of us. School lasted from Monday through Saturday noon, and we did get some vacation in summer to help with the harvest at home. The curriculum consisted of reading, writing, arithmetic, and music. We used slate boards since paper was too expensive. We did not get to write on paper until fourth-grade. We also had religious classes, since 99% of the students were of Lutheran-Evangelistic faith. We had to learn a lot of this by memory, by reciting the catechism, and through songs.

Of course we had some sports in the *Turnhalle* behind the schoolyard. There was a soccer field to one side that was used by the local soccer team. The schoolyard also had fifty to sixty chestnut trees, which provided excellent shade and beauty.

My second-grade teacher was Herr Kuebler. He was younger and new to the school in Moessingen. On the whole, I liked him better. By this time it was 1934, and I was going on eight years old. That meant we really had to pitch in at home whenever we were off from school.

Herr Bader was our third-grade teacher. He was an older man with rimless eyeglasses and a runny nose. He was strict and easy to anger. For no reason he would get out his three-foot-long bamboo stick and strike the girls over their open hands once or twice. He would pull the boys over the front bench and hit us on the seat of our pants. If my memory serves me right, my mother and all the Steinhilbers had him as a teacher.

My father died in 1933 following a hernia operation; consequently, my mother was unable to retrieve me from Germany. In 1935 she married my stepfather in Brooklyn. My stepsister Louise was born in December.

The year 1936 was an eventful year. I started fourth grade with Herr Bader again. We learned to write the Latin alphabet, and we started to write in ink on paper. Herr Bader was musical; he taught us many folk songs, some in the *Schwaebische* dialect, and accompanied us on his violin, interrupted often by his temper tantrums.

Nineteen thirty-six also brought me back to America. I remember going to see Herr Schrenk to make arrangements; he owned a hardware store in Moessingen and was also the agent for the North German Lloyd, a large shipping company in Bremen. Tante Martha, Grandma, and I saw him several times to arrange this trip. In preparation, we traveled to Stuttgart by train to buy Grandma new clothing for the journey at a large department store there. This included a new, matching hat—a first for Grandma; she had only worn a scarf previously. She was overwhelmed by all of this.

Leaving my grandparents, family, school, and buddies in Moessingen was hard for me as a nine-year-old. At the end of May, we walked to the railroad station in Moessingen. Grossvater presented me with a new pocket knife made by a local craftsman, a symbol of manhood. My entire class with Herr Bader were there and serenaded me with multiple folk songs, including *"Muss Ich den Zum Staetele Hinaus,"* a song later popularized by Elvis Presley while he was a soldier stationed in Germany. Tears were shed all around.

Grossmutter Steinhilber and I traveled to the port of Bremen. We stayed a couple of days at a hostel-like inn and got to know other passengers. We sailed from Bremerhaven on the *Europa*, a large, modern, German ocean liner. We stopped in Cherbourg and Southampton to pick up additional passengers and mail before traveling across the North Atlantic to New York, which took five or six days. We had some rough days on the sea, but the food was great.

We landed in New York on June 4. My mother and Tante Anna (my godmother) were there to meet us. At home in Brooklyn, I met my stepfather William Feuerborn. I started school right away in Public School 56 on Madison Street and Bushwick Avenue, a ten-minute walk from our house.

I was put into the first-grade because I couldn't speak English. Of course I did not fit the benches as a nine-year-old. This went on for about two weeks, and then summer vacation started.

Our neighbors Arthur and Shirley Mason, about ten and twelve years old, tutored me during the next few months to help me learn English.

Grossmutter had the vacation of her life. She had many relatives in the area and was on the go constantly. She had days of leisure she had never experienced before in her life. She stayed in the U.S. until September.

The day she left, I saw her off. I pleaded and cried for her to take me back to Germany with her, and I had the headache of my life. At my mother's I felt as if I was just another mouth to feed. When not at school, I was put to work doing housework, scrubbing the hallway, stairs, and bathrooms in this four-story, furnished rooming house that my parents owned. When neighbor boys came to the door, my mother chased them away. I was not allowed to play.

I continued to learn English in school and with good grades earned my way up into my proper grade level. One teacher stood out—Mrs. Doyle in fourth-grade. She was sympathetic to my struggles with the English language and worked with me to bring my language skills up to level. I also attended church in the next street, Our Savior Lutheran Church. On Saturday afternoons there was children's

George, dressed for a Hitler Youth march, 1944

choir practice and then Sunday School. This was the extent of my joy in life. I also helped in a family delicatessen on Saturdays for fifty cents, which went into my savings account.

My life at home deteriorated, relieved somewhat by good relations with Aunt Anna, her husband John, and their son Henry, who all lived in the Bronx. I was allowed to visit them, and when life became unbearable at home, I ran away to them, where I sought refuge. By late 1938, they were willing to adopt me. My mother would not permit this, so it was decided that I go back to Germany. In April of 1939, Tante Amalia took me along with her on the *Bremen*. She escorted me to Tuebingen by train, and I arrived in Moessingen alone around April 23.

When I got off the train, I dragged my suitcase the best I could to the home of my grandparents. I was a pale and hungry twelve-year-old, lonely boy delivered from evil. I was welcomed by my grandparents Steinhilber and the entire family, friends, and neighbors. This meant working as an equal alongside the family on the farm on a daily basis except on Sunday.

Of course I went back to *volksschule* and was reinstated with my class that I left three years before. I was now a seventh-grader, and I found the going tough. Teacher Herr Schnepf was a middle-aged man who had a drinking problem. He had little sympathy for me and made life in school rough for me. I had a lot of catching up to do on my own, and I prevailed.

Four months later, on a Saturday morning in September 1939, World War II started. Uncle Adolf was re-called on that first day. He had just come home from active duty and reported to Ulm to an engineering battalion. Many others from Moessingen left that day, including a few teachers. Return to school was delayed by one week due to the war.

Herr Schnepf did not get drafted at that time. However, to support his drinking habit, he was later caught taking money from the students' savings program and was inducted immediately into the German Army. He was a Nazi Party member, which perhaps helped him avoid going to jail.

Our new teacher was Herr Batheldt. He realized that I needed extra attention to catch up with the class. He helped me with assignments. It was a blessing for me and made life more comfortable at school.

I also had religious instruction in school as well as confirmation class in church during the week and on Sunday mornings. I joined the Hitler Youth and did track and field activities.

In early March 1940 I was confirmed in the Peter and Paul Kirche (church) in Moessingen. Tante Martha presented me with my first wrist watch. With the moneys I received for confirmation, I bought myself a pair of skis and bamboo poles. Shortly thereafter, I broke my thumb skiing. Worse yet, I also broke one of the ski tips, but that could be repaired by glueing.

That spring I was promoted to eighth-grade with my class, and we were able to stay with Herr Batheldt, which was good all around since I had made good progress and had gotten caught up.

With the war entering the third year, everything was rationed and in short supply. Tante Martha worked at the town hall and was in charge of distributing food, clothing, and shoes. She was fair, and we received no preference. But we had milk, chickens, a pig, lots of fruit and vegetables on the farm, and milled our own flour, so we did not go hungry.

In 1941 when I was in eighth-grade, we had to fill out forms in school for the state employment office. We were all fourteen years old and had to decide what we wanted to do for a living and then find a place as an apprentice. I put down "mechanic or toolmaker." Herr Batheld also had to write his evaluation; then it was sent to Tuebingen, our county seat approximately ten miles away. Of course Grossvater Steinhilber also had to sign off on this.

A few weeks later, I received a letter from the Trade and Commerce Board directing me to be tested and interviewed by MONTANWERKE WALTER in Derendingen, a suburb of Tuebingen, for an all-day affair. We were sent to a large room in a fairly new, white building. About twenty boys from the surrounding towns were to be tested. This procedure lasted all day. We were told that more boys would be tested, and we would be notified later of the results.

Some time later I received a letter from MONTANWERKWE WALTER stating that I was accepted into their apprenticeship program. On March 29, 1941, I graduated from the eighth-grade *volksschule* in Moessingen, and a few days later I started my apprenticeship. The first three months were a probationary period. Being cooped up in a factory from 7 A.M. to 5 P.M. was something to get used to! We were approximately twenty new apprentices in addition to forty boys in their second, third, and fourth year of a three-and-a-half-year apprenticeship.

For the first six months we were learning how to file, chisel, chisel and scrape metal on test pieces, as well as measure, lay out, and center-punch. I did well in trade school and was put into an advanced grade in the second semester. This meant I had an additional half-day of school and additional homework.

The war advanced, and in December 1941, following the attack on Pearl Harbor, the U.S. declared war against Japan, Germany, and Italy. The bombing of German cities began by England and the U.S.

By 1943 some of my classmates were being drafted into the German armed forces at the age of seventeen. The result was that in August 1943, after two and a half years' apprenticeship and trade school, we took the journeyman's test early. One half was practical and one half theoretical. I passed both and continued working at MONTANEWERK WALTER. We received increases in our hourly pay, but you could not buy anything in Germany during the war. Food, clothing, shoes, etc. were rationed; all manufactured goods went to the war effort.

After I turned seventeen in November 1943, I volunteered to go into the *Landdienst* (Agricultural Service) through the Hitler Youth. I was sent to Poland to a camp for two and a half months in the town of Burgstadt. A girls' camp was also there, across the frozen lake. The barracks we stayed in were not heated, showers had only cold water, and it was an eye opener to be away from home and its comforts. Food was rationed, and only on Sunday at noon you got to eat your fill of potatoes, onions, and gravy.

I was made a camp leader and re-assigned to Uttenhofen, near Schwaebisch Hall, about two hours from Moessingen. After a couple weeks furlough at home, I reported there, and in April about fifteen boys arrived with their parents—fourteen-year-olds to be assigned to farms in the surrounding area. We stayed in a barrack with bunks and were clothed with uniforms. I had my own room, and we shared a large washroom and toilets.

All of these boys were away from home for the first time,

and here I was, seventeen and in charge of these boys. It was a challenging task. The head farmer for whom I worked helped make the job assignments. His wife was a hardworking woman and an excellent cook. There was also a French POW, who was difficult and not very ambitious. My job was only half days, but I worked mostly full days. I had to visit the farms where these boys were assigned. I had one difficult boy who ran away to his home.

In June 1944 the Allies landed in Normandy, which changed the war in the West. The Russians were also on the offensive. Americans bombed German cities during the day, and the British bombed at night. This resulted in a turn for the worst for Germany. In September I was called to arms and notified to report to the Ninth Armored Division in Stralsund on the Baltic coast of northern Germany. Before I reported, I had to wait for my replacement at the camp.

Well, this was a rude awakening—eight weeks of basic Infantry training in rain and snow, little rest, and sparse food, then an additional four weeks of heavy Infantry weapons training, i.e. mortars, heavy machine guns, and sharp shooting. After that I was selected to go to a tank destroyer school in Czechoslovakia for ten days. Upon returning to Stralsund, our training was complete.

Christmas 1944 was approaching. Germany was bombed day and night, and the Allies were approaching German borders on both sides. Things started to look grim. I received ten days leave to go home to Moessingen over the New Year holiday. The trip through Berlin, Nurnberg, and Stuttgart was treacherous. These cities were bombed around the clock. The trip home took three days; with train stations and tracks in ruins; we had to walk for miles around the bombed-out stations, with little or no food.

As soldiers "on the march" so to speak, we were not supplied with food, so we helped ourselves. We took coal from the steam engine's tender to fire up a potbellied stove in the freight car. We stole potatoes and sliced them on the side of the stove. In a freight car we found big wheels of cheese, spaghetti, and marmalade. We were searched but always kept one step ahead in order to avoid bone-chilling hunger.

We came through the East German city of Dresden, which was bombed mercilessly. By the side of the tracks lay the Blue Train, the *Flying Dutchman*, that was used between Hamburg and Berlin.

We traveled across Czechoslovakia to the west side of Vienna, where we were held up for a couple days and were fed a watery green soup and some rye bread—pathetic, to say the least. Next we headed toward Hungary. During the night we were ordered off the train, and the next morning all hell broke loose when Russian troops with many tanks, artillery, and air cover hit us. We were ill-equipped—no armor, artillery, or ammunition. We were supposed to be the stop-gap against a Soviet force that had just taken Budapest. The Hungarian Army had surrendered to the Soviets, and here we were—five to six hundred young soldiers on our way to Vienna. We were almost entirely annihilated.

It was early April, perhaps Easter Sunday. The Hungarian peasants begged us to stay and defend them. Then we got the order to retreat to Schoenbrunn, summer palace of the former Austrian emperors.   I caught my first lice there!

Vienna was bombed daily, and I was in the center near St. Stephen Cathedral. Russian fighter bombers and heavy artillery blasted us. Trying to get across the Danube River was almost impossible. Withdrawing German troops had dynamited the bridges. Fire engines from Vienna were dangling from the ruins there.

We were ordered to withdraw to the city of Linz. We went on foot through Lower Austria and were fed by the people as we went through the villages—a band of about thirty troops led by an Air Force corporal. This was late April 1945. On our way to Linz, we observed German soldiers hanging by their necks from trees. They were considered traitors for deserting; placards explaining this were attached to them.

When we arrived at the Auhof Kaserne above Linz, we observed American bombers that were bombing Linz unabated in broad daylight, along with the Herman Goering Works—a large complex of munition factories. There was no German Air Force by this time at the end of the war, only German flack cannons shooting at several of the bombers.

We continued our march toward the city and passed a group of shot-down American POW airmen. For them the war was over.

We were loaded onto freight cars heading east towards Vienna. At the Enns River we were told to get off. We slept in an abandoned factory. It was early May, and we found out a few days later from the locals that the war was over on May 8. So we headed back west to where we came from. On the Enns River, near the city of Steyer, we came upon American soldiers, who told us to lay down our arms. We were now officially prisoners of war.

They led us to a huge green meadow where the river made a big bend. There were thousands of us German soldiers and a large number of nervous Americans guarding us. They segregated officers from the enlisted men. We pitched our small tents there, and the Americans on the road above had their jeeps parked with 30- and 50-caliber machine guns mounted on them, pointed at us. During the night they fired over our heads, at times hitting some of us lying on the ground.

Among my personal belongings, I had my report card from Public School 56 in New York and pictures of my American family. After a few days of standing for hours in the blazing sun, I identified myself as an American-born German soldier. They used me sparingly then as an interpreter for a few days in a farm house. Then they turned me back to the general prisoner population.

They moved us by truck to a camp next to some planted fields and a forest. We were kept very hungry and dug up the old potatoes and cooked them with water and dandelions, which caused us to have dysentery and weakness.

We moved by train further west in cattle cars and arrived in Ebensee on Lake Traunsee in Austria. This happened to be a concentration camp site. As we walked up a hill towards the camp, we were pelted by rocks and sticks by the former inmates. They roamed freely, harassing us and the local population. Several loads of American MPs came by truck to drive off the assailants.

On the way into the camp we had to abandon everything but the clothes on our backs. Inside the former camp were many wooden barracks that were vandalized and destroyed by the former occupants. We slept on the floor, huddled together. Food was sparse. We were ordered to clean the barracks the best we could. We loaded onto trucks to get some raw lumber and fix things up, like whitewash. The camp commander, an American captain, told me if typhus broke out, he would hoist a yellow flag and let us die.

The guards of this camp were combat troops of the Oklahoma National Guard. I spoke with them (in English) and was offered a job to work in their mess hall as a dishwasher. It was my salvation from 6 A.M. until 8 or 9 P.M. They gave me soap and a can of DDT powder to rid myself of body lice that I had contracted back in Schoenbrunn. Now I was clean with the help of some of my barracks buddies who washed my clothes, and in turn I fed them what I could bring with me into the camp.

By now it was August 1945. They started to discharge some of the youngest prisoners of war, the seventeen and eighteen-year-olds. I happened to be one of the eighteen-year-olds. I was interrogated, and the next day I found myself on my way—not to freedom but to prison in Mauerkirchen in solitary confinement as an interned person by the U.S. Army's CIC—Counter Intelligence Corps.

After a few days I was trucked under guard to Braunau on the Inn River into the local jail for solitary confinement. I guess I was considered a dangerous war criminal by the CIC. In this jail were many Austrian men such as doctors, teachers, and state employees, that belonged to the NSDAP (the Nazi Party), a requirement of intellectuals and state employees.

After a couple days in jail, I was taken for interrogation to the Braunau Public Library, which just happened to be the house that Adolf Hitler was born in on April 20, 1889.

These CIC agents of the U.S. Army happened to be young second lieutenants with German accents, sons of German Jews that had left Germany in the 1930s to escape the Nazis. They were in their early twenties, and I was eighteen. They interrogated me for hours for a few days. They felt very superior to me and finally returned me to the local jail.

One day they cleared everyone out of the jail and trucked us to a camp in the woods near Hallein in Tyrol, Austria. I saw there the entire intelligentsia of Austria locked up, probably to age seventy —and me the only American, at age eighteen. I got to know some, as well as the group from Braunau that came with me. Bedbugs dropped from the ceilings at night and sucked on us. We remained in the Hallein camp until October.

One day we were loaded onto trucks in the direction of Salzburg, to a complex of cement block buildings—a former Army engineering garrison on the Salzach River town of Glasenbach. The prisoner camp was called Marcus C. Orr. Each building was two to three stories high made of raw cement blocks in and out, cordoned off with barbed wire. There were bunk beds three high, thirty to a room.

Inmates were the same group I had known in Braunau, along with some from Vienna, Burgenland, and the surrounding area. There were barely enough bed-slats where I laid my canvas shelter, half of it to sleep on, and an army blanket for cover. I had an old toothbrush, washed-out small towel, and barely any clothes. Food rations were sparse, divided up fairly by elders of the room. By Christmas the locals received packages from home, and they shared some of it. Many of the local inmates had families with children, who also suffered while being locked up. Karl Hartelmeyr, who was a young railroad officer, and Leo Bodingbauer, a private school teacher, Ph.D. professor of English, Greek, and Latin, were close to me.

Close to a year went by as I stared daily at the Unterberg and Castle Hohensalzburg. When some guards appeared to get me, I had ten minutes to gather my few measly possessions and say goodbye to my roommates. Under guard I was transported to Gmuden, on Lake Traunsee, on the back of a three-quarter-ton Dodge truck.

There I was taken to the attic of one of the lakeside villas. It was unfurnished, with chicken wire walls—CIC headquarters for the American zone of Austria. The personnel there were pretty much the same that I encountered in Braunau. More interrogations followed.

One day they took photographs of me, and a couple days later they came to take me under guard to Vienna, through the Russian zone in Lower Austria to the American zone of divided Vienna. There I was housed in the Rossauerlande Jail for a few days. While there, I was taken to the American Consulate to make an application for a new American passport. A few days later I was returned to Gmuden.

While there I met a few GI interpreters, including Milton Giese and Egon Schreiner from Brooklyn. It turned out that Egon's family bought Uncle John's delicatessen where I worked as a boy.

I turned twenty years old on November 19, 1946, sitting in a cold attic. I was befriended by an American soldier named Russell DeChristina, also from Brooklyn, who sometimes gave me a candy bar. He also forwarded a couple letters I wrote to my mother in Brooklyn, so the family would know where I was. Tante Frances, my father's oldest sister, sent me a package at Christmastime, the contents of which were only labels from canned goods and a pint can of cod liver oil; the rest was stolen, probably for resale on the black market.

Over the Christmas and New Year's holidays of 1946-47, I was put into a trailer-like, small room on site. It was brightly lit and over-heated. Guards marched back and forth twenty-four hours a day, beating on the door with a baton around the clock.

After New Year's, I was back in the attic and was told by one of the interpreters that I would be discharged in the next few days. On January 13 I was driven to Braunau, where I had been interned, and released onto the street—cold, hungry, with no money. I went back to the people at the local jail, who were kind enough to put me up until I got my bearings. While in Braunau, I sold my watch at a pawn shop, which was then handed back to me as a personal belonging. Then I decided to go to Vienna to the consulate and get my passport.

During my stay at the CIC villa in Gmunden, I had befriended a man named Josef Durst from Vienna. He was an Austrian Jew who had survived the war in Vienna and the Nazi persecutions. He was arrested by the American CIC at his home and taken to Gmunden. He was perhaps fifty years old and very sick with ulcers. Somehow he heard that I was going to Vienna in the American zone. Since he had no contact with his family since his arrest, he wrote his name and Vienna address in case

I would get back there, and I should let his family know of his whereabouts and that he was "well."

I took a bus from Braunau to Linz, then to Vienna. Before we got to the Russian zone, I met an elderly man, and we spoke about my journey. At the Lower Austrian/Russian zone border, we were stopped. Russian soldiers demanded identification. Fortunately, I had the discharge paper from the Americans. This old man heard my ordeal and began explaining in Russian (which he had learned during the First World War as a prisoner) that I was going home to my mother. That said, they let me go on, and I arrived in Vienna late that afternoon. I made sure I stayed in the American zone.

I got on a streetcar to the district where Josef Durst's family lived. I found a large villa, rang the doorbell, and an older gentleman, servant of the Durst family, came to the door. I showed him the paper that Josef wrote for me. He took me outside of the house and directed me to another address, telling me that I would find Mrs. Durst there. I found the address, which happened to be her parents' house, and I learned what happened after Josef's arrest several months before. They were given forty-five minutes to pack their personal belongings and leave. The American CIC wanted their house and took it over, arresting Josef's wife's father and evicting the family.

They were happy to see me, invited me to stay with them. I slept on the couch, bathed, they fed me, and gave me one of Josef's shirts—of Egyptian cotton, the finest I had ever had. The next day we spent visiting and my telling them (with no details) that Josef was well, as he had instructed me to do.

They offered to chauffeur me to the American Consulate. They had a car when others barely had shoes. So off I went. I identified myself, but there was no passport. My file had been sent to Stuttgart!

Somehow I telegraphed my mother from Vienna. TWA Airlines had just opened New York, Paris, Vienna service. Mother was willing to pay for the ticket, but I had no passport. So what was there left for me to do but return to Germany to my grandparents in Moessingen. By now it was late January 1947.

So the Dursts gave me some Austrian currency and drove me to the train station to catch the express to Salzburg. All went well until we hit the Russian checkpoint in Steyer, before crossing into the American zone entering Upper Austria. The train halted at the bridge that crossed the Enns River. The train conductor came a couple compartments ahead of the Russian soldiers. I showed him my discharge issued by the American Army. He told me to quick get out, or "You will be held by the Russians." Without hesitation I left, with nothing but the shirt on my back, jumped off the train into cold darkness, crawled under the train onto an axle and held on, freezing, scared to be apprehended by the Russians.

Thank God they had no flashlights, and after their looking around, the train started to roll across the bridge, with me holding on below for dear life! The train stopped on the other side in the American zone. I was safe and very cold. As I returned to my compartment, the others were surprised to see me, glad I had escaped.

The train continued on to Salzburg, where I got off. I went to the Red Cross there hoping to get something to eat, but no food was available, only black coffee. So I hungered and waited for daylight to continue my journey. I still had some cod liver oil, so I took a sip.

When the train arrived in Bavaria I had to report to a soldier repatriation center for a physical exam as a returning prisoner of war. I had to strip naked and be subjected to examinations by a multitude of former military doctors. After about two hours I was declared healthy and fit to work. I received something to eat, but before that I had to be deloused with DDT. I had had no lice since summer 1945, but this was routine to make sure.

I was provided with a rail ticket to Moessingen. In the compartment were an American soldier and his German girlfriend. We were joined by a tall man in dark clothing. The American told him to get out, then explained to me that he was a Jew, and he should ride in another car.

My journey continued, not without incident. The destruction of cities and towns on the route was shocking. Trains were few, and there was no schedule. Tracks were sparse, and ruins as far as the eye could see. Locomotives were patched together, and passenger cars often fitted with wooden benches. My thirst and hunger continued, and at one point I bought a bottle of mineral water, which made me quite sick.

When I got off the train at Moessingen, I was recognized by the dispatcher, my uncle Otto's brother-in-law. He greeted me heartily and telephoned Tante Martha. It was late January 1947, nearly two years after the war had ended.

As I walked home from the station, many people recognized me, and the entire neighborhood came out on the street to welcome me home. Grossvater Steinhilber cried when he saw me. Grossmutter Steinhilber had died eleven months before. Three of my uncles had come home from the U.S. and England. Uncle Adolf was still a prisoner of war in Russia. (He returned home in 1948 very ill, but he survived for several more years.)

It was all so overwhelming for me, I don't remember the feeling, or if I had any, after almost two years of hunger and abuse. It took me at least a month to adjust into this new life style of family gatherings, abundant food, and security.

Moessingen was in the French occupation zone and had about a hundred French soldiers in town. The French took everything—the entire contents of factories, which the Germans were forced to load onto trains going to France. The American zone was far better for the survivors of the war, after the Marshall Plan, but that came later.

In March I started a job as an auto mechanic for eighty-five pfennigs per hour. The Reichsmark was nearly worthless, and there was nothing to buy. Food was rationed as well as clothes, shoes, etc. A week's work and wages could buy a pack of cigarettes on the black market.

There was plenty of work to be done on the farm, and I worked along with numerous uncles, aunts, and cousins. We had good harvests, and with all this going on, I started to fit back into daily life. My mother wanted me to come back to the States. I gave it some thought. In March of 1948 I finally went to the American Consulate in Stuttgart, which got the ball rolling. The family and my girlfriend were not sure if I should go, but I decided to in the hope for a better life and future.

One more trip to Stuttgart, and I acquired a passport and one-way ticket for travel direct to the U.S. I left during April for Bremen. Grossvater Steinhilber pulled a small wooden wagon with my suitcase on it. My buddy Gauger took me to Tuebingen by car, then I had a long train ride to Bremen. There I was placed in a compound with displaced people from all over Europe. I had caught a severe head cold on the way to Bremen and kept much to myself, with my suitcase made of cardboard. I was called and taken to an off-site office; since I was an American, they offered me a return trip to the U.S. on a passenger freighter. A few more days went by, and I boarded the *American Scientist* in Bremerhaven—a ship of the U.S. Lines in service to bring the families of U.S. occupation troops to Germany.

The passengers were an interesting mix, including a business executive, a Lithuanian refugee who had lost his wife and children, a young Polish kid who shared my cabin and hid away the entire trip, an American heiress who paraded around in a mink coat, a German woman whose husband was at sea with the U.S. Lines, who was returning home to New York, and a German war bride going to Tennessee. The ocean was kind to us, and I ate my way across. We were allowed to help ourselves to the officers' pantry. I must have gained a pound a day!

When we were part way across, the captain received orders to land in Boston instead of New York. Upon landing, I was greeted by two FBI agents to be interrogated and fingerprinted, then let go. Eventually I made my way to New York to be greeted by my mother and sisters Louise and Joanne. I also had a four-year-old sister Hilde.

After a few days, Uncle Martin came to offer me a job at a machine shop in Brooklyn. I had long, six-day weeks of fifty-seven hours at eighty-five cents an hour, which amounted to forty dollars a week with overtime and deductions. I had to pay off the balance on my passage ticket to my stepfather plus for clothes and a toolbox, and I paid my mother for room and board.

The shop consisted of mostly Europeans, and the foreman was a hard-driving Swiss national. His motto was "Right or wrong, I am always right!" I got used to the work environment, learned a lot, worked hard, and got raises often. I made friends, bought a car, and had an active social life. It was a great difference from being a hungry prisoner of war two years ago. I took pictures of myself and the car and sent them to Germany. They couldn't believe it!

Through friends, I met my future wife Vi, and we were married in January of 1952. The Korean War was going on then, and I received a draft notice in August. After only seven months of marriage, I had to report to Camp Kilmer in New Jersey on August 19, then for basic training at Camp Gordon in Georgia. Vi continued to live and work in New York, while I was sent to Korea. I missed her very much and wrote to her every day. She wrote too, as well as sent me CARE packages.

Time dragged that winter of 1953-54, and we dreamed of building a house on Long Island upon my discharge. There were many detours before that happened. Final mustering out took place in July 1954. We built our house, worked at new jobs, and became parents of Baby George in January of 1956 and Christine, born Dec. 29, 1957. Other shifts occurred, upward promotions, and life was good for us.

In 1966 I went to our class reunion in Moessingen for our fortieth birthdays. It had been eighteen years since I left Germany. I saw relatives and longtime friends, although I had serious health problems while there, and it was good to get back home. Vi, Christine, and I returned for a visit in 1976.

In 1963 I took a job with IBM and eventually transferred to the new IBM facility in Boulder, CO—a dramatic move that involved a great deal of introspection and evaluation in terms of impact on the family. Moving west would involve real cultural shock for the children, but we were excited about having acreage and horses outside the city. Young George in particular, at age twelve, had real problems adjusting.

In 1979 we moved to Sydney, Australia, then to Singapore, still with IBM. We returned later to Boulder, built a house in Loveland, and retired in 1987. I have been back to Germany a few more times and traveled extensively elsewhere on the planet. Except for some serious health problems treated satisfactorily, we are enjoying our senior years in Loveland.

God bless America!

⊷ ChristelPfeiffer ⊷

Christel has written three separate accounts of her wartime and postwar German experiences. They are indeed unique—another example of how the entire population was caught up in the tragic and dramatic events of those times. At the same time, readers will note that several subjects' descriptions of prewar, more "normal" family life and childhood could often seem to portray an American setting as well, and Christel's account does that. Not just American parents expect good behavior from their children, exemplary performance at school and on the field, and all want their children well-educated and suitably prepared for the adult world. And "normal" doesn't necessarily mean "Leave It to Beaver" compatibility and congeniality—not in Germany, America, or anywhere else.

Christel was born in Berlin and grew up near Dresden, barely escaping the disastrous Allied phosphor bombings in February 1945. This was followed by a daring escape from the approaching Russians in May of that year, which she describes separately here. After the war she supported herself in Heidelberg, which was occupied by U.S. troops, as an interpreter/secretary.

In 1953 she emigrated to Montreal and later to Vancouver, British Columbia. She received her degree as laboratory technician there, saved her money, and began a two-year "working tour" around the world, with her first stop in Los Angeles, California. In L.A. she obtained a good-paying job that allowed her to buy a used car, and she started saving for her next stop, which was to be Guadalajara, Mexico. Then something totally unexpected happened; she met her future husband Augie Pfeiffer in Pasadena, California, and that was the end of the world trip—some fifty years ago. Augie and Christel presently live in Fort Collins, Colorado.

My Father

He was intelligent, gifted (he painted quite acceptable water colors and was an accomplished pianist), entertaining, and extraordinarily charming if he chose to be so. On the other hand, he was spoiled (an only child), impatient, and demanding. People loved him and I adored him. He called me his "walking question mark" because I would bombard him with a great variety of questions, which he would be only too happy to answer. He had been in the First World War, serving as a medic on the Eastern front, and later he studied medicine. Upon graduation he married my mother in 1924.

Christel's father circa 1920 as a medical student and member of the dualing fraternity. Academic fencing was considered to develop character and personality. Facial dualing scars were proudly displayed as a sign of courage and social status.

My father considered himself a socialist; that is to say, he would not tolerate any behavior that could possibly be interpreted as appearing superior to others. I remember when I was about twelve, I dreamt of wearing a chic little cap, red with a black brim and an insignia identifying me as attending the "Quinta,"— the second year of high school. He pointed out that this was showing off, because it would designate me as a student whose parents could afford to pay for higher education. In those days high school attendance required tuition as well as an entrance examination after four years of grammar school.

Not surprisingly, my father welcomed Hitler's ideas, while my more cautious mother was overheard to say, "I hope this young man knows what he is doing." During her lifetime she never expressed enthusiasm for the new regime, while my father joined the Party early. But to my knowledge he never actively participated in any political actions.

My mother died at age thirty-seven from complications following a gallbladder operation, leaving behind a bereaved husband with two young children—me age ten, and my brother age three. Father's mother came to live with us, which was a necessary but certainly not ideal arrangement. I vaguely remember that Oma always seemed to be the center of some turmoil. There had always been tensions between mother and son, dating back to the times when she wanted to accompany him to student affairs and be introduced as his sister. She was a handsome woman, widowed early in life, and left in very comfortable circumstances. She acquired a much younger boyfriend who talked her out of her last jewels and then merrily went on his way. She also disliked my mother, who, however, would become a saint once my father's second wife entered our lives.

At the time of my mother's death we lived in a small but lively city in the mountains bordering the former Czechoslovakia. It was to the southeast of the provincial capital of Saxony, Dresden. Dippoldiswalde, commonly known as just "Dipps," was the county seat, and my father headed its medical services.

The young widower must have appeared to be a tempting catch despite that *Anhang,* that is, his two young children. A twenty-two-year-old former secretary emerged as the victor, a smalltown girl with a teenage attitude and a stick-thin figure. They were married exactly a year after my mother's death. Father was forty-four years old, and the year was 1939.

War broke out in September 1939, and my father served briefly in the army but was released after a few months, being reclassified as "vital to the home front." By that time I was attending boarding school and returning home less and less frequently. Grandmother lived with us under the same roof, and the tension between the two women was tangible. Everyone noticed it except my father, who had developed to perfection a philosophical approach to troublesome matters known as the "Ostrich Technique." I was safely out of harm's way, but my brother and half-brother still bear the scars of their dysfunctional childhood to this day and neither ever married.

During the latter years of the war, my father apparently began to realize that all was not well with the Nazi regime. What bothered him most was the treatment prisoners of war received. As District Chief Medical Officer, it was part of his job to make periodic inspections of the camps in his district, and he found appalling conditions. He began to complain. Whether or not he actually left the Party is unknown. In any case, punishment was swift, and he soon found himself facing the Russians on the Eastern front. He was not to return until Christmas 1945, some eight months after the war ended, to assume his old job but this time in a Russian-occupied country loosely ruled by inept and ill-trained Communist loyalists. By this time his mother had died, and egged on by my stepmother, I had escaped to the promising West.

It is unknown just how well my father adapted to the new regime, but in any case, his relief of finally being home again was short-lived. One morning an article in Dresden's major newspaper accused him of having partaken in the infamous Kristallnacht, which resulted in the persecution of Jews and destruction of their property. The article was signed by the vice president of the state of Saxony. My father rushed to Dresden to confront the vice president, only to find out that he was on vacation and therefore could not have signed the article. What had happened? Eventually it emerged that one of his former secretaries, presumably a rejected girlfriend, had persuaded a Jewish relative of hers who held a high-ranking position in the

Saxon government, to write and publish this as a news item.

My father was cleared, but the damage was done. His reputation was tarnished, and he was transferred to Dresden, where he taught at the university for a while. His request to open his own medical practice was denied, and eventually he wound up being the company physician for Wismuth, a Sowjet (Soviet)-German company mining uranium. He never joined the Communist Party, which was a must (refusal to do so resulted in severely restricted salaries). But as he told me, he managed to coast along by writing plays leaning heavily towards praise of communism while criticizing capitalism and western imperialism. These plays would then be presented on suitable occasions to further the education of loyal workers.

By that time I had been thoroughly "Westernized" and inwardly shuddered when home on a visit, I had to attend one of these plays. However, this apparently put him in a strong enough position to keep my older brother out of jail when he went AWOL from the East German Army because he "didn't approve" of their practices.

Father was no longer alive when my younger half-brother got into trouble. After having had a few too many beers in a pub, he called then-East German President Walter Ulbricht a "dear old granddaddy but incapable of running his country." My brother wound up in a mental institution for a month and a couple years probation—a reduced sentence after pleading guilty, as advised by his court-appointed attorney.

As is quite often the case, experts neglect themselves as well as their families in the areas of their specific knowledge, and my father's health was not the best by the time he reached seventy. He developed diabetes, which he chose to ignore. At that time it was discovered that he suffered from acute kidney failure. Eventually he developed prostate problems requiring surgery. Death was imminent.

The hospital faced a dilemma. According to undocumented rules enforced by the Communist regime, any hospital would acquire negative points if it lost a patient who was still in the work force, particularly if this patient happened to be a practicing physician belonging to a job category where such candidates were always in demand. Hospital authorities decided to transfer their patient to Leipzig, Saxony's second largest city, approximately a hundred miles west of Dresden. The Leipzig hospital was fortunate to possess the only artificial kidney in the entire state. Authorities there protested heatedly; considering the patient's age and with both kidneys affected, they could not afford to tie up their one and only machine while neglecting those patients who could still be helped. Dresden apparently panicked; they immediately packed my father into an ambulance and rushed him to Leipzig, where a few hours later he died, just a month short of his seventy-third birthday.

This story only came to light because doctors in Leipzig were so enraged that their emotions took over and made them tell my stepmother about it. By then I was living in San Diego, totally unaware of what was going on. I was not to be informed of my father's death, let alone the circumstances, until I visited my stepmother the following year.

The Forgotten Children of Dresden

They began arriving the day after the third devastating attack within twelve hours had turned the inner city into a broiling inferno of heat, fire, and smoke, with phosphor dripping down blackened walls, imprisoning survivors and barring their escape. But the children did make it, all twenty-five of them, some on their own, others being handed over by mortally wounded mothers to those with better chances to reach safety. Their ages were from a couple months to about eight years, with the exception of an eleven-year-old girl with severe phosphor burns covering all extremities and part of her face.

The time was February 15, 1945, and the city mercilessly destroyed during the night of February 13/14 was Dresden, population 400,000. It was known as "Florence on the Elbe" because of its numerous museums, art galleries, churches decorated with elaborately carved sandstone figures, the world-famous Semper Opera House, a spectacular palace, and many more attractions. The estimated number of those who perished (mostly women, children, and elderly men) is estimated to be 130,000.

I had been in Dresden's main train station shortly before the first raid started on the evening of February 13. For the preceding seven years I had attended boarding school in a city a few miles east of Dresden, and I was on my way home to "Dipps," a small town in the mountains to the west. Winding my way precariously from platform to platform, I tried to avoid stepping on small children crawling on dirty, cold cement floors, watched over by older children while their exhausted mothers tried to catch a quick nap, surrounded by all their earthly belongings. Every available space was taken up by these families, who were refugees from Germany's eastern provinces, with the Russians snapping at their heels. There were hundreds of them. They had come with dreams, expectations of a better life, perhaps to join relatives. Little did they realize that this would be the end of the line for them. I venture to say that none survived.

When the first alarm sounded, signaling enemy planes approaching, all passengers with tickets were asked to quickly board their trains, which then pulled out ahead of schedule. I arrived home safe and sound some twenty miles and forty minutes later, to find my family sewing knapsacks in preparation for our expected flight from the Russians, who were as close as fifty miles to the east of Dresden.

Almost immediately the fatal bombing of Dresden started, and we watched its destruction helplessly—a sight all of us will have to live and deal with until the end of our lives. Soon the sky was illuminated to a bright orange, reflecting buildings on fire, accompanied by the dull impact of more bombs.

Except for occasional strafing planes, we felt relatively safe in our small city of Dippoldiswalde. It was and still is a lively medieval town, dominated by a castle which at that time housed the county judicial system and is now a museum. There were extensive public health services, a post office, a very ornate Renaissance-style city hall, and a bustling twice-weekly market— a typical example of doctor, lawyer, beggarman, thief, butcher, baker, candlestick-maker community.

This peaceful existence was suddenly and cruelly shattered by the arrival of the children and with them the permeating smell of smoke, lingering chemicals, and early decay. Who brought them? How did they manage to get there? Orphans or just temporarily lost? Who knew?!

With dark clouds of smoke framing the horizon to the east, the city somehow managed to set up emergency quarters in the auditorium of the school. Cots and beds appeared out of nowhere, as did clothing and food. The only help available were high school and gymnasium students on leave of absence from their various educational institutions, which had been closed down in order to serve mostly as hospitals for wounded soldiers or provide housing for refugees. Space had become extremely confined, with heavy artillery fighting some fifty miles to the east on the Russian front, and U.S. troops approaching fast from the west.

I don't remember just how I was notified to report to work, but I soon found myself joining several other students in taking care of "our" children. We worked every day in shifts, under the loose supervision of a school teacher. There were two and a half months left until the end of the war, but no one had time to give a thought to the future. It was a happy time for me, never realizing it would be the last of my youth.

There were about five students, and each of us had approximately five kids to look after. They seemed to get along very well with each other. They never cried very much, perhaps still too traumatized by past experiences. Even the older ones did not appear to miss mothers or siblings. In retrospect, they were not like children as we know them today.

There was one little boy, perhaps four years old, blond and blue-eyed, with finely-chiseled features, who never uttered a word. He reacted to sounds but not to words. We tried in vain talking to him in several languages. Whatever his problem, it remained his.

Christel Pfeiffer

And then there was Baby, a few months old, with an occasional bout of diarrhea. If I remember correctly, she had been found with a note tucked into her shirt giving the address of relatives in the West. Another delightful little girl was Emma (our name for her), about a year and a half, always smiling, always happy. We were so enchanted with her, we would "lend" her to each other so all of us could benefit from her happiness. There were also those two strange little girls of about six or seven years old. They would cling to each to other and talk a bit of German with a Slavic accent. Had they known each other before? We never found out where they originally came from or what had happened to their families. Occasionally, we would take a couple of the children home and treat them to a special meal. They generally seemed to be happy, but then that is from the viewpoint of an inexperienced, seventeen-year-old.

We never minded the various cases of head lice, and the only treatment I remember is diligently combing heads in search of nits. Then quite a few of us developed sore throats and fever. With no doctors or nurses available, we treated ourselves with cold wet compresses and gargled with salt water. Not until a month later, when I had bicycled to the city where I had been in boarding school and had lunch with a school chum at her parents' house, did I find out the cause of our illness. Both parents were doctors, and her father noticed that my palms were peeling and asked me what the problem was. I mentioned the sore throat and fever. He became agitated. We had had scarlet fever, and at this point I was in a most infectious state. I had to leave the house immediately!

It had fallen upon me to look after the ailing children—a couple cases of diarrhea, the above mentioned sore throats and fevers, but in general the kids were healthy; they were survivors. There was one exception, however. I never knew why this eleven-year-old badly injured girl wound up with these young kids; probably because there simply was no other place for her to go. She suffered severe chemical burns all over her extremities, and some areas of her face were affected. Anna was thin, pale, blondish, and must have been in perpetual pain. She complained little but screamed when an occasional visiting nurse changed bandages. Intravenous drips were unavailable. Her bed, a "real" bed, had been placed away from the hub so she would have some privacy to attend to more private matters. She was certainly unable to get up, wash or feed herself. No such luxury as a draped curtain. I would attend to her as best as I knew how—carefully dab her face and uninjured finger tips with water, give her a sponge bath, feed her, and if time allowed, read to her. I cannot remember giving any pain medication to her. This was before antibiotics became available, and I imagine that very little was on the market to treat phosphor burns. She grew visibly thinner, and it is doubtful she survived.

Being carefree and young, this didn't bother me at the time, not until much later, and it still does. Whatever became of her and all those other children?

The map of Christel's flight

Christel's Heroic Flight from the Russians, May 1945

All this came to an end, as expected, in early May 1945. Dresden was still smoldering, with many corpses decaying in the ruins—some not found until decades later.

The once distant booming of artillery fire now sounded like it was in our own back yard, and we foolishly decided to pack whatever would fit into and onto a little wooden ladder wagon (now sought after as an antique) and joined thousands of similar poor souls traipsing to the West. We started about twenty-five miles northwest of Saxony's capitol Dresden, on the only road out to what is now known as the Czech Republic.

On a gorgeous spring day, in a home in the Ore Mountains, a young woman of twenty-eight huddled with her five-year-old son Frank, ten-year-old stepson Juergen, and seventeen-year-old stepdaughter. I was that irresponsible, happy-go-lucky teenager. Our father was somewhere on the Eastern front.

A distant but constant, full, booming noise floated through the open windows—artillery fire from the fast approaching front and a sign of the heavy resistance by struggling German troops against the Russian Army. We were debating what to do—should we wait for the Russians' arrival and hope for the best? We had heard horror stories about rape and plunder. Should we hide in the mountains, and perhaps the Americans would arrive soon? Or should we start marching west, where rumor had it that U.S. troops were occupying Czechoslovakia and the Sudetenland. We made the fateful and illogical decision to trek through the mountains to join the Americans.

We knew the war would be over soon, and we were aware that our region was probably one of the last parts of Germany that hadn't been conquered yet. What we did not know was that just about sixty miles away to the northwest, the American

Army under General Patton had advanced to the city of Leipzig but had been ordered by General Eisenhower to stop there. Patton had already advanced some hundred and fifty miles into pre-determined Russian territory. Later in 1945, this entire area would be surrendered to Russia as a trade-in for establishing the Western Allied occupied zones in Berlin.

On May 7, one day before the end of the war and with the artillery fire much nearer, we loaded clothes and some food into our small ladder wagon, placed young Frank on top of it, and off we went!! Each of us also carried a hand-sewn backpack.

It was noon when we reached the one and only road through the mountains, which was clogged with hundreds of people with similar intentions, mostly women, children, and elderly men, as well as an occasional soldier. Most of them were on foot, pulling their wagons like we were. The center of the road was left free for an occasional passing vehicle—private cars, military trucks, and a few German tanks. The pace was slow, and people

German "ladder wagon" (hand-drawn cart) used by Christel when fleeing from the Russians, May 7, 1945

stopped along the roadside to rest and have a bite to eat. Water was available in the villages. I found it rather peaceful, as the boom of artillery fire had discontinued. I have no recollection of what we did to take care of life's necessities.

No sooner had we joined the trek when the *deichsel* (handle) of our ladder wagon broke. Some kind soul gave us a metal chain, which we tied to the wagon, but from here on someone had to walk behind and steady the cart, which had assumed a life of its own.

Several hours later in the afternoon, almost everyone suddenly stopped moving and pulled to the side of the road, and so did we. The word was, that in this particular village, there was supposed to be a warehouse of sorts where food and other supplies were handed out. When I left to investigate, little did I know this would be the last I was to see of my family for several months to come.

By now it was late afternoon of May 7, and the afternoon sun warmed the resting crowd, while others, like me, explored in search of food. I passed a couple of large tanks (*Panzerwagens*), with the crew giving me a happy wave, as well as some obviously stalled civilian cars and trucks. But there was no sign of food. Eventually I decided I had better find my way back, and once again I passed the tanks. This time a conversation ensued, during the course of which I was told that there was absolutely no hope to escape from the Russians on foot. But I was invited to join the tank crew, as they had been able to obtain fuel and were leaving the area immediately. I did not hesitate.

What an adventure—or so I thought. On the way out of the village, I may or may not have looked for my stepmother and siblings. When I was to see them again in September, the episode of our flight and consequent separation was never discussed. I do not know what happened to them, and they don't know what happened to me. At the time, this was a very typical German reaction to problematical situations.

I found life on the tank fascinating. The front of the vehicle contained two compartments—one for the driver, and the adjacent one for the radio operator. It was roomy enough for me to ride quite comfortably. The rest of the crew was tucked away in one single space behind us, which also accommodated a large gun. Food, or rather delicacies, appeared almost immediately: a variety of chocolate bars and other candies, cookies, sardines and crackers, canned fruit, salami and cheese—items I had not tasted in many months, if not years! I felt like being in *Schlaraffenland* as the Germans say, roughly translated "in a paradise catering to food."

It was still full daylight when I noticed that the scenery was changing. Villages had disappeared, and the forest became increasingly more sparse as we were gaining altitude. Also, fewer were the stragglers along the road. Most of them had apparently settled down for the night.

Some appeared to have simply collapsed; I sometimes had the impression they might have been dead. Many abandoned vehicles were simply left along the roadside, which was strewn with household items, clothes, sacks of what looked like sugar, broken down carts—anything that weighed down a weary traveler.

Our column of three tanks and a few cars stopped almost on top of the mountains. The road was deserted, and it was beginning to get dark. The tank following us was in trouble and blocking the way. I suspect it ran out of fuel. The third tank could not pass, but passenger cars did. The crews of the two stalled tanks were distributed among the other vehicles, and off we went once more. The horizon was lit up like a Christmas tree, indicating still heavy fighting going on, but we did not hear any sound.

We drove all night. I kept myself entertained talking to the radio operator, a young fellow from Hamburg. Among other things he confided in me was that he had a distinct feeling that he would not survive the war, and that his death would break his mother's heart.

When daylight came, our caravan had picked up a few more tanks, several military vehicles, and quite a few civilian automobiles. Where they came from I don't know; they must have been hiding somewhere, emerging when they realized we were Germans. It was a beautiful, sunny and warm morning when we arrived at the bottom of the mountains, according to maps in Czechoslovakia. The silence was ominous. No sound of any shots or artillery fire, no traffic on this road, which was, after all, the one and only main artery into Germany. It was decided that everyone pull off the road and park all vehicles in a lovely and peaceful little valley, while one of the automobiles should proceed to the next large intersection and reconnoiter.

The report was stunning. On the major road running east-west (we were heading due south), individual groups of German soldiers on foot were straggling west, while trucks loaded with Russian soldiers were moving east without seemingly noticing each other! The war was over!

Immediately, frantic activity began. Various food items, blankets, water bottles, and clothing articles were gathered and haphazardly packed into any type of container that was light and could easily be carried either on one's back or wrapped around the waist. I was told not to bother with anything.

Left on my own, I simply wandered about watching what people were doing. I was delighted to discover that I was not the only female in the group of approximately thirty. Another girl, slightly older than I, had joined us some time during the night and would remain with us for the next few days. I think we were the only civilians. Of all things, she lugged about a heavy fur coat and refused to part with it. It looked like rabbit to me but could have been mink.

It was at this time that I discovered that most of the soldiers were members of the Waffen SS, although all wore the olive green uniforms of the ordinary soldier. I happened to come across a small cluster of men who, to my great astonishment, appeared to be inflicting cuts to their inner upper arms. I was told that they were removing SS identification signs. It sticks in my mind that those could have been tattooed blood types, but I cannot be sure. However, the majority of the men did not do this.

These were also the times when women did not wear trousers. Consequently, I had donned my new and only suit of dark blue wool, consisting of a blouse, skirt and jacket with enormous pockets, very fashionable at the time. I must have worn some type of stockings, certainly not nylons; I don't remember. I was fortunate to wear my only pair of comfortable leather shoes, hand-me-downs from my favorite aunt, and a rarity in times when one was lucky to possess clunkers covered with cheap cloth and nailed haphazardly to wooden, platform-type soles. These were all the earthly possessions I owned, and they were to last me for a long time.

We were getting ready to leave and begin our march to the West, where somewhere the Americans must certainly be hiding. Explosives had been placed in all vehicles, including the tanks to be detonated after everyone had cleared out. Mounds of weapons were to be destroyed as well. I shall never know what prompted me, unnoticed by anyone, to bend down and pick up a lovely shiny pistol, just large enough to fit into one of my huge suit pockets. It turned out to be a Luger.

It was decided to split into smaller groups in order to draw less attention. In my group of ten were the girl with the fur coat, still hanging on to it, and my friend from the night before, the radio operator. Our unofficial leader was a sergeant from the state of Thuringia, who had assumed the role of my protector and to whose home all of us were now headed.

I knew little about the area we were to travel through, the Sudetenland, other than that the majority of the population was German, dating back to the Middle Ages. After World War I when the country of Czechoslovakia was created, the Sudetenland was included. The border to the west was Germany's state of Saxony, with the Ore Mountains (*Erzgebirge*) presenting a natural barrier. Although I venture to say that Czechs and Germans were not exactly in love with each other, they managed to get along quite well.

This was to change when Hitler invaded Czechoslovakia in 1939 and managed to encourage a possibly inherent dislike between the two factions residing in the Sudetenland, furthered by atrocities created by the Nazis themselves. This dislike for the Czech people actually spilled over into the rest of Germany. I remember distinctly having been under the impression that Czechs were inferior and could not be trusted. Whatever the case, at the end of the war, the antagonism felt by the Czechs, now fully justified, had resulted in the Germans being not only intimidated but outright afraid. However, I was innocently unaware of all this, and not until much later would I understand the ill feelings toward us by seemingly quite ordinary people.

We left the scenic little valley with the detonation of charges disturbing its peace and tranquility. Our pilgrimage on foot began just south of the city of Bruex (now called "Most") and a short walk brought us to the intersection and the road to the West. It was indeed an amazing sight that greeted us—a steady traffic of Russian trucks loaded with soldiers moving east, while uniformed Germans dragged weary feet on the sidewalk going west. Civilians, presumably Czechs, were occasionally seen among them. We inconspicuously blended into the crowd and soon lost track of our fellow travelers. It was fortunate that we two girls were surrounded by at least eight able-bodied men. Quite often shouts from passing trucks would direct attention to us: "Frau! Frau!" None of the vehicles ever stopped, but it made us feel uncomfortable. It is true that many rapes occurred at that time, usually in outlying areas with no officers present and certainly not sanctioned by the authorities.

There were Czech civilian checkpoints every so often, less to check identification but to search for weapons and to show who was in charge now. We and everyone else had destroyed our IDs, mainly because they all bore the image of a *Hakenkreuz* (Swastika), which might have provoked more ill feelings. Quite often they confiscated whatever articles might be needed; blankets, food, and particularly water bottles were in demand. Once I witnessed someone being left without boots. The first of many of these stops proved to be almost disastrous for my group. One must remember that I still carried the Luger in my jacket pocket. When the guard ran his hands down along the side of my body and pulled out the gun, a stunned silence ensued, followed by excited chatter among the Czechs and loud protests from the Germans that they had not known about this. In the end, I was severely admonished by both sides; the guard kept the gun, and we were allowed to be on our way.

The next few days were spent walking. The weather was glorious and warm. We slept either in adjacent woods, huddled together for warmth, or in barns provided by sympathetic farmers. After all, the majority of people in that area were of German origin. We never went hungry, being supplied with food by these same farmers. There are certain gaps in my memory; for example, I cannot remember how we took care of ourselves as far as keeping clean is concerned. I do remember washing my hair in a little stream next to the roadside. Occasionally we would also use these clear streams to drink from, because more often than not we had just lost our newly-acquired water containers— perhaps given to us by some kind farmer at the last checkpoint.

The road we were on led through some villages and ran parallel to the Ore Mountains, on the other side of which lay Saxony and eventually the state of Thuringia, our destination. The Czech people did not bother us, but their unfriendly demeanor was clearly evident. We never even asked them for directions. Russian soldiers were not evident other than in military vehicles.

In the vicinity of the city of Karlsbad (now Karlovy Vary), we turned north toward the German border. At this point it must be mentioned that unbeknown to us, U.S. troops were only a few miles away in Karlsbad, and thousands of German soldiers were surrendering to avoid becoming prisoners of the Russians. In retrospect, this was most fortunate for me. Had my companions surrendered, I would have been left stranded in a foreign country under most undesirable conditions. As it turned out, we were not bothered by anyone until reaching our final destination.

Somehow it was known that we had to pass through one final checkpoint at the border town of Gralitz (now Kraslice), before reaching German territory, and we hoped the American zone. This one was manned by Russians, and we needed an exit permit. We must have been on the road for some six or seven days, bringing us to about May 14.

I don't remember who came up with the idea that I should pass myself off as an English girl, in order to receive preferred treatment. At that time, German children began "high school" at age ten. One had to pass an examination, and there was a monthly fee. English was taught from the first year on, and I did speak some halting English and understood even less. But I didn't care, and so our "English adventure" began.

Upon reaching Gralitz, we were directed to the city center, a very pretty public square of grass with inviting benches and lined by tall trees displaying their new leaves in this special, pleasing, yellow-green color we call "May green." With the early afternoon sun filtering through the branches and Czech families milling in the square, it was a most peaceful sight. The reason I am mentioning this is because this tranquility would soon be very cruelly shattered.

We joined a short line of Germans waiting to enter a one-story building in the square. A few were allowed in at one time, and eventually I found myself, accompanied by my mentor the sergeant, in a large room with several desks, each manned by a Russian in uniform. Some of them had civilian interpreters with them. My companion immediately launched into a spiel about this poor English girl stranded in Germany and wanting to go back to her homeland. Our Russian spoke German fluently and was fascinated by the story. I never opened my mouth. As agreed upon previously, the sergeant asked if we possibly could have a couple blankets as well as water containers. These were produced out of nowhere (no doubt taken from one of our poor fellow travelers). We were handed our exit papers and proceeded to the exit where there was stationed a "Kommisar," a ranking Russian officer, whose signature would finalize the exit permit.

While we were waiting to see him, the girl with the fur coat entered the building. When she saw me, she threw the coat at me saying that she was afraid it would be taken from her, and that just in case, the address of her aunt in Thuringia was tucked into the pocket. She was accompanied by my new friend the radio operator.

The Kommisar turned out to be a good-looking, very young man to whom I was introduced once again as the "English girl." He gave me a big smile (what a rarity among the usual grim-faced Russian officials) and said in heavily accented English, "I also speak English." Can you imagine my shock! I started mumbling something in English, when suddenly there was a very loud blast that made the ground shake and almost knocked us off our feet. When we looked toward its source directly across the square, we saw the entire front of a large, three-story building tumbling to the ground. The noise was ear-shattering, followed by screams, cries, and shouting. The Kommisar acted quickly and told us in fluent German, "You must get out of here quickly. I will arrange an escort." Immediately two Russian soldiers grabbed us and marched us through the hysterical crowd to the outskirts of the town before turning us loose. Still stunned, we climbed up the hilly countryside and settled down in a lush meadow to wait for the rest of our group. We waited and waited. We heard shots—quite a few of them.

An hour passed before the first one of our people arrived. Eventually there were about five of them. Here is the story they told: The large building where the explosion occurred had previously housed German soldiers, and it was suspected that they left behind several unexploded bombs called *Blindgaenger.* Subsequently, after the Germans left, Czech families were temporarily housed there, and it was thought that children had found and played with these devices and set one off.

Presumably there were injuries and even fatalities. The people in the plaza simply went wild; they attacked and beat up anyone German. Every male within the inspection site was supposedly shot, and the women arrested and taken away. However, this must be considered hearsay. But we did hear shots, and I know that when some three weeks later, I delivered the girl's fur coat to her aunt, she had not heard anything from her niece. The premonition of the radio operator may or may not have been fulfilled. We never found out.

By midday the following morning, we came across our first German village. No one can imagine the relief we felt. I no longer had to fear being snatched by Russians, and the German soldiers by far preferred becoming POWs of the U.S. Army. As a matter of fact, it was a miracle that they had made it back into German territory and not been arrested previously.

Our much-anticipated encounter with our first Americans proved to be disappointing, although very fortunate in its outcome. The villagers told us that American soldiers were stationed "just beyond this huge wheat field and across the road." We took a short cut through the knee-high plants when suddenly something went bang! bang! Dust sprayed around us, and before I knew it, I was the only body still standing; the rest were on the ground and hissing,"Down! Down!" I followed their example, finally catching on that we were being shot at. And there we were. What were we to do?

The shots stopped, and after some time it was concluded that we had not been meant to be hurt, but that this might have been merely entertainment for bored soldiers. I am certain this was so, because when we got up we were not bothered again.

We reached the road, crossed it, and there was the first American check point. I practiced my minimal English, much to the delight of the Americans, and we were quickly waved on.

We stopped in the next, larger town and presented ourselves to the local mayor. Remember that none of us had any type of identification nor a single penny. Obviously, we were not the first ones he had encountered. The mayor was well-prepared. We stated our name, age, and last address, and VOILA, we were once more documented Germans. I imagine that many "wanted" people took advantage of this extremely haphazard procedure and thus were able to live under cover for many years to come. I seem to remember that each of us also received a small amount of cash.

The rest of our journey was relatively uneventful. We still slept out-of-doors, begged for food, and a few days later reached the small Thuringian town near Rudolstadt where the sergeant's family lived. I stayed with them for a few days while the rest of the soldiers proceeded to their individual destinations. It was the latter part of May 1945, and curiously enough, no one showed the least interest in any of them.

I managed to obtain some used clothes and immediately started looking for a job. When I was a teenager, there was a time when I had informed my father that I wanted to quit school and work on a farm. I loved animals. Obviously, I had been dissuaded. And now my time had come.

I hired myself out as a farm hand! The farmer and his family were very kind people who quickly realized that getting up at four A.M. and cleaning stables before breakfast was not exactly my strong point. They gave me other duties, allowing me to sleep until seven A.M. I lasted about a week and then took on another job as companion to the train stationmaster's married and very pregnant daughter. We were very compatible and enjoyed each other's company.

One morning we woke up, looked out the window, and there to our horror were Russian soldiers in marching formation six abreast carrying rifles across their shoulders. The Americans had disappeared overnight. At the Potsdam Conference, General Eisenhower had negotiated with his Russian counterpart to exchange the territory actually assigned to Russia but conquered by General Patton, for the right to create the American, English, and French zones in Berlin.

After arrival of the Russians in August 1945, I considered returning home to Dipps. However, no trains were running yet, and I had no money. I answered an ad for household help with free lodging, food, and some monetary compensation. Thus I was introduced to the arts of house-cleaning (including moving furniture weekly), as well as dodging a pinching husband.

By mid-September I had saved enough money and returned home. My stepmother and the boys were fine; my father had not yet returned from the former Eastern front. All higher educational institutions were still closed, and what was I to do? I had just turned eighteen, and encouraged by my stepmother, I packed a suitcase, donned a backpack, and made my way by train to the Russian/U.S. border. A second and final escape from the Russians, not quite as dramatic as the first one, but nevertheless with its own highlights, brought me to the city of Kassel.

Almost immediately I got a job with Special Services, the entertainment branch of the U.S. Army. Eventually I wound up in Heidelberg and worked there at the 130th Station Hospital (where General Patton had died a few weeks earlier of a blood clot following an accident) as a medical secretary until emigrating to Canada in June of 1953.

Christel Pfeiffer

◄ Anita Griffith ►

Anita's story is far from ordinary but it is an example of how ordinary German civilians were impacted by the horrors and complexities of the war while attempting to live normal lives. She comes through it all without bitterness or self-pity and is grateful for her new life in America.

I was born in 1930 in Dresden in East Germany. I had one brother, Gaston, who was thirteen months older than I. My father was a successful medical doctor. Mother came from an affluent family and had a privileged upbringing. Consequently she was quite helpless; she couldn't even cook. We lived in a very big house, and one wing was my father's practice. We had servants to do everything—cooks, upstairs and downstairs maids, a gardener, chauffeur, and nannies to care for us. They all lived in a separate house in the back of the main house, except the governess. She had her bedroom upstairs between my brother's and my bedroom.

Anita and her brother Gaston, 1937

We rarely interacted with our parents and saw them only in the evening at bedtime or in the morning, when we were "presented" to them formally. We had to curtsy and bow and

61

say "Good morning" or "Good evening—Herr Papa and Frau Mama." My mother seemed to be disinclined to be bothered with us children. However, she was very strict and insisted that we learn to WORK.

My grandma died when my mother was two years old. Grandma's older sister raised her in the traditional way: a "lady" does not work, and she marries an older, well-established gentleman, not merely a nobleman. (My father was twenty years older than my mother.) However, my grandma's sister married a commoner and was shunned by the family.

My father also had two ranches in Nackel, near Posen in the Polish corridor. On one ranch he bred Arabian horses and Lippizzaners on the other. So I think we must have been well off. Those properties got disrupted during the Polish War in 1939.

Now and then we visited my paternal grandparents in Nackel. But my mother didn't keep in contact with those grandparents after my father got picked up. It happened that my mother was a great admirer of Adolf Hitler. However, my father thought he was a joke and made fun of him. A "friend" overheard his jokes and reported him to the authorities. So the SS picked him up and sent him to a concentration camp. (I must have been about four or five years old.) He was in Buchenwald and Dachau and had to do experiments on other prisoners, which saved his life but not for long. The Americans set him free and got him to a hospital. He had heart problems and tuberculosis and lived only six weeks after he came home in 1946.

In the beginning, just about everybody liked Hitler. He got Germany out of the Depression. We all had work, food, and a good time. There was morality, honesty, discipline, and order. Crime was almost non-existent. Yes, it was dictatorship, but it was very good until he started the war. I was only nine years old, but I thought that tiny little Germany fighting against that big Russia and then England and France, even Africa, were all around us and against us, but politics was never my thing.

Hitler's hatred against the Jews I will never understand, that an intelligent country like Germany could find people who would commit such incredible cruelty against anybody. My father was in the concentration camps not only with Jews; there were also gypsies, Poles, Hungarians, criminals, and other "misfits." But nobody knew there was such a thing as concentration or extermination camps; we thought he went to jail or prison. Germans sure could keep a secret!

I think when they picked up my father, my mother snapped. She did not know how to work or take care of children. Because there was no more income from my father, eventually she had to let the servants go. She hated us, especially me. So she sent us constantly away to strangers in Children's Homes or to my grandma's in Rodebeul. It was nice there at Grandma's; there were lots of kids to play with and make friends. I made friends in first grade who are still friends today. However, one thing I didn't like at school was each time Hitler gave a speech on the radio, we were required to write an essay about it, and I hated that.

After my father left, my mother moved around a lot, and so I was in thirteen schools in my eight years of schooling. Often I was at Grandma's in Rodebeul near Dresden. I figured because my mother didn't know how to work she was often fired. I don't know; I never asked, and she never told. That was none of our business, she said. So we practically raised ourselves. Sometimes we lived in the big house in Dresden but often somewhere else. I went to many school reunions later and loved it. We all cried when I had to leave again. Now we are all over eighty, and it is hard to get together. Many have died or can't get around so well anymore.

I belonged to the B.D.M. (*Bund Deutscher Madchen*) group of twelve-to-eighteen-year-old girls. Everybody had to belong. I loved it. Our group went to soldiers' hospitals and sang or played theatre. We went marching, on little trips, and other things, and we had fun.

On February 13, 1945, we were in the house in Dresden when the alarm went off. We were not really concerned about it because the alarm went off just about every night. We went up to the attic. There were some windows in the roof, and we watched as they set off what we called "Christmas trees," which are flares in a square to mark where they were to drop bombs. They dropped phosphorous bombs, and they were very close to the house. Everything was burning—streets, houses, people, everything. So my mother wrapped us in wet blankets and we ran—to where, I did not know. Then I tripped over a dead woman. She had her mouth and eyes wide open, and her hair and clothes were all burned. That must have shocked me so much I don't remember how we got to Meissen. We probably walked, because there was no transportation. It was about thirty-five or forty miles from Dresden.

There was no reason to bomb Dresden. We had no industry. Dresden was a beautiful city and admired for her art, historic architecture, and cultural life, but the city was 100% destroyed by American and English bombers on the 13th and 14th of February 1945. This act was severely criticized by postwar analysts from both sides. Since the Russian occupiers left, all those major buildings have been rebuilt, and they are better than ever. Some that were several hundreds of years old have been improved with modern materials, electricity, underground garages, etc.

In Meissen we found a little two hundred-year-old fieldstone house with two tiny little rooms. My mother found a job at the hospital, even though she was not a trained nurse yet; she studied later. But nurses were desperately needed, because of the wounded people from Dresden.

In March 1945 I graduated from eighth grade. We had only eight years of schooling, but we went to school on Saturdays and had only four weeks of summer vacation. Hitler made a law that everyone had to work one year in a household or on a farm, so we would really learn to work hard. "R-I-I-IGHT!" After that nothing was hard anymore. So, the next day after graduation, I was on a big farm. The next farm was about a mile away. The farmer where I worked had seven kids, including a baby nine weeks old, one a year-and-a-half, and a three-year-old, all in diapers. They were my responsibility. I had to milk fourteen cows by hand morning and night, cook for fourteen Polish war prisoners working on the farm, and cook for the whole family. Very simple meals—soup in the morning , for noon a big pot of potatoes in the peel and a big bowl of cottage cheese; that was it. Every day, no milk or butter. I had to wash the clothes and the whole house on my knees, scrubbing with a brush and a big bar of soap, from the attic to the downstairs, do field work, everything by hand. Grass was cut with a scythe and turned with a rake. Hay was put on a big horse-drawn wagon with a hayfork. I had to feed the pigs and three hundred chickens, a bunch of geese, and I had to milk. This went from four in the morning until 10 P.M. every day with no pay.

On the 6th day of May 1945 the first Russians came; actually they were Mongolians. They were told to do with the Germans what they wanted, and they did. Each Mongolian company consisted of twenty-one men, and they did everything in company strength: rape, from babies to grandmas, stealing everything, unbelievable cruelties, murder, whatever. A fourteen-year-old girl who lived on the farm next to us was raped twenty-one times by a unit of twenty-one soldiers. I was thirteen at the time and plenty scared but managed to hide whenever I felt threatened. They never raped my mother either, although she wouldn't have told me if they had.

I was in charge of the babies. One Mongolian hit the farmer's wife on the head with a vodka bottle. Another one hit the farmer over the head with the end of a gun. The farmer's wife told me to sneak out to the chickens' incubator and hide with the youngest baby. I went, and the baby started crying, so I put my sweater around his head so the Russians couldn't hear him or hear me praying that I wouldn't suffocate the baby.

That was the first group of Russians that came. They left after a few hours. But a new troupe came, and we hid in the rhubarb. One of our Polish prisoners told the Mongolians where we were, and some of the Mongolians shot through the field, killing an old man, a young woman, and a child from the farm next door.

They stole everything in sight, like doorknobs, light and water fixtures, rings, watches, vodka, horses, pigs, chickens—whatever they could get their hands on. We were told that they sent those things back to Russia. The water and light fixtures they would take home and thought if they put one in the wall or ceiling of their mud hut, water and light would come out. They washed potatoes and socks in the toilet, and everything disappeared when they flushed.

My brother picked me up from the farm at the end of July 1945. Although the war was over, there was still shooting going on, because there was no radio, and nobody knew the war had ended. All the bridges were blown up. My brother had an old bike with no seat, but a luggage rack. The tires were pieces of garden hose. We drove the bike until it fell totally apart. It took us a week to get home to Meissen, about forty or fifty miles away.

Everywhere there were dead horses, cows, and people. The horses had been mostly shot; the cows died because no one milked them, and there were dead civilians and soldiers of both sides. We stole everything we could find to eat. Chaos was everywhere.

When we finally arrived in Meissen, the Russians had occupied the town. My brother, a friend of his, and a girl were standing on the street, and one of the boys said, "That red flag does not belong on the mayor's building very long." We still believed we would win the war, because Hitler said he had a secret weapon. Anyway, the girl squealed on the boys. The Russians picked them up and imprisoned them in Albrechtsburg Prison, accusing them of belonging to an underground organization. The boys didn't even know what that was. They tortured them and gave them nothing or little food, in order to force them to confess.

My brother did not confess to belonging to the underground, and they let him go after a month. The other boy could not take the torture and confessed, so they put him to work in a uranium mine, where he died of typhoid fever. The boys were only fifteen and sixteen years old.

My brother fled to West Germany, but he wanted to be home for his seventeenth birthday on the fourth of June. There was no coal for the trains, so it took a long time for him to get home, the train moving every ten days or so. Consequently, the train was over-loaded. People hung onto the steps or bumpers between cars, or sat on the roof. My brother sat on the roof and hit his head on a bridge during the night. It was four days before his birthday in 1946. They picked him off the train in a little town called Kragenhof on the border between East and West Germany.

When I got back to Meissen from the farm in July 1945, all the bridges were still blown up. The Russians ordered one bridge rebuilt in two weeks, and the Germans did it, so we could go to the other side of the River Elbe. This bridge is still in good service today.

My mother found work for the director of the Singer Sewing Machine factory, and we moved out of the tiny two hundred-year-old house and into his beautiful villa, right on the river. I found a training place in a fashion atelier to learn dressmaking. I love to sew and started sewing for my teddy bear when I was five years old. When I was seven, I made the first dress for myself and wore it to school. No one believed I did it myself, all by hand.

When I was eight, I was allowed to use my grandma's sewing machine and sewed a little cape for her from an old jumper she didn't wear any more, and she wore it with great pride.

At this time I joined the Free German Youth Group, which was actually Communistic, but I didn't care. I wasn't interested in politics and didn't know about the Communists. I wanted to be with other young people, and these people played mouth organs, like me, plus other instruments. But, as you know, my mother loved Hitler, even though he was dead, and she did not like my associating with these people, so she told my master that I had joined the Communists, and she fired me.

That was OK. I was tired of being hungry all the time, because the Russians stole everything. We had one pound of bread that was mostly sawdust, one hundred grams of sugar, and one hundred grams of cream of wheat to last for ten days. No meat, no butter. We picked dandelions and made spinach or salad out of it, and we stole from the fields. That was very dangerous, because the fields were posted with people with guns. But the farmers did not give us anything if we did not have something to trade.

The Russians continued to rape and murder, and we always lived in fear. So I sneaked away to West Germany—many, many miles to walk. I got a job as a maid for the doctor who wrote the death certificate for my brother. He was buried in the town where the doctor lived. The doctor's wife was a bit mentally off. She was fifty-two years old and I always had to tell her that she was beautiful. She wore a pink teddy with a black belt and a big gold rose on the belt, a big cigar in her mouth, and walked around the town pond. I was only seventeen at the time; that meant I was under-age. My mother gave her the right to punish me if I did something she thought was wrong. For example, I was supposed to kill a beautiful rooster (I couldn't kill anything!) and save the blood. She slapped me because I did not kill the rooster, so she did it herself. She put dried plums and dried pears in the blood and forced me to eat it.

I worked there for almost two years and never had a day off. That was for ten Deutsch Marks a month. Housework, yard work, tending to the geese and chickens, cooking, sometimes helping in the practice giving ether or preparing medications.

One day there was a Fireman's Ball in town, and I was allowed to go with the next-door neighbors and their daughter. By 9:30 they wanted to go home. I was supposed to come home with them. So I did, and it was not far from the dance hall. I made like I went into the house but went back to the dance and danced until the end. The next morning she asked me if I came home with the neighbors. I said "Yes." I did not lie, because I did come home with them. But she had watched when the light went on at the neighbors, and I did not come in. So she beat the living h- - - out of me, and I was never allowed to go anywhere again. But I had fun; dancing was my life. (I danced ballet until I was forty-eight years old. I even danced in the Dresden Opera Children's Ballet.)

I left the doctor very soon after. His wife was too mean and crazy. She had a son twenty-six years old, and he was not allowed to have a girlfriend, so he killed himself.

From there I picked up my mother from East Germany and went to nursing school in Kassel, on the American side. My mother got a job at the hospital there. Nursing school was another place where you did not get paid but had to work long hours and very hard. Those long hallways had to be washed and waxed by hand on our knees and buffed with a heavy brush, every day. The beds had to be washed with Lysol every day. Especially the first year there, we were nothing but cleaning ladies. The second year we had to watch operations. I could not see blood and passed out. They said I would get used to it, but it did not work for me. In the third year, I quit.

Then I went to designing school for fashions and learned cutting all kinds of fabrics, designing, and all the tricks of the trade. I graduated after two years. From there I went to Austria to marry my husband (more about that later).

Now and then I sneaked back over the border. On one of these trips, I got caught by the Russians, and they locked me up with some other people in a very small cellar with nothing to eat or drink. There were sixty-five people, and we did not even have room enough for us all to sit down. Every two hours a few people were allowed to go to the bathroom. They kept us there for almost three days. Then they drove us back to the East German border. There were four Russians with guns walking with us, two in front, two in back. I saw a big haystack on the side of the road and made like I had to tie my shoe and fell back from the group. They kept on going, so I jumped behind the haystack. For some strange reason, they did not seem to miss me.

I walked until I came to a train station in the West zone. There was a young man there, and he said, "Oh, you are here too. I saw you in the cellar." He was very good-looking, and I wondered that he even looked at me, because I was used to being ugly, according to my mother. We rode a bit on some train; then he had to switch trains to go to Austria, where his sister lived. We exchanged addresses and wrote to each other for five years. Four years after we met, he invited me to come to Austria. I went for two weeks, and we got engaged. In February 1952 we got married.

Big mistake—it was very bad. He was a control freak and beat me up constantly. I was not allowed to talk, only when I was asked. The night before the wedding, he called me a stupid goose and beat me. I had to go to my wedding with a black eye. Because I did not fight back, he kept it up. I wanted a divorce, but in Austria it is allowed to beat your wife, and he threatened to kill me if I left him.

One day he sent me shopping, and I forgot the money and had to go back home. There he was lying in bed with a fifteen-year-old neighbor girl. I was so shocked and called him a "pig." He beat me unconscious; I was all colors from top to bottom. As he slapped me, he said if I told anyone he would kill me. But I told his parents what he did when they came to visit, and his mother wanted to beat me too! I didn't care any more if he killed me. That was no life anyway.

After six years of marriage, I found out he had a child with someone else. The lady we visited where he was stationed during the war said, "I saw Sibile the other day. That kid looks like somebody ripped it off your back. You cannot say it is not yours." So I asked him about it, and he slapped me right in front of that lady.

That was the night I left him. I thought that if he finds me and kills me, so what. I put in for divorce right away. We lived at the time in Frankfurt. It took three years for the divorce to become final in March 1960. In the meantime, he kidnapped our daughter Anita and took her to his mother in Austria. I never got her back, because she had Austrian citizenship, and if I would have tried to take her to Germany, I would be arrested.

I worked for a time in an American laundry, where I did alterations. Bob Griffith, a young American serviceman, used to come in to work pressing uniforms. He always winked at me and flirted. But I did not want anything to do with an American because you got a very bad reputation if you did. (My mother called me an "Ami whore.") He took me home every night after work, although for six weeks I did not speak a word to him. I didn't speak to ANY American serviceman. One day he said, "If I marry you, will you speak to me?" I had to laugh and thought 'the war is long over, and he was much too young to be involved in WWII.' He was only twenty-six years old. I was thirty but he thought I was seventeen because I only weighed ninety-eight pounds and had a long blonde ponytail.

Anita and her daughter Bobbie

He gave me a little German-English book so I could look up what he said to me in English. He said such very nice things to me. All of a sudden I was pretty and sweet, not worthless and ugly any more. I just ate it up; I felt so good. And I fell madly in love with him. He was in the Military Police and stationed in Frankfurt.

When I took him home to meet my mother, I insisted he wear civilian clothes so she wouldn't know he was an American serviceman. Of course she recognized him as American once he spoke, and she had plenty to say to him. I was so embarrassed! However, Bob and I got married the same year, in September 1960, in my apartment. My mother was there and a few friends of his and a priest. I didn't understand a word they said, and I just said "Yes" and "Amen."

In August 1962, my daughter Bobbie Jane was born. In February the following year Bob got transferred back to the States. I had to wait until my papers were processed because I was born in East Germany; they had to know if I were a Nazi or Communist, a prostitute, or whatever. In August 1963 I followed him to Fort Ord in California. Everything was very well organized; a lady picked me up in New York and took me to a place where Bob picked me up. In all, it took thirty-six hours, and I had one-year-old Bobbie in a box on my lap. It was all extremely tiring.

When we got to Fort Ord, he set me up in a little motel and

said he had duty and had to go. I was so tired, I only wanted to sleep. He said that our little white house he always wrote about was not quite finished. I was too tired to care.

The next morning at eight o'clock there was a knock on the door. I was very sleepy and thought 'they sure wake up people early here.' I opened the door, and there was a lady with three kids. She said, "I'm Mrs. Griffith." I said, "Oh, I'm Mrs. Griffith, too." I thought it was his sister, because he told me there was only his sister and grandmother by the name of "Griffith."

She continued, "I'm not giving him a divorce; I need him for my kids." I had to look in my little book to find out what she was saying, and I almost fainted. What happened here? He had a wife and three kids?!! The youngest was eight months older than my daughter with Bob. Dear God, what now!?

I had sold all my belongings so I would have enough money to come to the States. I had to leave my older daughter behind, because my ex would not sign the papers I needed to take her along. I didn't have a home; my mother didn't want me, and I never told her that the wedding was a sham. She never believed me anyway. She often made up things, then beat me for things I did not do.

So, now I had no money, no home, and a husband who was really not my husband. But he swore he loved only me and wanted me to stay. He sent his wife and kids back to New York. I was in total confu-

Schatze, the most adorable pup you can imagine, is a rescue from an abusive situation, fortunate indeed to have found a new and loving home with Anita.

sion; how can I trust him after he did what he did?   But I had no money to go back to Germany, and I still loved him. I was his wife for almost three years, and we had a child. He was always so good to me and said all those nice things. So he convinced me to stay and get really married, although it took a few years, because his wife didn't want to give him a divorce.

Bob retired from the Army after fifteen years, and we moved to upstate New York. I kept busy with my own fabric store and sewing professionally. Later, I closed the store because the landlord was after me, and I turned him down, so he did not renew my lease. Then I worked in a mental hospital. Nineteen seventy-six was a hard year: I divorced Bob because he could not be faithful, I broke my neck when a patient attacked me, and my house burned down, losing everything. The following year I moved with Bobbie to Colorado Springs, where I had a good friend who encouraged me.

My first husband, Karl the control freak, is eighty-six years old in 2013 and living in Austria. He is separated from his latest wife. Our daughter Anita lives in Majorca, Spain, where she works with horses—dressage, jumping, riding, etc. I have always stayed in contact with her. Bobbie lives in Virginia and has two children of her own. Bob remarried, but that wife died. We stayed friends until he died in 2007. He asked me to come when it was close to the end. He apologized for all he had done to me and died with my hand in his. I still live in Colorado Springs, and at eighty-three years old, I am happy here.

All that I went through was because of the war. It was not easy, but it made me stronger. And, I did find out that you can love your enemy, even **MARRY** him. So, why in heaven's name do we make wars?! and haven't learned that wars only bring death and destruction, incredible heartache and misery, and **NOBODY WINS.**

⊰ Gernot Heinrichsdorff ⊱

Gernot's account gives a complete and detailed description of life on the front and his training that preceded it. Were his experiences as well as anxieties much different from those experienced by his American counterparts?

The author has known Gernot for at least fifty years in Colorado Springs. He is a highly respected landscape designer and artist. Gernot and his talented wife Ava are active members of the cultural community of that city.

I was born in Munich to Irma Franzen in 1925. I had an older sister, Waltraud, and we were both born out of wedlock. My mother was a unique individual for her time; she always said she'd been born in the wrong century. She consorted with freethinkers, sometimes lived in a nudist park, wanted to work for a salary, and believed in women's equality. All this was outrageous for a "girl of good family."

She dreamed of having a landscape architect's firm and asked her family to support and finance it. Unfortunately, they did not approve of her ambition, although it would have made her self-sufficient. She did

Gernot's mother, Irma Franz

A younger Gernot

have a profession, having studied landscape architecture and worked in England, and she became the first female landscape architect on the European continent.

When I was a few months old, we moved to Dresden, where she worked for the city as a landscape architect. From Dresden we moved to Klingberg, on the Baltic Sea. There my mother worked for the famous landscape architect Harry Maasz. We lived in a "nude park," a community of nudists.

In 1929, when I was four, we moved to Nordseebad Dangast, a fishing village and summer tourist village on the North Sea. Mother's family bought her a decrepit house there, where she would live far away from the family in Witten so as not to embarrass them. However, in Dangast she had no opportunity to work as a landscape architect. It was far from any city, with no market for nursery stock.

The house we lived in needed a lot of repair, with no indoor plumbing, minimal heating, a leaky roof, etc., yet she managed. She started a *Kinderheim* (children's summer home like a summer camp) and opened a vegetarian restaurant. These were difficult years for her, a single mom with two children. I remember that one summer she had seventy-two guests to cook for besides the summer children. I found myself in a different world, where the population spoke Low German, barely understandable to my High German. It was difficult for me to make friends, and I frequently got into fights with other boys.

In 1933, Adolf Hitler came to power. At the time, I was visiting family in Witten, and I joined the *Hitlerjugend* (Hitler Youth). I was eight years old. In the *Hitlerjugend* I started to become a good athlete. I was good in most sports, especially track events, and advanced to regional leadership in the youth group. The Hitler Youth in Dangast never felt "political." We had games, sports, and nature study, and in our village it was similar to Boy Scouts. I even taught sports in addition to my own track specialties—playing soccer and European handball. After the war, I realized how different the *Hitlerjugend* was in other regions, especially in cities.

In Dangast, I went to public school. Unfortunately, the teacher in Dangast neglected the academic subjects and stressed only sports. Therefore, my mother put me in private school to catch up on my education so that I could qualify for *Gymnasium* (high school). At age fourteen, children are tested; college-bound students go to *Gymnasium;* others go to trade schools. But this private school was not the best either, and it didn't prepare me well enough for *Gymnasium*. I couldn't qualify but it was too expensive anyway, located in a town ten miles away, and transportation was difficult. Since I couldn't go to *Gymnasium*, I went to the *Handelsschule*, a school for commercial trades people, and I earned my *"Mittlere Reife,"* the diploma that let one enter a trade.

Around 1938, Peter and Jochen Wuerfl came to Dangast for

the summer in the *Kinderheim,* and for some reason could not return to their home in the fall, so they became part of our family. At the time, I did not know why. When some summer sessions ended, sometimes certain children could not be sent home because they had no home to return to; their parents had disappeared. I learned in 1940 that Peter and Jochen's mother was Jewish. These boys' parents had sometimes visited my mother as her guests for several months, when they were hiding from the Berlin government. They were without ration cards since Jews didn't get those. Then they vanished and afterward died in a concentration camp.

Kotja Kaal also came and could not go home to Estonia because of the war, so he too joined our family. All three were a bit younger than I. My mother received little compensation for their care, sometimes none at all. She kept them as her own and raised them to adulthood. However, she did remove them from membership in the *Hitlerjugend*—"for medical reasons." The entire village protected them, including Edo Pille, their teacher in Daganst's one-room schoolhouse, who was in the Gestapo and SS. There was one eager SS man, Vogel, whom my mother and others in the village somehow managed to appease in this situation. My mother often had to entertain and placate high-ranking Nazi Party members and Gestapo. For years she risked her life for these children. After the war, during warcrimes trials, my mother testified on Herr Pille's behalf, and he was released. Few Americans realize that some Germans were human enough to not follow the Nazi Party's dictates about Jews.

During vacation from the *Handelsschule,* I joined a special section of the *Hitlerjugend* to learn to build model airplanes, since I was most interested in airplanes. Then I went to a *flugschule* to learn to fly *(Segel-flugschule)*. First it was gliding, then further sailplane training. After the *Handelsschule,* I applied to a school in Leipzig to become a commercial artist. But the *Arbeitsamt,* the Department of Labor, did not allow that. "Germany needs blue-collar workers!" they said. Unfortunately, I had only my

Mittlere Reife, not the Gymnasium diploma that would have let me go into a more intellectual profession.

So I started as an apprentice airplane mechanic at an airplane engine factory at Varel, ten miles from Dangast. At least I loved airplanes. From January to July of 1943 I had to join the mandatory RAD *Reicharbeitsdients* (working force). We built roads for military installations. After RAD, I returned to the factory and worked my way up to be certified as a *Flugmotorengeselle.*

In September of 1943, shortly after becoming certified, I was drafted into the army at age eighteen. But I was sick with hepatitis so was deferred. After I recovered, people looked at me strangely, since I was of draft age yet still running around at home. "What is wrong with him?" they wondered. So I went to the draft board in Oldenburg. They looked through a heavy file and found to our astonishment that by my name was no entry date at all. I had been overlooked. But now I had been "found" and was drafted, the day before Christmas 1943.

After meeting a *Ritterkreuztraeger* pilot, (meaning one who had been awarded the Knight's Cross medal), I was "discovered" as one who should be receiving pilot training. That changed my life! I had been doomed to be a blue-collar worker, but I was moved right away to a different unit and railed to Angiers, France, for basic training. After basic training would be the opportunity to go to the *Luftkriegsschule* (Air Force Academy), which was like going to college or university. It would give me better chances in my future.

From Angiers we were moved to Auxerre for further basic training. "I hope you don't get 'The Tiger of Auxerre' for your sergeant!" I was told. That man was known as the toughest and meanest basic training sergeant in all of France.

Of course I was assigned to him, and he was all that was said of him—small, with a heavy pig-face and a stubble beard.

One day our group had decided not to take our gas masks into the field, since we had never used them in training. Then he noticed. "Who told you to leave your gas masks behind?" he shouted. No one stepped forward, because it had been just a general agreement among us. I knew what was coming to the entire group, so I stepped forward. I got the treatment—crawling and running and more for an hour around the wet field. But after that he became friendly toward me and favored me in whatever we were doing. He respected my "confession."

From Auxerre we were sent to the most northern part of Denmark for pre-pilot training with sailplanes (gliders). I was in paradise; my dream was coming through. As a pilot, I would become an officer, elevated to a higher level in my life.

After a couple weeks our instructor was not satisfied with our landings. "You come down like a ship in the water! Are you afraid? Come closer, brake, and land!" So I decided to show him. When I was flying from Frederickshaun in Denmark I could see Sweden. Exhilarating! Approaching my landing, the field was coming closer. "Wait!" I said to myself. "Did he not instruct us, 'Come close, put the landing flaps out, and land.' Still too early, "OK, NOW!" Going down, flaps engaged, I saw my group running frantically away. I looked around; maybe another plane was close? We had had a problem a few days previously when two planes collided. But everything looked okay to me. I leveled out but overestimated my height, hit the ground, and bounced the glider thirty feet into the air. Then I landed all right and came to a stop. I looked down. Damn! I was standing on GRASS! The entire undercarriage of my plane was missing.

It must have happened when I bumped and adjusted my forward direction. I had destroyed the plane. The angry instructor ordered me to spend the entire day and evening running, pushing a dolly from one group to another around the airfield, saluting each group and announcing, "I destroyed a plane." We had few planes, and none to spare.

But I was alive, and they let me stay. I was luckier than eight others in my group, who were released because of casualties or inadequate skills. At the end of our academy training, eighteen of our group of thirty-six had made it.

After pre-training, I entered the *Luftskriegsschule,* the Air Force Academy in Oschatz, near Dresden. In my first piloting of a motorized plane, with my instructor on board, I just flew around the airfield and landed again, three times. Then he said, "You are ready. Go!" He meant I should go solo, and he got out of the plane. I was scared of course, but in the air I caught myself talking to the empty seat next to me. "Jawohl! Yes, Sergeant! Keep the plane level; stick to the right to make that curve! Jawohl!" I was flying!

Unfortunately, it took a long time for half of the group to fly solo, and when my turn finally came again, I was worse than a novice.

One time on an overland flight, I suddenly saw little white clouds around my plane. Looking down, I saw a bunch of Messerschmidt Me 363s and knew I was over forbidden territory. The little white clouds were anti-aircraft flak. I flew down fast through openings in the woods below and found my way out of their range. I never reported it; I would have been dismissed.

The academy did a lot of sports. In October of that year, there was a big sporting event in Oschatz, and I was allowed to participate, representing the Academy. I ran the 100-meter sprint in 10.2 seconds, so I was put on the Armed Forces' list to participate in the next Olympics, if and when those games would ever take place again. I had equaled Jesse Owens' best time at that point in his career; he surpassed it after that.

Then we were transferred to another Air Force Academy near Vienna for more training. There I learned to fly the Messerschmidt Me 109, the famous fighter plane. But Germany unfortunately ran out of gas that month, and that put an end to all flying.

Consequently, in late 1944 we became Infantry soldiers, without any knowledge or training for that. We marched forty kilometers to Vienna and were placed near the *Westbahnbruecke* (West Railroad Bridge), where our job was to keep the Russians from crossing the Danube River.

We dug in on the north side of the river. An elderly soldier appeared—we didn't know from where—and helped us in a fatherly manner. He must have realized that we had no idea what we should be doing. He went up and down among our groups and instructed us.

During the night we heard the Russians progress on the other side of the river. We heard only a few shots fired back and forth. In the morning we found our "father-friend" dead. He had been shot in that little exchange of fire. He was our first casualty; it was a sobering start to our Infantry experience.

In the early morning, we dug in on a table-mountain, a "mesa." The mesa overlooked a flat area with agricultural fields. In the middle, about half a mile away, was a farm village. We watched. In the afternoon, a Russian tank came to the village center, very much in my view. It stopped, and a figure appeared on top. Then other vehicles came and went frequently. I realized that it must be a command post. It was far away, actually out of my range, but I had tracer ammunition, and I tried. My first shot was far short. The second was better; I aimed far over my sight and came close. After a few shots the fellow on the tank must have realized that he was in a dangerous spot, and the tank moved out of sight.

At dusk, I heard engine sounds and a Russian tank appeared on the road below me. Some soldiers of a different German unit shot something at the tank and crippled it. After a while, a Russian soldier appeared on the tank, jumped off, and disappeared into the night.

In the middle of the night, I woke up in my hole hearing voices down below the slope. They weren't speaking German. I threw a few hand grenades downhill, shot a few shots with my rifle, and the voices stopped. It became eerily quiet.

After a while, figures appeared all around me in the dark. I dug down in my hole; to my left and right, figures passed me. Then more approached. I realized that I had been overrun by a Russian attack, but still there was no shooting. All was quiet except for the dark figures' voices. Where was my company?

What to do? I was behind the enemy lines! I could not go forward toward the Russian lines or they would shoot me. But if I went toward our own lines, I would be shot by our own troops. Everything was still quiet. I took the second choice and jumped out of my hole, hoping for good luck. On both sides, figures and a line. I moved slowly, let some pass, moving to the right. After a while, no more figures, no voices, but off to the left where I had come from, gunfire began. What a strange war. Fighting was only in spots, between empty areas—that was my luck, so far.

After the war I found the address of the lieutenant who was our company leader, and I visited him. He was surprised to see me. "I thought you were dead! We had to take the front line a quarter mile back, but we couldn't find you to tell you that. Then we heard the shooting in front of us, which must have been you."

I hurried farther and farther in the German line direction. Just before daybreak I came to a busy road crowded with Germans who were moving back, chaotically. I "mingled."

We approached a village as it grew light, and I saw soldiers hanging from trees. Signs on their bodies said "Deserter." "What is going on?" I asked. No one answered. One tree bore a sign *"Auffangslager"* (Reassignment Center), and I was directed there. Sitting on the ground were soldiers waiting to be interrogated and reassigned. I joined them.

When it was my turn, I went into a room where two stern officers sat behind a table. I told them what had happened to me and asked to be directed to my unit. They asked me, "Have you deserted?" I realized that these men were the hangmen. I was in real danger. I pulled my rifle closer to me and said, not knowing if it was true, "General Wessely has his headquarters nearby." Noticing my gesture, they stopped questioning me and ordered me outside to wait for an assignment.

An hour passed. Then the Russian artillery started firing at the village. I saw the two officers and a small number of soldiers get into two trucks that were loaded with furniture. In the front seats were some women. They drove away. Then I knew that *they* were deserters, covering their retreat with *"Auffangslager"* and the hanging of soldiers.

After a while the truck arrived for us who were waiting. It took the eight of us to our newly-assigned unit—an Infantry battalion. As a cadet, I had the highest rank and so became the leader of our tired, frightened group. We were of many ages; one was just a boy, and one had gray hair.

We were ordered to scout the woods in front of us, without making contact, to see if the Russians were advancing. We took an old wagon road into the forest. I told the group to spread out just far enough so we could still see one another and communicate. I started out, but soon found myself walking alone through the woods. Almost at the end of the woods, I'd seen no enemies, so I rushed back and found my group huddled by the road almost where I had left them. "We took cover," they explained. So much for my first assignment.

Late the next day we came to our destination. The earliest we could expect contact with the Russians was the next morning, we were told. That meant a good night's sleep. It was only February but we had lovely, fragrant, spring-like days; the trees were in bud. I made myself a comfortable bed of autumn leaves and bedded down. It was peacefully quiet. Then, above the slope where I was lying, I heard singing: *"Auf der Heide blueht ein kleines Bluemlein. . ."* (In the Meadow Blooms a Little Flower . . .). I remembered lying on the branch of my favorite "leopard tree" at home in my childhood, listening to the sounds of the village. The singing went on for an hour, and I could tell that the soldiers up there must be drunk.

When morning came, quiet and beautiful, little drops on the twigs looked like diamonds in the rising sun. A patrol came down the hill and reported that the entire group of soldiers up there had disappeared. Either they had been taken by the Russians during the night, or they had deserted.

A motorcycle drove up to us from below, and on the back seat sat a Russian soldier. "I picked him up on my way," said the driver, a German ordnance officer. "He probably got lost in the woods." That Russian became our company's "mascot," riding wherever the driver had to deliver orders. What a strange, welcome, and humorous disconformity in this dangerous setting of a deadly war!

Like a scene in a film or in a Grimm fairy tale, that afternoon a *Gelaendewagen* (VW jeep) drove up, and a general stepped out of the passenger side. He wore a coat, binoculars hung from his neck, and he carried a map under his arm. He talked to our commander, walked up the hill in plain sight of our enemies, returned to his car, and drove off. With Russians all around us, he strolled as if on an outing, as if immune to danger. And he didn't even wear a halo.

The village before us, Losdorf in Czechoslovakia, had been taken by the Russians. It was nestled in a valley between two mesas. We were ordered to counterattack. On our way toward the village we had passed a company on foot. They were in Air Force uniforms. I was sure they were from the Air Force Academy, but I was now with a different group.

We were supposed to take the left flank, the hillside on the village's east. It was house-to-house combat. During a little break in the gunfire, I looked to the opposite hillside to the west and saw a group of Russians advancing, bent on encircling our troops in the village. I shot over the valley to the other side to discourage their progress.

That became my worst memory of the war. It gave me nightmares, and occasionally still does. As if I were sitting in front of a war-game machine in a game parlor, I shot one soldier after another. Like the clay figures in a game machine, they fell one by one.

At that time, of course, I was thinking only of my comrades in the village about to be surrounded by the enemy. But in my nightmares, I was a murderer. Each of these soldiers had a mother, wife, sweetheart, or children. I ended their lives; I was a murderer, a murderer even though they would have done the same thing if they had encircled us in the village. The strange facts of war. War gives you not only the license to kill but the order to kill, and to feel justified. It reminded me of the last words of "Cornet" by Rainer Maria Rilke: *"Ich hab eine Mutter winend gesehen."* I saw a mother in tears when her loved one did not come back.

The German Army was in retreat and disorganized. My rank from the Academy did not fit in the Infantry, but we muddled into battle anyway. I was more or less equal to an Infantry sergeant or higher rank.

Late that afternoon, just before dark, I was wounded by shrapnel in my thigh. Blood filled my boot. I yelled to the guy next to me in the noisy gunfire, "Take over, it got me!" Slowly I crawled back and just by luck found a Red Cross station behind our lines.

They moved me to a field hospital, and from there I was transported to a hospital in Linz, Austria, for surgery. When I entered that hospital, a doctor tapped me on the shoulder and said, "Now you can leave your rifle here. You will not need it any longer." But I clung to it. It had saved my life at the *Auffanglsager*, and I did not want to let it go from my side. Yet, I finally did let it go as the doctor ordered.

ODE TO MY RIFLE

In war your rifle is your closest companion
Your partner, your comrade, your cohort, your mate
You talk to it, handle it as tenderly as a sweetheart.
Your rifle is the one thing that can keep you alive,
And you keep it alive.
A silent partnership.

G.H.

In the hospital I met a wounded friend from the Academy, and we stayed together until we were released by the Americans in July of 1947.

We got papers ordering us to report to a recovery center about forty kilometers from Linz. But the Russians were marching from the east in that direction, so we thought this was not a good idea. We put our papers into our socks, and would say, if anyone asked, that we had lost them. We wanted to get as far west as possible.

So we stood on the highway hoping to hitchhike. A troop convoy came by, and we boarded the last truck. "At your own risk!" the driver told us. He took us out of pity, because my leg and my friend's arm and head were heavily bandaged.

A night, a day—we were going west. But at nine o'clock that second night, the driver abruptly stopped and came to the back. "A control! Get out!" Quickly we rolled into a trench next to the highway. The control men checked down the line and then stood by our truck, the last one, not leaving until every other vehicle had gone on.

All night we hid in the ditch. The next morning we went to the nearest village, Woergel. A schoolhouse there had been made into a hospital, and they took us in.

Shortly after we "settled" in Woergel, the war ended. The Russians had stopped five kilometers east of the village, so luckily we were in the American Zone.

Released from the hospital, we were transported to a "Holding Area for Prisoners of War" south of Munich. It was about a square mile in size, without many guards. Food from the Americans was brought in by truck. About 20,000 of us POWs were held there, I was told.

I was put to work in the kitchen. Some of that square mile was forested, and I collected mushrooms for our meals, *Lowendzahn* (lions' teeth), dandelions for our salads, and other edibles.

One day strolling through the woods I came onto a surprise— airplanes covered by netting. These included the latest models of Messerschmit Arados, and others—all the latest jets. Did the Americans know about these? I wondered. No guards, just trees. The planes looked like a bunch of dogs tied to trees, sad, lost, forlorn. What a sad sight! I kept it to myself.

Writing about this now, it reminds me of the remnants of the Mayan civilization in Guatemala, a civilization that had once existed, but no more.

Germany was divided into French, English, Russian, and American zones of occupation. In July of 1945, my friend and I volunteered to work for the Americans, because we couldn't go home yet. My home, like his, was in the English-occupied zone, and no transfer from one zone to another was allowed. So in July of 1945, we joined the Volunteer Company of Prisoners of War to work for the American Depot Company of the 44th Air Squadron. It was housed in the BMW plant in Munich. We formed an entire company in the German tradition, from captain to soldier, with loose though voluntary discipline.

We had been allowed to send just one postcard home to say that we were alive. But my mother never received the one I sent, and until July of 1947 she did not know if I were dead or alive.

I volunteered as an office clerk because my leg was still too weak for heavy work. I was put in the office as a typist, managing transfers of everything from heavy equipment parts to cloth—everything the American Air Force could need. But they soon found out that my typing was not the best, and I was afraid I'd be ordered to work heavy labor. I had visited around the BMW plant where some German civilians were still work-ing, and when talking to a girl in the printing office, I got an idea. I suggested it to the master sergeant in our office. "All those different documents and papers are confusing. Why not use different colors of paper for different jobs?"

"Excellent idea!" he said. "I can arrange that," I offered. It saved my office job. As a matter of fact, I was elevated to a VIP.

This was in the days of segregation of the American Armed Forces, and the entire 1951 Depot Company was Black. When I became acquainted with some white officers in their Officers Club, I could not believe how they spoke about the Blacks in "my" company. I was shocked and puzzled. I became good friends with our Black master sergeant, our office boss, and invited him for dinner in our room at the plant. He complained, "We fought together with the Whites in Monte Casino in Italy, we were friends, we saved each others' lives, but now we do not exist for them. We only work for them. No communica-tion with each other at all."

Yet, unbelievably, this man was an admirer of Hitler. Hitler, who despised Blacks? Why? What "information" had he been given? Later, when I moved to the United States, I wished that I had his address. I would have liked to see him again; he was a fine person.

Cigarettes were more valuable than money. All of us in the company gave our cigarette rations to the captain, and in return he got us the best food—officers' food. He traded cigarettes for food from the country.

For days, a jeep stood forlornly in front of our office. After a week I ventured to get into it and drive it through the plant. Somehow it then became "my" jeep. People would ask me if they could borrow it, and I insisted that the borrower fill it with gas before returning it.

One day it was very low on gas, so I put three sticks of gum in my mouth to disguise my accent, drove to the filling station inside the plant, and said in my briskest English, "Fillerup!"

"Okay, open the gas tank, I'll be right there."

But where the hell was the gas tank? I couldn't find it. The attendant looked at me strangely, pulled up the right-side seat, and uncapped and filled the tank. Live and learn.

The main gate was serviced by Polish guards. I was itching to drive out that gate into the city of Munich, so I wrote myself a trip ticket (these were now pink), signed it "Sergeant Heinrichsdorff," gassed up, and drove my jeep to the gate. Again with three sticks of gum in my mouth, of course. We prisoners wore American uniforms that had the big letters POW on the back, so I leaned back against the letters, flourished my pink ticket, and was waved through without any problem.

I didn't drive far, afraid of being stopped by military police. I didn't dare go to the important Munich "sights." I just enjoyed the temporary freedom of being outside the prison camp BMW plant.

In Munich, there was some underground movement activity, so the American soldiers were instructed to take weapons with them on their days off duty. One hundred-sixty pistols were delivered to our office for their use. Since all American office personnel were overloaded with work, the master sergeant said, "Gernot doesn't have much to do; he can take care of it." So I became the "guardian of weaponry" of the 1951 Depot Company. On Saturdays I signed the pistols out. They had to be returned by 10 o'clock sharp on Monday, and I threatened the soldiers with drastic late penalties. They respectfully obeyed. A good job for a POW.

Behind our living quarters was a convenient and frequently-used hole in the fence, but I did not have to use it. The guards at the main gate recognized me and always waved me through.

Ruth Essig had been my family's neighbor in Dangast. I don't know how she knew I was in the BMW plant, but she and I went every Tuesday to the Unitarian Church to attend a discussion group. We had some great times at those discussions.

In July 1947, I was released from the 44th Air Supply Squadron and released from being a prisoner of war. I was sent home to Dangast by railway. What a surprise for my mother and sister, after not hearing a word from me for a great many months.

Our home was surrounded by a Canadian military camp, so I needed special permission to enter that area. Only a few days after I arrived home, the Canadian police came to our home and arrested me for having been in the *Freicorps Adolf Hitler Verdaechtig*—a postwar underground movement. I told them that I had been on the front, not at home at all, not in any underground. Later I found out that people who wanted to "make friends" with the Canadians had turned me in. "You are a Nazi

Party member," they told me, and I denied it. Then they even gave me my Party number. Later, I found out that leaders of the *Hitlerjugend* were automatically enlisted in the Party, so that must have happened when I was still in the Academy or at the front.

So I was arrested and interned in a former concentration camp in Westertimke for more than seven months.

Every morning we had a line-up. Sometimes we had to stand for an hour or more in wind and every kind of weather. Several prisoners who had been arrested at night were without shoes and had to stand there half-dressed and barefoot, with just a rag around their feet. We were about 250 prisoners in camp and were given very little food. I lost fifty pounds in just a couple of months and developed the heart trouble that one gets from starvation.

To avoid going crazy, we created meetings for learning, learning anything from skills to literature. One *Oberst* (colonel) gave lectures on poetry and could recite Goethe's "Faust" from memory.

One prisoner was an American, perhaps a deserter, perhaps Jewish. We didn't know how he ended up in this camp. He had not been released when the war ended, and of course he complained bitterly.

After seven months I was told, " Tomorrow you are getting out." That was on a Monday. But on Wednesday the colonel was reciting "Faust," and I was eager to hear that. I went to the commandant and asked him to release me on Wednesday after the recital. The commandant looked at me for several minutes, disbelieving but curious. Then he said, "You better get out while you can, "Faust" or no "Faust." So I left on Tuesday.

I later found out that Peter Wurfl, the Jewish boy my mother had protected and who had lived with us, had gone to the camp to argue for my release. The Polish commandant told him,

"Leave right now, or we will keep you here, too."

Two months after my return home, I was almost arrested again. A Canadian officer with a Frau Wegbner, who had been hired as interpreter, came to accuse me of burying weapons in the garden. A Canadian who came with them said he had seen me burying these and showed the exact place. I had planted some seedlings in that area, using a planter that had a pistol handle, and this planter was still stuck in the ground. So we parted with a laugh; they were satisfied.

I found work at a nursery but had to quit after a week because it was too far away. It took five hours to bicycle there and back, so I could work only about three hours. But while I worked there, I had to report to the police every seventy-two hours in a different district. I never changed back, and everybody forgot I was supposed to make these seventy-two hour reports.

In January of 1948 I got "De-Nazified" and was erased from the Nazi list. That year and in 1949 my mother and I established a perennial nursery. Since she was a landscape architect, she got permission to be my "master," although I had to work three days a week in another nursery in Varel. I also had to attend business school in Oldenburg. In 1949 I became a Certified Gardener and attended the Horticultural Research Institute in Bonn-Godesberg, which was part of the University of Bonn. Passing my exams there, I became a Certified *Gardentechniker*—a garden technician. I had to find temporary work elsewhere because I couldn't find work in horticulture, but later I did find summer work in landscape construction at a nursery in Godesberg. I designed several gardens there, including part of a garden for the American General Clay and one for the Vatican Embassy, so I did well.

I had applied for immigration to the U.S. but there was a law at that time that prohibited my going because of my *Hitlerjugend* involvement. Peter and Jochen had already moved there in a special program for surviving Jews and others. Before I was allowed to emigrate I found temporary, relevant employment in Switzerland and in Sweden. Finally, in 1952 I received a letter from the American Embassy stating that the law which had prohibited my going to the U.S. because I "had been a Nazi" had been nullified, and I was free to go.

Jochen got me a sponsor in Baltimore, and on November 26 I boarded the *Italia* at Bremerhaven, bound for New York. But when I saw the shore of Europe disappear, I had goose pimples. Peter and his fiancée Elsa met me in New York. I still wondered if I was doing the right thing.

For more about Gernot and his remarkable mother Irma, see SAME WAR DIFFERENT BATTLEFIELDS (beginning page 256), previously cited.

Gernot, as handsome as ever

Alex Baumgartner

Readers may get the impression from reading Alex's memoir that everything that happened in the rest of this collection of memoirs also happened to Alex. And surely, repetition serves to reinforce the situations and conditions being described throughout the book; there was enough adversity, drama, and suffering to go around, and around, and around.

I am a German from Russia but not *"Volga Deutscher,"* a term with which American readers may be more familiar. *"Volga Deutsch"* refers to the Germans Catherine the Great induced to settle in the Volga area under similar terms and situations as the later settlers described below. I am a "Black Sea" German, born just west of Odessa, five miles north of the Black Sea, in the Ukraine. There are many Germans from Russia in the High Plains states, but only Colorado is home to the "Volga" immigrants; the Dakotas, Nebraska, etc. contain the population from the Black Sea.

A brief background history follows. In a series of campaigns against the Turks in the late 1700s, Russia obtained vast territories north of the Black Sea. Czar Alexander I, grandson of Catherine the Great, realized the need to develop these territories, and in 1803 he extended an invitation to foreigners, particularly Germans, to settle on the virgin steppes of New Russia, in the southern Ukraine. Like Catherine's original offer in the late 1700s to settle German immigrants around the Volga, the terms were generous: religious freedom, exemption from taxation for ten years, and exemption from military service. In the late 1800s, some of these concessions were withdrawn, and times grew hard for descendants of the original immigrants, which brought many to America.

The last picture of Alex Baumgartner's family, August 1944. Standing - Ingrid, Alex, Anna. In front - parents and Hedwig.

My ancestor Johann Friedrich Baumgartner settled with his family in Grossliebental, a small German colony/village in the south Ukraine near Odessa, in 1806. Grossliebental means "big, lovely valley." The settlers were from the Stuttgart area and spoke the Stuttgart dialect. My father Alexander, born in 1899, worked for the railroad as a young man, doing manual labor, but in 1927 he had the opportunity to attend a German, teacher's college in Odessa. He made a career of teaching and also served as a principal in a nearby village. The village was located outside the political activity during Stalin's years of terror in 1936-38, which probably saved him from being arrested during that time.

I was born in 1926 and had three younger sisters. We had German schools in our colonies, with Russian and Ukrainian language classes starting in the fourth grade. Beginning in the 1936-37 school year, everything was converted to the Russian language. We continued to learn German, but as a foreign language. That made school hard for the farm boys, who did not speak Russian. Even some of the teachers did not speak Russian very well.

In 1939 my father was transferred back to Grossliebental,

where the family had continued to live, and life was very hard at that time. I had one pair of trousers, which were probably made by my mother from hand-me-downs. I had one pair of shoes that were glued together, so when they got wet, the sole separated, and the shoes had to be glued again. There was a shortage of everything, but the government would not admit it and did not issue ration cards to distribute the few available products evenly. When a delivery was made to one of the local stores, the news spread like fire that something would be available the next morning. People started to form lines the night before, although many times you did not know what had arrived, but whatever it was, you could use it. Sometimes the announced quantity ran out before the quota was reached. We suspected officials confiscated it for their own use or sold it on the black market.

The assassination in Leningrad in 1934 of Sergey Kirow, Secretary of the Communist Party, triggered the beginning of Stalin's reign of terror. The trials and executions that followed Stalin's accusations of "conspiracy" worked themselves down to every village and to every family. In our village of about 3,500 people, over 600 men, along with a few women, were arrested. The distance of my father's work from that political ferment perhaps saved him from being arrested.

During the night between one and four o'clock, the police car would drive through the town and pick up men. They would knock on the door and say that the man of the house had to come along to the police station to answer some questions. Everyone knew they would never come back. They were taken to the local jail, then transferred to Odessa. One time I was standing in the schoolyard nearby and saw how these men were loaded onto the truck to be transferred to Odessa. They walked to an open truck and had to lie down so they could not be seen. Two police officers with guns sat at each end of the truck, and it departed.

After a few weeks, the wives would be informed that the men had been transferred to a different division of the NKVD, which claimed they had no information about where these men were at present. (The NKVD was a Russian political and domestic department of security, similar to the FBI.) Only after the collapse of the Soviet government in the 1990s did we learn that most of these men were shot, and some of the younger ones were sent to Siberia.

My uncle Viktor, a college professor who taught languages, was arrested in the winter of 1937. He owned a short wave radio receiver and was accused of listening to German stations. Two years later, his wife, Tante Martha, received a letter from him saying that he had been sent to the camp of Magadan, north of Japan near the Kamchatka Peninsula. This was one of the largest and worst camps in Siberia. Thousands upon thousands of prisoners died there. Uncle Viktor wrote that he had lost the use of both of his legs and could no longer work, so his food rations had been cut to the bare minimum; he did not expect to live much longer. This was the last we heard from him.

In 1939 a non-aggression pact was signed between Russia and Germany. Overnight, we Germans became the best friends of the Russians.

The following summer of 1940, at age fourteen I got my first job at the railroad station, taking samples of wheat from deliveries from the collective farms, before the wheat was shipped to Germany. We worked twelve hours a day, sometimes eighteen hours, seven days a week. At the end of the summer I was only a skeleton; I had lost a fourth of my weight. I dreamed of locking myself in one of those railroad cars and escaping from Russia.

The school year of 1940-41 was my last year of formal education. This was the eighth grade in our system, but because we started school when we were eight years old, we had accelerated studies; eighth grade is comparable to the tenth grade in the U.S.

The summer of 1941 I worked in the Grossliebental town library. On the morning of June 21, I met with friends at the library to play cards. When I got home, my parents told me that the Germans had bombed four major Russian cities that morning and had declared war on Russia. I was excited, thinking that now we would be "liberated."

A few weeks earlier, in April, an airport had been built outside our colony. It was nothing special; there were no paved runways, just flat land and a few barracks. The military officers were stationed in our town, and an Air Force doctor and his wife moved into one room of our house. The doctor's wife told my mother that there was going to be a war.

The day following the declaration of war, bombers came to bomb that airport. It scared us, and that night we slept in the cellar. From then on, Romanian and Italian bombers flew over our town almost nightly toward Odessa, which was about twelve miles east, to bomb the harbor and the city. In August, three Romanian bombers flew over our colony, dropping bombs and killing six people. There was no Russian military presence in our town at this time. Soon the Romanians were four-to-six kilometers north of our town. By the end of August we no longer felt safe, so we left to join friends in a town by the Black Sea.

By the end of July, the German Army coming down from the north had cut off Odessa from the Soviet mainland, and the area around Odessa was left for the Romanians to occupy. In October, the Russians gave up Odessa and left the city by ship. The Romanians established their headquarters in a former NKVD building in Odessa. Three days later the building exploded, and 220 Romanians, mostly officers, lost their lives. It was thought that before the Russians left, some timed device may have been set to destroy that building and its occupants. In retaliation, the next day the Romanians picked up anyone off the streets who looked like a Jew. Odessa had a large population of Jews. They took roughly three thousand people outside

Father Alexander Baumgartner with his 3rd grade class, all boys, about 1943 in Grossliebental. Note the sober, smile-less facial expressions and lack of shoes.

the city into abandoned military barracks, poured gasoline over the barracks and set them on fire, killing all the people inside.

Later, life in our colony returned to normal. The *kolkhozes* (collective farms) were dissolved, and farmers received their land again. In fall of 1942, schools were re-opened. Some of my friends and I decided to go to school again, but there wasn't much to learn other than improving our knowledge of German. Harvests of '42 and '43 were good, and our farmers prospered. My father worked again as a schoolteacher, and I worked in the grocery store. Pastors of the German Army baptized and confirmed the local children.

This good life ended in March of 1944. A community meeting was called; we were told that the Russians were only about two hundred kilometers away, and we would have to leave our homeland. We were advised to get our wagons in good shape and to cover them with carpet, plywood, or whatever was available, to slaughter the pigs and chickens, then cook the meat, put it in jars, and cover the jars with lard in order to preserve the meat. It was recommended that we take our cows with us, as their milk would provide us with much-needed nourishment. It was also suggested that we organize into groups of six to ten families who would help each other.

Since my father was a schoolteacher, we did not have horses or wagons. We were given a wagon from the community for carrying our personal belongings; it also carried some important community records on it. We were thankful for the wagon, as we could use the rest from walking alongside a separate, loaded wagon. All this was done under the supervision of the German Army.

The day of our departure was set for March 23. It rained the night before, and mud was knee-deep on the streets. It was a wet and cloudy day. Our colony's refugee train consisted of 540 wagons. All we could accomplish on the first day was to get the wagons lined up in the direction of Ovidiopol, a town on the Dneister Bay, so we had to stay another night in our cold, empty houses.

The next morning there was a frost, which helped us get on our way because the ground was firm. I still remember clearly that day we left Grossliebental. I had always wanted to get out of Russia, and this was my chance. The departure of the Jews in the film "Fiddler on the Roof" reminds me very much of the way we left our town.

At Ovidiopol, the Dneister Bay is approximately three kilometers wide. Barges from the German Army transported us across the bay. On the other side of the bay was the city of Akkerman. We were told that some women and children could stay here, and they would be transported to Germany by train. My mother and sisters stayed in Akkerman. However, the train never came, and my father had to go back by horse and wagon a week later and pick them up.

The roads in Bessarabia were paved, and we made good progress. By April we had reached Belgrade, which is in western Bessarabia and close to the Danube River. Here the German Army had to negotiate with the Romanian and Bulgarian governments about whether our route would go north of the Danube through Romania or south of the Danube through Bulgaria. As a result, progress was halted for about a week.

One morning we were told to march as fast as possible in the direction of Galatz, on the Pruth River. This was the longest single-day march on our journey. At about five o'clock in the evening, after we had walked sixty-six kilometers, a German soldier on a motorcycle came along and told us to turn around, because the Russians would be at the bridge ahead before we could get there. We turned around and walked in the direction of Reni on the Danube. During the night the Russians bombed and damaged that bridge by Galatz. At Reni, ferries from the German Army once again brought us across the Danube.

After we had crossed the river, we walked for one day, then took a two-day rest. Local governments had assigned empty pastureland every twenty or thirty kilometers for us to camp on overnight. There were other colonies ahead of us, and we had to camp in the same places they had left in the morning. When we came to these places, before we could spread our blankets, we had to clean the ground of lice from the previous occupants!

The next thing we had to do was to find a place where we could cook. Some housewives even baked bread. My job was to lead our cow from one camping place to the next and let her graze along the road. She was young and healthy and provided us with milk both morning and evening.

At Ruse in Bulgaria, about six weeks after we had left our home town, we received some supplies from the German authorities for the first time. Farther on, close to the Danube River, we could see far into Romania. We heard bombing in the direction of the famous Ploesti oilfields there. Soon we could see the fires in Bucharest and Ploesti. One time, American bombers flew close over us but decided to leave us alone after they saw that we were civilian refugees. On a hill, several Bulgarian girls were working in the fields. As the planes flew by, these girls lifted their long skirts over their heads and started to run up the hill. They were wearing nothing under their multiple skirts. With one eye I watched the airplanes, and with the other I watched the naked bottoms of those girls.

While in Bulgaria, we received more supplies from the authorities, but not enough to feed both the people and horses. The number of cows started to dwindle, as they could not endure the hardships of this difficult journey.

Early in June, while still in Bulgaria, we received news that the Allied troops had landed in France. I realized that this was the beginning of the end of the war. On June 20 we entered Yugoslavia and camped for about a week. Our wagons, horses, and cows were taken from us, and we received a worthless "receipt." With our remaining belongings, we were loaded onto railroad freight cars, and the train began to travel toward Hungary. We noticed that the Yugoslav partisans were active in the area, as we saw many railroad cars lying at the side of the tracks.

After four or five days of traveling through Yugoslavia, Hungary, Slovenia, and Tschechnia, we arrived in Lodz, in Poland. There we were cleaned of lice, then sent to the county of Turek. This was on July 2, 1944, three months and ten days after we had left Grossliebental. We were assigned one room with a Polish family in their one-family house. We shared the kitchen with them and we all got along together very well. I made friends with Polish youth my age and went along with them to steal cherries on a nearby farm.

Recruiting of young men by the German army began immediately after our arrival. The Nazi government did not trust foreign-born Germans *(Volksdeutsche)*. There were two armies in Germany—the regular army (the *Wehrmacht*) and the *Waffen SS*. The *Waffen SS* was under the control of Heinrich Himmler, a close associate of Hitler. Therefore, the Nazi Party had closer control over the SS, and for this reason all men whose loyalty was questionable were called to the *Waffen SS*. The SS consisted of two separate divisions: the political SS, which was in charge of internal security, including concentration camps, and the military *Waffen SS*. The latter was created some time near the beginning of the war as a private army for Hitler, in case the *Wehrmacht*, the regular army, revolted. Hitler didn't trust the *Wehrmacht*. The *Waffen SS* received the latest weapons and were known as a tough fighting unit, similar to the American Marines. At the beginning, it was an all-voluntary army, but later, young men were called to service, just like the regular army.

The *Waffen SS* also had divisions of foreign volunteers who wanted to fight the Communists. They were not fighting to support Hitler but they felt the Communists were a greater threat. I know that there were divisions from Norway, Holland, Estonia, Russia, and probably from other countries.

Men in the SS were told that the Allied soldiers, especially Russians, had been instructed not to take SS prisoners, but instead to shoot them immediately. So they should not allow themselves to be taken prisoner but to fight to the last bullet and shoot themselves if necessary. One of our distant cousins, Viktor Baumgartner, did just that on the Russian front in Hungary, and after he realized that there was no way out, he killed himself. Life expectancy of an SS soldier was six months after he had been called for duty. I had no desire to become a dead hero and was constantly thinking about how I could avoid being called to the SS.

In late August 1944, I received a call to report to a labor company that was building a defense line along the Weichsel (Westula/Vistula) River. We were told to bring clothes for one week. We were shipped to the city of Leslau to build a bridge-head on the east side of the river. We started to dig an anti-tank ditch six meters wide and about four to five meters deep. We received a spade and were told to get to work. All of the work was done manually.

We were housed in a big barn without any washing or toilet facilities. The weather in September was tolerable, but later on it got cold. The food was not enough for eighteen-year-old boys doing hard manual labor. We supplemented the small amount of food with sugar beets we dug on nearby farms.

After four weeks there was still no sign that we would be going home soon. There were about two hundred men in this barn, and at the end of September some of us decided to take an unapproved, short leave of absence and take the train "home" for a few days; home was a refugee camp where my parents were near Posen. I was able to go home at the beginning of October and again at the end of November.

During October, my parents received a summons for me to report to the SS recruiting station. They returned it with a note saying that I was not at home. During my last visit home, on about December 1, another summons from the SS came. I quickly decided to return to Leslau and had my parents return the summons with the same note—that I was not home. As I departed, my parents, sisters, and I felt that something was going to happen, and we all cried. This was the last time I saw my parents and six-year-old sister Hedwig.

When I arrived back at the work camp, I was told that the police were there to pick up men like me who had left the camp without permission. My name was on their list. I was also told that a recruiting officer from the Todt Organization was there to gather volunteers. The Todt Organization was established in 1936 to build the western defense line—the Siegfried Line, along the French border. These workers wore uniforms but were not armed. They continued to build defense lines behind the front.

This organization looked a lot better to me than the SS, and when they came about three days later on December 9, 1944, to pick up volunteers, I asked if I could join. I was accepted, no questions asked. We boarded an overnight train to Berlin. The organization had a training camp at the Berlin suburb of Britz. We were supposed to be trained to defend the organization's men and projects against the partisans. During my forty-day stay there we were taken to a shooting range twice, but did not receive weapons.

The camp was located on the southeast side of Berlin, and although the city was bombed almost every other day, no bombs fell on us. The British bombed the city for two hours on Christmas Eve, but we survived.

In January 1945, the Russians started an offensive from Warsaw, overrunning the rest of Poland and coming into East Germany. On January 20 we were ordered to leave for Posen in East Germany. We were loaded onto freight cars and headed off toward the East. By the time we reached Frankfurt on the Oder, the Russians were in Posen. We were unloaded and sent to some barracks on the south side of the city.

In the evening, our commander came into our room and asked for a volunteer to deliver a letter to the downtown Todt Organization headquarters. I volunteered; he showed me the location of the headquarters on a city map, and I received a bicycle and left. In less than two hours, I was back and reported to him that the letter was delivered. He was very impressed that I was back so soon and told me that from now on, I should keep myself available for special assignments from him.

At this time, most of Germany east of the Oder River was in chaos. Day and night, refugees and soldiers crossed the Oder

River bridges in Frankfurt. (This is a smaller city east of Berlin, not the large city by the same name, "Frankfurt-on-Main" in western Germany). Our assignment was to stand at every bridge and collect men belonging to the Todt Organization coming across and direct them to our camp. From there, new companies were established and sent out. My assignment was to get the daily food supply and mail and to run other errands. As the Russians approached the city and no more refugees came across the bridge, our company's assignment was to dig ditches on the east side of the river at night, just behind the front line. I was lucky that I was never once out on the front line.

At the beginning of March our company was ordered back to a village about sixty kilometers east of Berlin. Our assignment was to build a temporary bridge across the Spree River. We worked on this assignment until April 20. On a beautiful spring morning, I heard machine gun fire very close to us. We were ordered to destroy the bridge we had just built. The Russians were advancing on the north side of the river, and we were on the south side. By noon we returned to our quarters in the village to await further orders. The village consisted of about twenty houses south of a small highway. Aside from a soccer field, only forest surrounded us.

Communications with our headquarters had been completely broken and no orders came. At two o'clock we were ordered to put our belongings into our wagons. We had one tractor with a trailer and two horse-drawn wagons. The wagons were ordered to start moving west on the highway, as men were ordered to get together on the other side of the soccer field. As we crossed the soccer field, I noticed some common, flashily-painted German tanks moving west. Then it was quiet for a moment, and two black tanks came along the highway. I got suspicious and started to run. At the same time I saw that they were turning their machine guns toward us, and they began to shoot. Everybody started running into the woods. Somehow I got separated from the other men, but I kept running until a German soldier yelled,

"Stop! You're in the middle of a minefield!" He directed me out of it. I had gotten lucky once again.

We regrouped at the next village; only eighty men were present out of the one hundred-twenty in our company. We walked until about midnight, when we decided to camp in the woods off the highway. Early the next morning, explosions awakened us. We had camped next to an airport, where a soldier was blowing up airplanes because there was no fuel left to fly them.

We continued marching westward. The road was full of refugees. On April 26 we were in Berlin and were instructed to wait near the Olympic stadium for new orders. Our commander went to the Todt headquarters to get new instructions. The rumor was that no man was allowed to leave Berlin, because all had to stay to defend the "Fortress Berlin." We all knew that this would be the end of our lives. I cannot describe how relieved we were when our commander returned with orders to march to Denmark. We immediately broke off and walked northwest.

We did not walk together as a company; instead, each man was on his own. I got a little behind, and nobody was around me. I still had my bike, and my assignment was to stay at the rear and direct lost men in the proper direction. I was in no hurry and did some sightseeing. All of a sudden, grenades began exploding near me. I pedaled as fast as I could westward. About a kilometer later, some German soldiers were lying in ditches and asked me where I was coming from, because the forest was full of Russians. I must have been one of the last men who got out of the city before the Russians encircled Berlin.

Northwest of Berlin we were in the airspace controlled by the American and British Air Forces. We could not walk during daylight hours because enemy airplanes were shooting anything that moved. During the day we stayed in farmers' barns, and at night we walked. During the night of May 1-2 we marched through the city of Schwerin. In the early morning hours, we pulled into a large farm north of the city. The first rumor we heard was that the Russians would be there by noon, then that the Americans would be there in the early afternoon.

We also received news that Hitler had died defending "Fortress Berlin." My reaction was one of relief, that the war would soon be over.

In the afternoon, two American tanks came out of the woods about a kilometer north of us. They started to shoot toward the farm with their machine guns, but when no one returned fire, they continued eastward. Then an American jeep driven by two soldiers approached the farm. I was surprised to see around two thousand German soldiers come out of various barns to greet the Americans. They collected our revolvers and asked us to break all rifles.

The next morning, we received instructions as to where we should go. Our commander released us of our oath, and from then on we were on our own and could go where we pleased. Some men from East Germany headed east but most of us went west. During the preceding few months, I had befriended two schoolteachers from around Odessa. The three of us were some-what better educated and unofficially became the sergeants of the company. We three had civilian clothing in our backpacks and decided that this was the time to get rid of our uniforms and change into regular clothes. We still had our tractor and trailer with our belongings on them. I still had my bike. The next morning we started to walk northwest, without worrying about airplanes.

We came to an intersection where a British soldier was directing traffic. As I came to the crossing, some Polish boys jumped on me to take away my bike. I was about to tell them that I was a Russian, not a German, when I saw a car with a large red star (Russian) on the side come from the east and stop at the intersection. This was a shock to me, and without saying a word I abandoned my bike and walked away.

Toward evening, we pulled off the road to camp for the night. There were hundreds of people at this camping place. About an hour later, British soldiers came. They told everyone in uniform to follow them. The others were asked if they were soldiers. When they came to us, we told them we were not soldiers, just workers. They left us alone.

I decided to go to the village for water. The well was at the entrance to the village, and as I got close, I saw men from our company coming from the other side toward the well. They were already with British guards. I turned around and waited until they were gone, as I did not want to be recognized.

The next morning, farmers with trucks came looking for workers. We tried to find out whose farm was the farthest west so we could go with him; we naturally preferred to go in that direction. We had no intention of working, but we wanted to get across the Elbe River as fast as possible. So we connected with one farmer who took us across and to his farm. Early Monday morning, before the farmer got up, we were on the road.

We walked until late afternoon and decided to find a place for the night. We entered a village and immediately American soldiers waved us over. They told us to unpack our backpacks and lay everything out. There were some Polish boys waiting for this again, and they looked through our belongings too and took anything they wanted, like pocket knives, money, watches, razor blades, etc.

The soldiers did not ask us any questions but took us into a camp for prisoners. This was a fenced-in cow pasture, and over a thousand men were there. We asked them how the food was. They told us that most of them had been here for over five days and had not received anything to eat. We asked to speak to the commander. A German college girl who spoke English took us to him. We told him that we were Russians and did not belong here. He apologized and told us that we were in the wrong camp. He said that on the other side of the village was a camp for foreigners, and we should go there. A soldier took us there.

This was on the yard of a good-sized farm. The owner was probably a former Nazi and was willing to do anything he could for us and the other twenty-three foreigners that were sent to him. The farmer was instructed to feed and house us as well as he could. The people in this camp were from France, Belgium, Holland, Italy, Poland, and Russia. Life was bearable on this farm, as there was no work, and reasonably good food.

After about three weeks, the Americans came and told everybody from France, Belgium, and Holland that they would be sent home the next day. Then they picked up the men from Italy and Poland and finally came for the men from Russia. But we told them that we were not from Russia; we were from Ukraine. The officer thought they were the same thing, but we insisted that it was not. His knowledge of geography was not very good, and he left us alone. We knew now that it was time for us to move on.

Early the next morning we started to walk toward the Elbe River. We reached the river early afternoon, just south of Lauenburg. We were told that we could not cross the river at the bridge because there were guards on both ends, and you needed special permits to cross. However, five kilometers south there was a boat that was shuttling people across the river. The boat took fourteen adults; at every crossing, two people from the next group in line went along to bring the boat back. At about five o'clock, a Dutch military boat came up the river. They saw what was going on and used an axe to chop up the boat, which ended that operation.

So the three of us went into the woods to collect heavy

branches. We intended to tie them together and build a float, put our belongings on it, and swim across the river. The current of the river was very strong, and as soon as we got about fifty meters into the river, the current took our three-meter log float and flipped it over, throwing us out and leaving our empty boat floating down the river. One of the men, Schumacher, swam in to get the boat, but without oars he could not get it out of the strong current. I ran along the shore to see if I could help. But the boat got ahead of me, it got dark, and I could not see it any more. I heard some shouts and gave up. I never found out what happened to Schumacher.

Now only two of us, we camped in the woods for the night. It rained but wasn't too cold. The next morning a new boat arrived, and the shuttle service continued. We got on the list to go across and made the crossing. In the village across the river, we met some women with their children from the Odessa area. They told us that Russian officers told them to go home. When the women told them that they would like to wait until their husbands came home from the war, the Russians told them their husbands were probably already home. They also told the women that they would return the next morning with trucks to pick them up. We received two bikes from the women, and the next morning we started our journey south to the west side of the Elbe. The only address I had was that of Tante Rosl in Schwaebisch Hall. After bombs destroyed her apartment in Stuttgart, she found a temporary place in Schwaebisch Hall. My remaining partner Neumann and I rode together for a couple days, then we parted.

There were no military checkpoints on the roads, and I made good progress until south of Goettingen. As I was biking on a small highway, two girls coming from the south warned me that there was a checkpoint ahead. I thought I had better get off the highway for a few kilometers. After about an hour of walking in the woods, I thought it would be safe to go back to the highway. I found a path and followed it.

As I came closer to the highway, I noticed that the checkpoint was straight ahead of me. As I had noticed them, the British soldiers had noticed me. I was about two hundred meters from the checkpoint and had no idea what to do, so I sat down and opened my backpack and acted like I was taking a break. One soldier started to walk toward me. When he was close to me, he took his gun off his shoulder and pointed it at me and asked for my papers. He looked at them, gave them back to me and told me very politely that when I was finished eating, the officer wanted to see me. I was finished right away, so I went with him to see the officer. He talked to me in English, which I did not understand. He said something about papers, pointing to Goettingen and then to the village down the road and said something about the mayor of the village. Then he made it clear to me that I should go. He probably said that I should go and see the mayor of the village, who would give me identification papers.

I went to the village, asked for the mayor, walked into his office, and was told to wait for him. While I was waiting, I looked around and noticed a card on his desk with a passport-sized photograph and the person's birth date and home town. When the mayor came in, I told him that the British officer sent me to him to get an ID card like the one on his desk. He thought for a minute, took a photo I gave him, and had his daughter make me a card. When he gave it to me he said he wasn't sure he was doing the right thing, as this was his first day as mayor. I assured him he was doing the right thing, thanked him, and left. Now I had some real papers besides my book from the Todt Organization.

A few kilometers down the road was another village and another checkpoint. This time, two American soldiers were controlling the checkpoint, with the assistance of two German girls. I proudly showed them my new papers. When I told them where I was going, they said I had the wrong papers. As I was crossing the border between the British and American zones, I needed papers issued by the British office. I was supposed to go to the village, stay there over the weekend, then go back to Goettingen to the British authorities and get the right papers. I stayed in the village overnight with no intention of going back, and I left the next morning on a small road south of the village. Soon I was on the Goetting-Kassel autobahn, and there were no more checkpoints.

On the autobahn, I met a Russian family on their way to see relatives in France. I asked them how they got through the checkpoints. They said it was easy; all you had to do was speak Russian. The only thing they understood was that you were a "Ruski," and they let you through. And so, everything went well, with no checkpoints until the outskirts of Kassel. There I saw two Americans sitting on a railing on an autobahn bridge. They waved me over and asked for my papers. I showed them what I had and started to speak in Russian. They did not understand me; I did not understand them, and they let me go.

I stayed overnight near Alsfeld, where the local people told me that the American authorities in Alsfeld were generous in issuing travel permits. So I decided to go to the American authorities. I was led into an office with an American soldier sitting behind a desk and a German girl on his lap. I told them that I needed to go to Schwaebisch Hall to meet my parents and then go home to Russia. The soldier had some questions, but the girl talked him into giving this skinny young boy the necessary papers. I still have them.

On my way, I stopped to see some friends in Luedersdorf. They invited me to stay with them, which I did for two months. I worked for farmers and in the woods. By the end of August, I decided to go to Stuttgart to find something more permanent. I pedaled to Schwaebisch Hall, where I found Tante Rosl's house but was told that she had returned to Stuttgart, and they did not have her address. They also told me that Uncle Caesar was back and was working for a farmer near Forchtenberg. This was about thirty kilometers from Schwaebisch Hall, so I pedaled there.

I arrived at about six o'clock in the evening, but where should I look? I sat down in a ditch next to the road to think about what to do next. Two girls came by. One girl asked me, "Well, soldier, how far from home?" I told her my story, that I was from Russia, and I was looking for my uncle, who is supposed to be working here on a farm. The other girl said she knew of a man on a certain farm who said he could speak Russian. When I got to that farm, I saw Uncle Caesar standing on top of a hay wagon. I recognized him right away. Was my luck that good, or had somebody been leading me to this place?

Uncle Caesar and Tante Rosl were living in Stuttgart with her brother, but there was no room for me. We decided to find an apprentice place, a *"Lehrlingstelle,"* where I could work and live. A neighborhood butcher took me on. This was not exactly what I wanted to be, but I had no other choices. I began in September of 1945 and passed my butcher journeyman exams in April 1947. I took on other jobs, unrelated, until I finally emigrated to America in November of 1951.

Before the move to America, from February 1945 to the spring of 1947 I did not know what had happened to my parents and my three sisters. In addition to my aunt and uncle in Stuttgart, I also had an aunt in Texas, near Wichita Falls. In Germany we were allowed soon after the war to correspond with my aunt in Texas; however, my relatives in Russia were not allowed to mail letters to a foreign country until 1947. In the spring of 1947, another of my father's sisters wrote from Siberia to my aunt in Texas, and this is what I found out; all former citizens of the Soviet Union living in central and eastern Europe had to return to Russia.

During January of 1945, the Soviet army broke out from the Warsaw area and overran Eastern Germany up to the Oder River. At that time, my parents lived about two or three hundred miles east of the Oder. When the Red Army came through, it was chaotic, and people of German descent started to flee ahead of the army. My parents left their home with a wagon and two horses that had been given to them, in the direction of the Oder, to the city of Frankfurt. They made it close to a bridge over the Oder when they had to leave the highway to allow German military personnel to cross the bridge. The next day the area was overrun by the Russians. In March my dad was arrested by the Soviets, accused of cooperation with the Germans. During the German-Romanian occupation of our town, he had continued to teach, Germans of course, and this was the crime he was accused of. He was thrown into an unheated, damp cellar, released in May, and died two weeks later.

My mother, her older sister, and my three sisters were now all by themselves, still east of the Oder. In September 1945 this territory was given to Poland, and all people of German descent had to leave within twenty-four hours, across the Oder into East Germany, which was occupied by the Russians. The refugees were not welcome. The East Germans did not have enough food for themselves, and the refugees added another six to twelve million people. Especially the people from Russia were told, "Why don't you go back to where you come from?" Before he died, my father had told my mother not to go back to Russia.

However, life in East Germany became unbearable. The Russian Army insisted that all former Soviet citizens report to the Russian administration to be returned to their place of birth. In October, my aunt and my older sister, without my mother's knowledge or approval, went to the Russian authorities and requested to be returned to our home town, Grossliebental. In November they were all put onto a train. Soon they noticed that the train was not going southeast but northeast. They wound up in the Ural Mountains. They were placed in barracks that had housed German nurses, who had all died within six months of the end of the war.

My mother, her sister, and my three sisters had no warm clothes for this extremely cold climate. However, they were told to report to work the next morning, or "no work, no food." It was their job to clear the railroad tracks of two meters of snow. They had to stay outdoors as long as the temperature was above -40 degrees Fahrenheit.

During the following summer, my fifty-year-old aunt had to take one of the boss's cows to graze in the woods. She got lost and stayed in the woods three nights. When she was found, she had lost her mind and died two weeks later. My oldest sister was sent to rebuild Stalingrad. That left my mother and my two younger sisters by themselves. In the spring of 1947 my mother became very ill, and a Russian neighbor offered to take her to the hospital. My mother died shortly after, having starved to death. My sister told me that her last words were, "If I just had a piece of bread." I think of this every time I see how people waste food in this country.

My youngest sister, Hedwig, who was ten years old at that time, was separated from my second sister, who had to continue working. Hedwig was placed in a children's home, where she died three months later. Her cause of death was the standard Soviet "explanation"—pneumonia. It is more likely that she starved or died of homesickness.

I was living at this time, from 1947-51, in Stuttgart.

After Stalin's death in 1954, the prisoners were allowed to go wherever they liked, except they had to stay 150 kilometers from the place where they were born. My second sister, Irmgard, married a man from western Ukraine who had been sent out there to the same place in the Ural Mountains, Novosibirsk. He was a former Soviet fighter pilot. The Russians didn't take very good care of their veterans; driven by hunger, he stole a sack of flour to use to make bread. The penalty was to be shipped to Siberia, where my sister met him in Novosibirsk. After that release in 1954, together they wanted to move back to our home town near Odessa, but they were not allowed to stay there.

Consequently they settled in Donetz in eastern Ukraine, an active coal basin. Her husband worked in the Donetz coal mine as an electrician. He told me that he went down into the mines only to fix problems, then got out as fast as he could. He knew how unsafe the mines were.

In 1995, Irmgard, her husband and their daughter, emigrated to Germany. Irmgard died in Germany in 2009 in a car accident.

My oldest sister, Anna, moved after Stalin's death from Stalingrad to Taschkent, also in the USSR. From there she emigrated to Germany in 1992 and died in 2010.

Now, for the rest of the story—my move to America. In 1947 Germany was still in ruins. Jobs were scarce, and good jobs were not available. Australia and some states in South America opened their borders to German immigrants. I wrote to my aunt in Texas and expressed my interest in emigrating to South America. She had a son and a daughter, older than I; they all strongly objected to my moving to South America and suggested I consider coming to the United States.

I went to the American Consulate in Stuttgart, where I was living, and filed an application. I was told that at that time Germans were not being accepted for immigration, but they said they would put my paper on file. I did not hear from them until the summer of 1951, when I received a letter asking if I were still interested in going to the United States. If I were still interested, I was to come to a camp near Frankfurt for interviews. My health and political views were checked, and my health was deemed acceptable. At that time, the Korean War had started, and the man interviewing me was not interested in whether or not I was ever a Nazi, as I had expected, but he was very interested in my views on communism. I must have passed the examination, because I was informed that I would be notified later of their decision.

In 1950 President Truman had signed an immigration act, which allowed 300,000 displaced persons from Eastern Europe to immigrate to the United States outside the established quota. I qualified under this act, as did my future wife, Irene Scholl.

At the beginning of November 1951 I had to report back to the camp, ready to be shipped out. From Frankfurt we were moved to a camp in Bremerhaven, and from there we were loaded onto U.S. Navy transport ships.

I was on a ship called *General Taylor*. These types of ships were shipping supplies from the U.S. to Europe and on the return trip transporting immigrants to America. These ships were not luxury boats but regular military transporters. Adult passengers were required to work. For example, there were duties in the kitchen and bakery, doing painting, or some other light maintenance work. There was also a need for about forty "policemen." That job sounded like an interesting assignment, so I volunteered for it.

We were taken to the ship the day before the other eleven hundred passengers came on board. We were familiarized with the ship so we could help direct the other passengers to their assigned places. The loading went without any problems, and we were ready to leave the afternoon of November 23. We policemen were released from our duties, and it was suggested we retire to our own bunks.

A storm was brewing on the North Sea, and we were the last ship allowed to leave port. We acquainted ourselves with this storm very soon. At six o'clock supper was served. Passengers were asked to come to the dining room to eat. However, the ship was rocking so strongly that nothing would stay on the tables. People were vomiting, sitting on the floor, and feeling miserable. We policemen were asked to escort the sick passengers back to their bunks. They were vomiting on us, and this ship was a mess! I had no time to think about myself; our work was so distracting that I made it through this difficult time without any trouble. I was very proud of myself.

The next morning the ship was off the coast of the Netherlands, and the sea was calm. On the third day we made it to the coast of Portugal, and from there the ship was pointed southwest, in the direction of Florida. Our destination was New Orleans. Most passengers were bound for southwestern states, with the majority going to California.

As we crossed the open water, my job was to guard the railings on the left side of the ship. I was charged with keeping children from going near the railing. Because I was on the south side of the ship, it was sunny during the day, which was pleasant, as it was wintertime. On most days I could usually find a nice place to sit and read.

On the eleventh day of our journey, we saw the skyline of Miami. From there we went around Key West into the Gulf of Mexico. On the twelfth or thirteenth day we entered the Mississippi River. Our first view of America was disappointing. The houses on the shore were so small that the cars parked next to them appeared longer than the houses themselves. We thought these must be vacation homes, but we were told that some people live there year round.

On December 7 we were unloaded in New Orleans. My cousin and her husband, who had just returned from the Korean War, picked me up. As we drove through the city I noticed that the city was decorated with flags and banners. At first I thought this was in my honor, but later I found out that it was in honor of somebody by the name of "Pearl Harbor."

After brief stays in Dallas and Henrietta (near Wichita Falls), we returned to Dallas, where I began to look for work. At first I was completely lost, knowing very little English in addition to the new surroundings being too much for me. I worked briefly in Dallas and in Henrietta, then Wichita Falls, where my Uncle John unloaded me in the center of the city and said, "OK, go look for work. I'll be waiting for you here."

My first stop was at Safeway, where the manager of the meat department had recently returned from serving in the American Army in Germany. He must have had a positive experience in Germany because he was very friendly to me. I was hired and asked to start the next Monday. I assumed I would be cutting meat in the back room. A short time later, the manager came and told me it was time for me to start waiting on customers at the counter. With such little knowledge of English I should start serving customers?! He told me not to worry; if I didn't understand what the customer was asking for, he would be there to help. It must have worked out, because two weeks later, I received a new assignment, which meant I was by myself for several hours on the evening shift. This was in March of 1952, and my English was still very limited. The manager said if I didn't understand what the customer was asking for to just say, "We don't have it." It must have worked, as I only made one customer mad.

I also took classes in English and accounting during my time off. I kept in correspondence with my future wife, Irene; her story is told separately.

Her family came originally to South Dakota, then moved to Milwaukee where I joined her, and we were married in 1954. I continued my evening classes at Marquette University, and in 1957 joined the Harnischferger Corporation in Milwaukee as a cost clerk. I worked my way up to supervisor, then assistant department manager, and retired as a plant controller in 1989.

Our son Werner, after finishing medical school in Milwaukee, moved to Denver. Daughter Ingrid has a Ph.D. in pharmacy and works at Children's Hospital in Aurora, Colorado. We liked Milwaukee, except for the weather, so after I retired we moved to Denver and presently live in a retirement community near Boulder.

Alex Baumgartner

⊰ Irene Scholl Baumgartner ⊱

Irene's story begins as a "German from Russia" and emphasizes the disruption of ordinary citizens' lives as non-combatant civilians, caught in the politics of both Russia and Germany before and during the war. Parents reading these accounts will be mortified at the instability of some children's lives as well as the insecurity, fear, and physical discomfort that often accompanied their countless moves.

I was born in 1927 in Grossliebental, near Odessa and the Black Sea, and had an older sister Erika, born in 1924. Grossliebental was the largest German colony in the Ukraine. It was the educational and cultural capital of the other German colonies northwest of Odessa. Established in 1804, Grossliebental was located eighteen kilometers west of Odessa and eight kilometers north of the Black Sea.

My parents and grandparents were not originally from this colony but from other villages also near Odessa. My grandfather Konstantin Beck was a landscape architect, and he also grew wine grapes. He designed parks on the Crimean peninsula and others near Odessa. His only son, my uncle Anton, was shot by the Communists. (Families often did not know the reasons or circumstances of arrest and execution.)

My father was a physician, who studied in Odessa, Latvia, Estonia, and Heidelberg, Germany. He became chief doctor at Grossliebental Hospital. He was a very busy man—in addition to Grossliebental's population of 3500, he served the Russian town of Alexandrowka and six other German colonies. In every town there was a medical station, with a nurse always on duty. For more serious cases, either the patient was brought to Grossliebental or my father traveled by horse-drawn wagon to visit them. He performed surgery once a week and was often assisted by two other physicians from Odessa. Between four and eight surgeries were performed every week at that clinic. He sometimes gave lectures on contagious diseases, cleanliness, aging, and other health issues. He was well-liked, always willing to help, but he could also be very strict; he required that patients wash their feet before they came to see him!

In 1930 my mother was infected with typhoid, allegedly because she drank from a public water fountain. She died in October. After her death, we had a housekeeper who took care of my sister and me. We called her Katja, and she was very good to us, but she couldn't replace our mother. In 1935 our father married Katja, and she gave me another sister, Elvira. Father was disappointed, however—he wanted a son.

Beginning in 1929, living conditions of the German colonists, along with those of the Russian farmers, deteriorated. Stalin began the *kolhozification* of the farmers. Kolhozification meant that all farmland, farming machinery, and farm animals were to become community property. The Communists took away all property of the wealthy farmers and sent them and their families to northern Russia or Siberia. Churches were closed, their steeples torn down, and their priests sent to Siberia.

During the 1930s we got accustomed to the Communist lifestyle. Thankfully the practice of exiling people to Siberia had ended. But then in 1936-38, a new wave of terror began *[Details are described in Alex's memoir in this book]*. We were never told of the accusations against men who were picked up during the night, just that they were "enemies of the people."

On the afternoon of August 7, 1937, our father was asked to come to the NKVD office (Soviet Secret Police) and was detained. Erika and I were in Lustdorf with relatives, and we were not able to say goodbye to him. Our grandfather brought us home from Lustdorf and told us not to cry; our father would never abandon us. He was kept for four weeks in the local jail. Erika often walked back and forth by the building, hoping to catch a glimpse of him. On the third day, he opened a window. Erika was so shocked that the only thing she could say was to ask if he had a bed. He shook his head, and immediately she heard somebody behind him ordering him to close the window. The next day Erika went to the police station and asked if she could bring her father some clean underwear. After much deliberation, the NKWD allowed it. She ran home, collected underwear, socks, and shirts and returned to the station. As the policeman handed the clothes to my father, she briefly caught sight of him. What a sight! His trousers were torn, his socks were pulled down, and his legs were swollen. He had definitely been tortured. We found out in the 1990s that he was shot in December of the same year. The family never found out why he was arrested or what happened to him. The rumor was that a young doctor wanted his job and turned him in. Just being accused of giving preference to patients of German nationality was enough to have him shot.

During the process of expropriation of the wealthy farmers' land, our grandfather Scholl lost everything. His property and all the property of his children were taken away. He had no place to live except to stay with us. The house of our other grandparents in Lustdorf was also confiscated. They were allowed to stay in one small room, but after a few months this too was taken away. Even their furniture was thrown out into the street. Grandfather Beck had established beautiful city parks with trees, shrubs, and lovely flowers. He had done so much for the community, and this was the thanks he received.

Not long after my father had been taken away on August 31, 1937, Grandfather Beck was arrested. He was seventy-one years old at the time. He was brought to the jail in Grossliebental, which was only three doors down from our high school. During school breaks, children would run to the end of the schoolyard to see if any prisoners were being loaded onto trucks for transportation to Odessa. About three days after our grandfather was arrested, Erika recognized him as he walked to the truck to be transferred. He lifted one arm and waved before he was made to lie down in the truck.

After our father was arrested, we were forced to move out of the doctor's apartment near the hospital. One of Katja's sisters allowed us to move into two rooms of her house. Grandpa Scholl joined us while we were living there. We had a whole house full of furniture and no room for it. Selling it was not an option, because people had no money.

In November of 1937 at 3:30 in the morning, the head of the local NKVD came to take us to the police station. Grandfather Scholl was with us at the time and had an anxiety attack. The NKVD men didn't care about him; they just left him alone. The next morning Katja's sister came to the jail and handed us a large loaf of bread, milk, and some honey through the window so we could have something to eat. There were eighteen children in the room, and all of us were hungry. We shared with the other children and ate everything before the police could take it away from us.

On the first full day in jail, children were separated from their mothers. Small children were allowed to stay another day with their mothers, but eventually they too were taken from their mothers. The children would give a heart-wrenching cry, but that did not matter to the policemen, who no doubt were following strict orders (and some must have had children of their own?).

The next day all of us were taken to Odessa—mothers to the jail, children to an orphanage. Children under five years of age were taken somewhere else. We were told that they would be raised the "Soviet way." Erika was thirteen at that time; I was ten, and our little sister Elvira was under two. Erika pleaded many times to see Elvira, but her requests were always denied. Finally, after two weeks, Erika was allowed to go to the place where Elvira was staying. When she arrived, she was told that Elvira had died (probably from homesickness?). This news was a terrible shock, and we felt very helpless.

After about two or three weeks, we were taken by train to Kiev, capital of the Ukraine, approximately three hundred kilometers north of Odessa. At the railroad station in Kiev, we were taken by the NKVD truck to a large house in the woods. By now it was December and very cold. The house had high ceilings and could not be heated easily. (It had once been the summer residence of the Czar.) In my room stood a large iron stove in which we burned newspapers, which gave a lot of smoke but little heat.

The police confiscated our belongings and shaved our heads to prevent us from getting lice. Disgusting food was served, but we did eat three times a day. We were so hungry we could eat anything. In the morning they served cornmeal and a glass of milk; at noon we received cucumber soup, sometimes with chicken in it, and a slice of bread. In the evening we received fruit.

I was soon separated from Erika. Girls of her age had to work, mostly sewing bed linen. We were promised that we would be able to go to school, but that never happened. Because I preferred to be alone, I often walked in the woods, beneath snow-covered trees.

After a month in the house, we were allowed to write letters. We could write to our relatives so they could come by train and pick us up. One of Katja's sisters borrowed money from relatives, and she soon came to take us home. She had only one room where she lived with her two children, so Erika stayed with her, and I was taken to Grandmother Beck in Lustdorf. Grandmother did not have a place of her own anymore; she slept on a sofa at some distant relatives'. I was very happy to be with my Oma again. After two weeks there, my mother's cousin took me to her place in a suburb of Odessa. Her husband had been spared the deportations, living unnoticed in a small Russian town.

In April 1938 the imprisoned women, including Katja, were allowed to go home. When Katja heard that her daughter Elvira was dead, she could not believe it. She made inquiries about Elvira everywhere, but the only thing she was told was that Elvira was dead, and no one knew where she was buried.

With Katja we moved into Katja's parents' house. We had one room and shared the kitchen with two other families. Before we were deported, we owned a cow, a pig, and some chickens. Now they were all gone, along with our bank account.

The colony had quieted down, and there were no more night arrests. Katja began to work in a knitting plant, while Erika and I went back to school. However, there was no word from or about the men who had been arrested in the previous years, including my father and grandfather. With their absence, there was a large shortage of workers, so the women had to fill in.

On June 21, 1941, the war between Germany and Russia began. We knew the harassment of the Germans would begin again. During that summer, between forty and sixty people in our village were arrested, taken to Odessa and shot. Since the beginning of the war, the Romanians had been bombing Odessa almost every night. After school ended, I went to my Oma in Lustdorf, which was only a few kilometers west of Odessa. Every time the alarm was sounded in Odessa, the sirens went off in Lustdorf. Oma was deaf and could not hear the sirens, so I helped her take cover whenever the bombing began. Luckily, no bombs fell on Lustdorf.

By mid-August the Romanian Army was about four kilometers northwest of Grossliebental and a month later moved in to occupy the colony. For one whole month, the fighting front stood between Lustdorf where I was and Grossliebental where Erika was. During this time there was not much to eat; store shelves were empty. Sometimes the stores had bread for sale. People would find this out the day before the bread was available, so at six o'clock the evening before, lines would start to form. Grandma would stand in line all night, and I would take her place early next morning. Frequently all the bread was gone by the time we reached the front of the line. Fortunately we were able to live off what we had planted in our garden at home.

In October the Romanians began their occupation of Odessa. Russian towns came under the administration of Romanians, and the German colonies were under the administration of the German Army. Houses and landholdings were returned to their original owners. Oma had owned a large, beautiful house in Lustdorf. It was now run down and filthy. We cleaned it up as much as possible, and the entire Scholl family moved in with Oma.

German soldiers were stationed in Lustdorf to defend the shores of the Black Sea. Three soldiers moved into our house, and they were welcome guests. In the spring of 1942, everyone started to plant food in their gardens and fields in order to be able to eat during the coming winter. German schools reopened, and I began attending seventh grade. There was a shortage of teachers, so Erika applied and was soon hired to teach in the lower grades. However, schools in Lustdorf only taught the first seven grades, so for eighth grade I had to go to Grossliebental, where I joined my old school friends. During the week I lived with Katja's brother Jakob; on weekends I walked the eight kilometers back to Lustdorf.

During the summer of 1943, German authorities decided to open a high school in Hoffnungstal. I was selected to attend and was joined by many children of my age. We traveled there by train; it was about eighty kilometers north of Odessa. The school was not in good condition; twenty girls slept in a room, and the bathroom was outside. Food was sparse, and we were constantly hungry. Once we invited the town's mayor to eat with us. He was not happy with our conditions and the next day sent us a slaughtered pig. It didn't take us long to consume it!

During the winter of 1943-44, the German Army was in retreat. By January 1944, the high school was closed, and we returned home to Lustdorf. For two and a half years we had enjoyed freedom; we could speak freely and were able to revive our German culture. But by the end of February, the Red Army was only two hundred kilometers east of us. We knew we either had to leave or endure the oppression of the Communists. On March 24 we left our beloved colonies Lustdorf and Grossliebental forever. No tears were shed, however, because we knew what would happen to us if we stayed. In August 1941 the Soviet government had issued a decree stating that all citizens of German descent were to be deported to Siberia. About two million Germans from the Volga River region were forcefully resettled. Hundreds of thousands starved, froze, or died because of the inhumane treatments of the Soviet regime.

We left our home town, heading westward in the direction of Ovidiopol. Once there, barges belonging to the German Army transported us across the Dneister Bay to Ackkerman in Bessarabia. We walked for three months through Romania, Bulgaria, back to Romania, and finally to Yugoslavia. Once in Yugoslavia, we were put on trains and taken to Turek, in the western part of occupied Poland. Older people, such as our grandmother, were taken from Odessa by train straight to Turek.

We settled there temporarily. I was notified that all students from the Hoffnungstal High School should report to a school on the Silesian-Polish border, which was to be reopened soon. I obtained my German citizenship and left for school. Erika and Katja stayed with Oma, who was renting an apartment near Posen, in East Germany. At first, Erika got a job at a school but later sold tickets at the railroad station. Her connection to the rail system would prove invaluable when the Russians broke through German front lines in January 1945.

I hadn't been at school long when after Christmas the Russian front began moving closer and closer. In mid-January we had to flee the school; Russian tanks were only two kilometers from us. We students left the school and went to the highway, where German trucks were driving west. I was lucky enough to catch a truck that brought me with some other girls to the railroad station in Breslau. I arrived at Puschkau, in Germany, the next evening.

I was overjoyed to be with my family again. They had already packed their suitcases and wanted to leave the next morning. Erika's boss told her that in the morning the last train for mothers and children would depart, and he would make sure we were on it. When the train came it was very full, but Erika's boss pushed us in, and we left for Frankfurt on the Oder, near Berlin.

At Frankfurt we boarded a train that was headed in the direction of Munich. However, after a few hours the train stopped, and we had to walk to the next station, carrying our heavy suitcases. When the train arrived, it was already loaded with soldiers who were going toward Kempten in Allgau. Grandma, Katja, and I were pushed through the windows into the train. Erika had to ride outside on the steps, with our suitcases. When we arrived in Kempten, Erika was frozen stiff; she had to be carried off on a stretcher to a Red Cross center where she could receive first aid. Nurses gave her hot black coffee to warm her up.

From Kempten, a mailman gave us a ride to Sulzberg. From there we had to walk another five kilometers to the Steigers' house, hauling our suitcases. The Steigers' son was one of the German soldiers who had been stationed at our house from 1942-44. When we left in the spring of 1944, he told us that if we ever needed a place to stay, we should go to his parents' home. We stayed with the Steiger family until we found a two-bedroom apartment to live in.

There we began a new life. We still had two of the three suitcases we started out with in Posen; mine was lost somewhere in Poland. But we were happy to be alive and together. We were definitely the lucky ones; Grandfather Scholl and his daughter's family were attacked by Polish citizens outside of Lodz during their flight from Russian soldiers. All their belongings were taken, even their clothes. A Russian officer picked them up in a field and brought them to a nearby house. Grandfather's feet were frozen and had to be amputated. He died soon after.

We had to start all over AGAIN. There was no work for us in Sulzberg. During the summer we were able to work for farmers. They did not give us money, only milk and bread. The work was hard; we had to load and unload hay wagons.

In the fall, Erika got a job as a teacher in an elementary school. I was hired as a nanny for two children. I stayed there until 1949 and still correspond with them.

Although the war in Germany ended in 1945, the plight of its citizens did not. Most German cities were in ruins, and jobs and living space were hard to find. We continued to move around, and in 1949, Oma, Katja, and I moved to Stuttgart where Erika was living. Once a month, the Germans from the Black Sea living near Stuttgart would get together at a restaurant to talk, sing, and dance. At one of these meetings, I found Alex Baumgartner, a man from my home town Grossliebental, whom I later married.

By 1947 we started to receive letters from Siberia written by friends and relatives. The Russians had caught them in East Germany, and instead of sending them to their place of birth as was promised, they deported them to frozen Siberia. There they had to work under inhumane conditions in the woods or in coal and uranium mines. Many of them, especially the children, died on the way to or in Siberia.

We were happy that we had the opportunity in 1951 to emigrate to the United States.

Irene Baumgartner

◆ Herman White ◆

Herman's memoir brings the Holocaust into our collection of WWII stories; I've only included two Jewish memoirs. Herman's account describes an uneasy life outside the camps, and how its vicissitudes, including the disappearance of his father, made no sense to a young lad.

The following memoir is instantly distinctive for its poetic quality, and Herman is indeed a practicing poet. Keep in mind that English is Herman's third language; yet his command of it is impressive! This segment of his autobiography describes a small but dramatic portion of his long life. Readers, be prepared to shed tears for this young boy's challenges, while remembering that there were millions of survivors who were similarly traumatized by the tragic fate of their loved ones. Most didn't have the opportunity or skills to articulate their feelings about those losses as effectively as Herman has done.

H erman was born in 1931 in Munich to a Jewish father and a Christian mother. His Jewish grandfather owned a boys' and men's clothing store in Ansbach. After the Nazi takeover in 1933 and the enactment of anti-Jewish policies, SA squads were stationed outside the store, forcing the business to eventually fail and go into bankruptcy. Grandfather hung himself.

In school in Hungary, Herman's treatment varied. His first- grade teacher knew he was Jewish and

Herman's father Moritz Weiss, 1900 - 1943 or '44. Perished in the Holocaust somewhere in the Ukraine.

Herman's mother

treated him cordially. The second-grade teacher treated him badly, and he was frequently arbitrarily targeted for harsh treatment. Although not uncommon for students who misbehaved or performed poorly, it was not warranted nor appropriate for this innocent young lad, whose only crime was being Jewish.

Herman's father was arrested in 1942. By 1944 the Russians were entering Hungary as invaders, and it was time for his mother to return the family to Germany. At that point, many Germans in the Eastern populations had the same idea, and train tickets from Budapest were scarce and extremely difficult to come by. Herman describes his mother as "fighting like a lioness" to obtain tickets on the last train out of Budapest.

Returning to his non-Jewish, maternal grandparents in Ansbach, Herman's family was able to hide there until the Americans came in 1945. His sister hid elsewhere in Germany with his mother's sister.

During this time, Herman says his mother and father seemed helpless, faced with calamities he could not fathom for a long time. The Hungarian language, which he learned in elementary school and on the streets, was a barrier for them, especially for his mother. The result was impoverishment.

After "liberation," the family was able to return to Munich, where Herman resumed his schooling. He finished *realschulle* (which is between high school and college, providing training mostly for technical fields), then entered an apprenticeship in the automotive repair business. American GIs brought very welcome food and coffee. They came on a truck equipped with a kitchen, providing breakfast which included American cold breakfast cereal—the first exposure to such a yummy delicacy for this young German.

In 1946 his sister and her husband (a concentration camp survivor) came to America and settled in Houston. Herman also emigrated, in 1952, spending time initially in Houston, then San Antonio, and finally settled in Colorado Springs in 1975, where he was employed by an auto dealership.

To quote Herman, "My early experiences in the U.S., starting in the 1950s, were eye openers in every imaginable way, good and bad. Acquaintances at work quickly led to invitations into American homes and friendships. Yet I soon became convinced to leave the past and its heartbreaks hidden. There are too many sore spots in people's psyches, like fallen fathers in the WWII American Army's march into Europe and into Germany. I was considered to be German. My Jewish roots I kept carefully hidden, having seen how one Jewish recruit was mercilessly teased in the unit to which I was assigned in the (American) First Armored Division in 1954.

"After all is said and done, I have few regrets; I am alive and quite healthy, with a few things inside and outside giving in to time."

Herman presently resides in Colorado Springs, Colorado and has a daughter who teaches in Denver.

BREATHING TIME
A Topography of Dread — A Geography of Hope

My first attempts to put on patient paper some of my childhood's first encounters with fate occurred after a meeting with Elie Wiesel, who spoke of the Nazi times and his personal struggles with those years. This meeting took place about 1998 at the Antlers Hotel in Colorado Springs at a reception in his honor. He encouraged me to do this.

Through a child's eyes, the present's heartbeat renders past and future equally important, equally sharp, equally bitter or sweet.

Summers and winters are brief eternities of wind-worried green leaves, silent silver snow, lazy Sunday afternoons of roller-skating and raspberry ice cream cones, damnably difficult homework assignments, birthdays, holidays, and funerals.

Funerals. That life could and would end seemed beyond understanding. That a father's familiar face and voice could vanish with the final metallic click of a closing door—that was utterly beyond comprehension to a child of eight—ME.

Was I that child? The child of a Jewish father, born in Germany, both of us.

My father's fate and final days remain hidden to this day. There is in the archives of the K2 Dachau his name and that of his brother Armin, as they were arrested together in Budapest. My mother spoke of a Red Cross functionary in Budapest who claimed to have seen the transport of Hungarian Jews in cattle cars heading for Auschwitz and places east where other death camps were located, north of Zhitomir.

When and how the Nazi death-machine overtook my fairly young father, or where exactly, I don't know to this very day—

some time in 1943, somewhere near Zhitomir, in the central Ukraine. He had no grave-side service, no eulogy, no Kaddish. Likely, the sole ritual was a volley of rifle fire atop the rim of some grisly mass grave, or the crack of a bludgeoner's club against the back of his head—the same head I held between my hands when I rode on his shoulders as an infant, holding on for dear life. Just how dear I was to find out. So was he. Time was running out for a Father.

That something horrible was happening dawned on me in the second grade of elementary school in Munich. My father had fled to Hungary only hours ahead of a visit by the Gestapo. I remember the pounding at our apartment door, the sound of iron-heeled boots on the floor, the harsh clipped commands to "Open up!" and my mother's pleading voice. So began the almost endless nightmare that early morning in 1938: "Daybreak with Dragons."

We remained in Germany for one more year, my mother, my two older sisters, and I—a year of poverty, hunger, daily humiliations, tauntings, threats, and assaults. I was too young to make a worthwhile target on the street, but in the schoolyard and the classroom there was no end of verbal and physical attacks. The class bullies had a free hand, and so did the teacher, a faithful follower and member of the Nazi Party. She proudly wore its bloody emblem on her dress. I no longer remember her face, yet I'll never forget her grating voice or the stinging pain of the long bamboo rod on my upturned palms and fingers.

In Ansbach where we stayed for a time with my grandparents at the end of the war, I took chances by walking the streets and was "arrested" by some schoolboys for not participating in the weekly meetings of the *Hitler Jugend*. They took me to an office where a uniformed Nazi began to interrogate me. Then the sirens started to howl, and everyone ran for the air raid shelter. I ran for the back entrance and escaped amid the confusion and earsplitting explosions of the air raid, having had ample experience of such raids in Budapest. I was unbelievably lucky—the luck of the innocent. At the same time, I lived practically within sight of a uniformed SA man, who just kept to himself. Perhaps he realized how near the end of the war was, the end of his power over sub-humans such as my mother and I.

The worst part was that I could not make any sense out of it all. Why was this happening to me, to our family? No one even hinted at the reasons. At home, my questions on the subject went unanswered, though my two sisters seemed to know far more. They lowered their voices to a whisper when I approached and excluded me from their secrets. I did not realize, and could not realize, that as teenagers they were much more vulnerable, more of a target for the Nazis than I.

A few years previously, the Nazis for all practical purposes dumped the German Civil Code and put in its place a lawless monstrosity they named "The Laws of Nuremberg." Overnight, anyone with even one Jewish grandparent lost all civil rights, was branded a parasite on the body of Germany, and therefore to be exterminated—the sooner the better.

Now it became impossible for us to remain any longer in Germany; WWII was about to begin, which meant that all borders were soon to be closed. So we boarded one of the last trains leaving for Budapest, Hungary.

Penniless, we arrived in this strange city, where equally penniless, my father swept me up from the railroad platform. I thought we were all to be together and happy again. I was a child. Many sparrows hopped and flew all around us.

The following months saw us moving from one flea-bitten, bedbug-infested room to another. My two sisters became what can only be described as indentured domestic servants of the most menial sort, paid a mere pittance in exchange for a place to sleep and not a day off except on the second Sunday every month. After a year, they disappeared from my life altogether.

What befell them I could not even guess, for no one explained it to me. I was still a mere child, yet somewhat less innocent than before.

Few and fewer were the days my father was with us. He would hurry on, leaving us quickly at the sound of any approaching footfalls. We became experts at reading footsteps. I began to figure out what was happening, even if slowly and incompletely. The pieces of the puzzle were all around me: my mother's faraway eyes overflowing with tears, her hands shaking as she plucked the bloody chicken necks with heads attached—food for a day, brought by her husband, my father of short and shorter hours.

One of my last walks with him ended in a classroom full of Hungarian boys and girls who giggled, as children will, over my appearance, and I was mortified by such treatment. I wore lederhosen, the standard Bavarian boys' shorts made of leather. For six months I had spoken only with the young female teacher, in German. But I learned fast, toed the mark obediently; it was sink or swim. The Hungarian language became my life raft. As an "undocumented alien" and a Jew, my father was prohibited from seeking any paying job. So he bought small amounts of tobacco and a little machine for hand-rolling, and peddled cigarettes.

By 1943 Hungary was well under the iron thumb of the Nazis. German troops were soon to march into Budapest, leaving no doubt about who was in charge. I feared and avoided all uniformed men on the streets, but especially the "Green Shirts," self-proclaimed "patriots" in the Nazi mold. Followers of a corrupt politician named Ferenc Szalasy, founder of the Arrow Cross Party, they were the very dregs of Hungary's underworld. With full Nazi approval, groups of these young men and boys roamed the streets of Budapest, brutally beating and killing every man, woman, or child that wore the Star of David. By decree, all Jews were forced to wear it on pain of death.

We did not.

At about this time, American long-distance aircraft began to bomb the city. I had a last visit with my father at the gate of a detention camp. He was arrested during a police sweep and could not show a valid ID or an official permit of residence. The Nazis had finally caught up with my dad. Heinrich Himmler and Adolph Eichmann were waiting in the wings.

I can barely recall what we said that last moment, with an impatient guard listening in. Dad impressed on me a man's duty to stay alive and remember. I promised to take care of Mother. He embraced me tightly, then drew back, reached into a pocket, and handed me a little rubber tire Mercedes racing-car toy, a promised present. It was my twelfth birthday.

Now mother and I were totally on our own; she cooked and scrubbed floors for acquaintances in return for handouts. After school I carried buckets of coal and firewood in our neighborhood. I helped a dealer in such fuels, whose place of business was below street level down a dark, slippery stairway of narrow stone steps. I expected to meet ghosts in that gloomy cold cave underground; it turned out to be a place of safety when bombs began to fall from the night sky.

In the evenings I delivered lovely buttons by the boxful to retail shops. The little button factory was also below a building, but the steps going down were regular stairs, with several light fixtures to properly see by. No ghosts were there either, or kept their distance.

Men were bending over machines that ground the buttons from mother-of-pearl, with great gritty clouds of white dust hiding them. It wasn't but a week later when little was left of this place; it had taken a direct hit from a fragmentation bomb. Countless buttons were strewn all over the street, grating under my feet like the layers of glass-shards I had walked on with my father on the day after Kristallnacht, the Night of Broken Glass, in Germany years ago.

Food became almost unobtainable. Food rationing meant additional dangers for mother and me. The ration cards could only be received with proper Hungarian ID papers, and we possessed none. I had to find a way to get those cards.

Though most local officials submitted to Nazi rule, the police officer whose beat included my elementary school's vicinity was a friend of all children. In the customary way of Hungarian convention, I knew and addressed him always as *"Rendor Bacsi"*—Uncle Policeman.

This true humanitarian, this angel in uniform, affixed the official seal of his precinct on my mother's photograph, along with an explanation of why I, as a child, was to receive the prescribed amount of Hungarian ration cards for two persons.

He waved to me for a few more days or weeks, then disappeared from my life also.

We shared a couch, my mother and I, along a friendly family's kitchen wall. A narrow table marked our private space, such as it was. On the deeply-pitted cement floor a hen scratched, for what only hens can know. She often fluttered up and roosted on my chest at night with a soft, satisfied, drawn-out clucking.

Only through the open door could light enter our nook, but it did, in more ways than one. There was Gisella, daughter of the family that gave us shelter. She was older than I, somewhat more mature, as girls are at that age. We did homework together, and we played in the large bare courtyard where mounds of sand made excellent hiding places. Gisella attended middle school and wore a uniform that reflected the Hungarian traditional dress of old times. So did I when we were together. The few who had not forgotten how, smiled on us.

Gisella was my first love; she kissed me first. We had a secret code: when safely out of sight behind assorted building maintenance implements, and the caretaker's curtain was motionless, she whispered "sparrow," and her lips drowned any words I might have said, if anything like words had come to my mind.

Nothing else but those kisses. We were too innocent and did not know the ways to still our pounding hearts.

All to the good, for some weeks later I had to move out of that kitchen, if not out of her heart. And it was not spared me to see her—my boy's dream of first love, the girl I chased down sun-dappled sidewalks—lifelessly crumpled on bloody cobblestones. Sparrows were hopping around her, and a dusting of light snow slowly turned pink.

Blinded, I ran away. Am I still running?

As 1944 began, Hell advanced from all quarters, and from above. The German army occupied Budapest, aerial bombardment was almost constant, and Hungarian fascists (Arrow Cross Green Shirts) had taken over the government. There was hardly a place to hide.

I had just recently gotten away from a pursuing gang of young Green Shirts by somehow vaulting onto a moving tramcar that was packed with German soldiers. To my great relief, they were Infantry in field-gray uniforms, not the dreaded black garments of the SS. At any rate, there was nothing to do for me but shout that I was being pursued by bandits. Hands reached down and hauled me aboard—German soldiers' arms, attached to German shoulders and heads and faces, curious friendly faces under steel helmets.

Apparently the ruse had worked: my cry for help was in flawless Bavarian brogue, and I wore *lederhosen*.

It was a mistake to tell my mother of my narrow escapes on the streets of Budapest, for in her desperation she promised to kill me if I got us in trouble.

I was to do just that.

With the approach of Soviet armies from the east, some feeble attempts at resisting the Nazis and their Hungarian helps began to occur.

Some middle school boys were secretly putting up leaflets calling for a new government—a constitutional monarchy like that of Britain, or a democracy as in America. I understood little of these things, but knew our neighborhood and its connecting passages and parks to a great degree. I knew which tenements had doors that could be opened without a key, storm drains that led past several gated alleys to narrow spaces, and I could quickly climb trees. I was accepted as a "go-fer" in the group, not realizing fully what it all meant.

Andrassy Ut was a great, wide, tree-lined street of upscale shops, wealthy people's residences, and embassies. Two double rows of ancient trees grew on both sides, from traffic islands that ran parallel to but separate from the spacious sidewalks.

The German headquarters were located there, behind tall wrought-iron fences and other obstacles. It was tightly guarded and crawling with all sorts of armed goons—even green-shirted Fascists. The news of Hitler's failed assassination was all over town.

The lovely old trees adjacent to that building had been cut down, most likely to give the guards a free field of fire. But they stood rank on rank, densely overlapping and intertwined, as far as the eye could see, all along this spectacular avenue. Such a long urban forest had one drawback: millions of sparrows made it their home. Their chirpings were deafening and almost intolerable, and the rain of droppings beneath those trees was constant. In turn, mites were tormenting the birds.

I was up there among them.

The sun had set, the great city around me in total darkness; not a light showed anywhere. Air raid blackout was a permanent condition in 1944.

My job was to wait for the pre-arranged signal of three quick tugs on my sleeve. A thin thread was attached to it that led to another, older boy farther down in an adjacent tree, from which the area near the structure was in view.

My friends had in the darkness strung out thin, strong, almost invisible piano wire in places where Green Shirts or Nazi guards were known to walk at times, to pick up "whores," women whose occupation I could dimly imagine.

I half-sat on a thick branch, my feet in kind of a large ring, to which a wire was attached, leading to an upper bough. On signal, I was to slip quickly to a standing position, with my full weight in the ring, holding on for balance to the branch I had been sitting on.

That was the plan.

The air raid sirens began to howl and wail for a while, silencing the sparrows' steady, subdued twitterings. The droning of countless aircraft filled the night sky, and the sparrows answered at high volume, increasing even more to a penetrating screech as bombs began to fall not far away, making my tree tremble; the ground itself seemed to heave in waves as the carpet bombing took its inevitable course. By the red light of burning buildings I became aware of the frantic birds' incessant swarming. The sparrows perched for mere seconds in one place and immediately flew a few feet off to perch again a short distance away. Everything was in constant motion all around.

My urge to get out of that tree was about to get the better of me. Had I been abandoned by those boys I trusted? Where were they?

The next minute lasted almost forever. My sleeve jerked sharply three times. I let myself drop from the branch in a short, sickening free fall that came to an end as the invisible wire suddenly grew taut. My chest rested against a branch lower down. Bruised and scratched and in pain, I put my elbows across the excrement-splattered bark. There was a horrible peculiar motion to the ring I stood in; it started to jerk violently, then became still. Next I fell another few inches, recovered my balance, withdrew my feet from the ring, and pulled onto the branch that had held me under the armpits.

Within the time it takes to read a page from the Torah, I had ceased being a child and became the Angel of Death for another human being.

Herman White speaking to Alice Rosenberg's Middle School English classes about his experience in wartime Munich and Hungary as part of their studies of the Holocaust.

By the dim light of distant fires I made my way down, out and away from the trunk. Between the rows of trees, close to the curb, something lay on the dead grass—the figure of a uniformed man. A piano wire nearby no longer taut, nearly tripped me. It led to him. A large puddle surrounded his head, which was at an odd angle.

Had my father's head and body met the morning in a similar random repose?

153

Pursued by the clamor of birds and bombs, I ran—ran until my burning, bleeding feet would carry me no more. The quietly-flowing Danube cooled and cleaned them. The outlet of a hot-spring drain joined the river at that point, the water warmer than the air.

The furious bombardment continued unabated almost till morning. It seemed to me as if those planes equaled the number of sparrows, my companions of that monstrous night.

Well, Master of the Universe, were You pleased with Your most recent underage servant? Sparrow-splotched and mite-infested, I usurped Your thousand-eyed Dark Angel's huge meaningless power and avenged what can never be appeased!

You, whose Name may not be uttered, summon Your Chief Angel Metatron and his brother Sandfalphon. Command them to exhume the bones of my grandfather, grandmother, aunt and uncle. Find for me my murdered father's mouldering bones that I may hurl them at Your winged feet of awe, at Your blinding Face of a thousand suns! Or are You a million infinities away, building ever more universes and numberless eternities? Have you sought refuge from us in the innermost abyss of Your final flower's dark beating heart, to utter once more the fatal Words LET THERE BE LIGHT?

O God of my Ancestors, WHERE WERE YOU! In my dreams within dreams I erect tall towers of bones and stones—stones and bones I have turned over in vain for more than half a century. Yet I no longer search for You—now You must seek me out. I am breathing time under Your million billion trillion stars, enduring all the acceptable losses of a long life, even the unacceptable ones; loss is as perennial as the grass.

Epilogue

I am now blessed with grandchildren whose faces shine like the blossoming springtimes this lovely Earth fashions so easily from sunlight and birdsong every year. Time has taught me to defy the menace in the mirror of nighttime memory, and I believe again that Time itself is the Treasure, and Hope is the Gift of Gifts.

As it has always, this enchanting world turns under garlands of auroral starlight, around a sun that does not count the hour or the eons of its life-giving gifts.

Although everything changes and I've grown old, an immense music rises from the heart of things, calming my restless days. I can live with that.

Herman's family: paternal grandparents center, the rest of the many uncles, aunts, and various other relatives, one or two of whom survived. The rest perished in the Holocaust. Grandfather took his own life before the Nazis came for him.

⊰ Renate G. Justin, M.D. ⊱

Renate's account of her ill treatment as a Jewish child in prewar Germany is heartbreaking. However, her family survived the Holocaust by being able to leave the country before the war started. The family's complete story has been written in Renate's book, <u>The Last Time I Felt Safe</u>, available on Amazon and at Barnes and Noble sites.

Questions That Have No Answers

German anti-Semitism cast a shadow over my childhood as a storm cloud does over the landscape. There was no way I could defend myself against the constant onslaught of anti-Semitism.

My life as a six-year-old youngster, pre-1932 in a small village close to the Harz Mountains, was secure. Our neighbors were friendly, and I knew by name the mailman, the grocer, and the man who delivered ice. I helped turn hay so it would dry and harvested potatoes. As a family, we enjoyed hiking, skiing, and visiting relatives in Kassel, who in turn often came to stay at our ski hut.

My two sisters and I attended the school in Ellrich, along with our many friends. I liked school until the morning we were detained in the schoolyard. Our teacher told us that from that day forward, we would start each school day by saluting the swastika flag and singing the Horst Wessel song—*"Die Fahne Hoch! Die Reihen Fest Geschlossen!"* (The Flag on High! The Ranks Tightly Closed!) Raising our right arm in the Nazi salute was mandatory while singing. We wore aprons with ruffles to school in the early '30s, so I pretended to sing, while covering my mouth with my apron ruffles. But I could not avoid raising

Renate, right, and her sisters

my arm to salute the flag. This daily demonstration of support for the Nazi philosophy was humiliating to me, and I could not wait to get out of the courtyard into the classroom.

However, things began to happen there as well, that were hard for me to understand. In the morning it was our teacher's custom to shake hands with his pupils and greet them, *"Guten Morgen, Gretchen, Guten Morgen, Hans."* When it came my turn to shake hands with the teacher Herr Fischer, he did not extend his hand, stood stiff and silent until I walked on, embarrassed and close to tears. From that day on, I no longer stood in line to say "Good morning" but proceeded directly to my seat. Herr Fischer also failed to call on me any more, even if my hand was the only one raised. I was treated as if I were invisible, not present. My fellow students and friends took a cue from his behavior and stopped playing with me during recess.

"We won't play with Jews." They gave no explanation for this decision. I stood around, alone, watching my erstwhile friends play tag and hopscotch without me. I tried to remember—had I insulted my classmates or hurt their feelings? I could not come up with an explanation for the ostracism I was experiencing. Eventually, the behavior of my peers at school extended to after school. No one accepted invitations to come play in my sandbox or on the swings in our garden. Each year, fewer guests attended my birthday parties, until no one came when I turned eight in 1935.

I questioned my parents, "Why isn't anyone playing with me?" They answered with fear and anxiety in their voices. "Because they don't like Jews."

"Why not?" They had no satisfactory answer to this question.

My parents also experienced rejection by many of their life-long friends, who no longer accepted invitations to afternoon coffee or dinner. It was as if the plague had struck my family, and people were afraid to socialize with us—its victims.

One of the joys of my childhood was to make factory rounds with my father. My sister and I vied with each other to be allowed to go with him, holding his hand to keep us away from the machinery. My father would greet the weavers and spinners by name, ask about their families, and thank them for their good work. I sensed that gradually the tone of these occasions changed; they became less relaxed, less openly friendly. Eventually my father stopped taking us. I think he was afraid his young daughters might say something that would compromise his more and more tenuous situation with his workers.

My sense of isolation and exclusion was further increased by the fact that all our classmates joined the Hitler Youth and spent much time with that organization. Of course we had no desire to join them, nor were we invited.

In 1935, going to and from school became hazardous and painful. On my way, I had to cross a bridge. On one end of that bridge a display case was erected, one of many put up all over Germany, and behind glass the newspaper *"Der Sturmer"* was displayed. This paper pictured caricatures of big-nosed Jews, accused them of low-down, mean behavior and crimes, and called them intrinsically evil beings. A group of teenage boys hung around this display and jeered at my sisters and me as we passed. They called us "damned Jews," "dirty Jews," and other anti-Semitic names that were printed in the headlines of the newspaper, and they emphasized their disdain with well-aimed stones. My older sister clung on to my younger sister and me, urging us to speed up and not be afraid, and to hurry home. However, even our home no longer felt safe. The graffiti that appeared on our garden fence was as insulting as what appeared in the *"Sturmer."* And the garbage that came flying over the fence kept us from enjoying our beautiful garden.

One day, when my eleven-year-old sister came home from school, she noticed a large billboard that had been posted by the Nazi Party in the driveway of my father's textile factory. This board had the letters DAF (German Workers' Front) at the top, and it captured my sister's curiosity. She stood in front of the board and quietly vocalized her guesses as to what DAF meant, none of which were correct. She speculated in a whisper that DAF might stand for *"Deutsches Affenvolk,"* (German monkey folk, which of course is not spelled with an F.) She was overheard by one of the weavers, who had joined the Nazi Party and reported her to the commandant of the local Party unit. My father received a call in his office.

"If your daughter does not leave the country in the next twenty-four hours, both you and she will be jailed."

My parents panicked. They made desperate phone calls and were able to reach a boarding school in the Italian mountains, accessible only via funicular. The staff of that school was prepared to accept refugee children, and my parents put my sister on a train to Italy less than twenty-four hours after that threatening phone call. Anxiously we waited for a telegram.

Did she arrive? Was she homesick? We missed her constantly, worried about her, wanted her home but did not want her jailed. We found out years later that there was no telegraph office on that high mountain, that she did arrive safely, was very homesick, but survived.

I, too, was fearful that I would have to leave my parents. Because of my sister's experience, I became afraid to talk when I was away from home, but also at home we talked less at dinner because we all were sad, finding my sister's enforced and unfair absence hard to bear.

That year, the celebration of Rosh Hashanah, the Jewish New Year, was subdued. The police harassed us during the High Holidays service by marching up and down in front of the temple, making it difficult to even gain access without colliding with them. When we wished each other *"Shanah Tovah"* (a Good New Year), we were apprehensive about what the year might bring. But we had no premonition of the excesses of Kristallnacht, when our house of worship would be burnt down, or of the Holocaust, when our relatives and friends would perish.

By this time, signs had been posted all over our village and in the rest of Germany—*"Juden nicht erlaubt"* (Jews not permitted). The pond where we used to swim every summer and where I had learned how to do the breast stroke had such a sign. Again, I asked, "Why aren't we allowed to swim here any more?"

I was told, "Because Jews supposedly contaminate the water."

Childishly I asked, "How do they do that?"

Again I was told, "I don't know."

It seemed strange to me that none of the adults in my life could answer my simple questions. I expected them to know more.

I remember the May Day parade of strong, young, brown-shirted Nazis yelling, "Heil Hitler! Kill the Jews! Heil Hitler! Kill the Jews!"

By that time I had stopped asking why they wanted to kill us.

Then came the day when, as a Jew, I was no longer permitted to attend school. On that day, my parents decided to send me, and later my younger sister, to Holland. The American Friends Service Committee (Quakers) had opened a school for religious and political refugees in an ancient castle near Ommen, Holland. With the help of the Quakers, my parents were able to send us to this school. I was nine years old and petrified of traveling alone to a place where I would be unable to understand the language and could not trust the adults. I worried about my parents' fate, remembering that refrain, "Heil Hitler! Kill the Jews!"

The pain of our leave-taking has never left me, and I am sure it was one of the most devastating events of my parents' lives. They sent all three of their young daughters—eleven, nine, and seven years old—out of Germany in 1936. Only because of their courage did we survive.

As an adult, when I reflect on the years I lived as a child with the Nazi doctrine, I still cannot answer the questions I raised repeatedly.

"Why did our friends abandon us? Why did those who respected, even loved us, begin to hate us?"

I shake my head and repeat, "I don't know; I cannot find the answer to that query."

Renate G. Justin, M.D.

❖ Helga Kelly-Bach ❖

The story of Helga's family includes a description of how non-Jewish Germans were affected by the Nazis' anti-Semitic policies and practices.

I was born in 1927 and had one brother, Heinz. We lived in Frankfurt, where my family owned and operated a popular hotel of forty rooms. My grandfather Kasper Ilg owned the Hotel *Deutscher Hof*, where my family worked and lived. Guests came from many places—England, France, Italy, and Russia, and included Nazi officers as well as resident Jews. Space in the building was rented out to a candy shop and a liquor store, the latter managed by a Jew. My family had no Jewish prejudice, but the prevalent community anti-Semitic mentality as well as strategy was brought home to us on Kristallnacht, November 9, 1938.

On that horrible night, throughout Germany, Jewish synagogues were burned, Jewish-owned businesses broken into and plundered, store windows broken by organized Hitler mobs, and arrests were made. My father was handcuffed, arrested, and classified as a Jew-lover—called "Jew Mate," because of the Jewish manager in his building. In fact, after Kristallnacht, a sign was

Hotel *Deutscher Hof*,
March 22, 1944

165

hung at the hotel that read "JEW LOVER." A good friend who was a policeman released my father through the back door of the police station. The punishment for us having a Jewish manager of the liquor store was that the government confiscated the hotel.

Signs hung over many local businesses that said, "This store owned by Aryans." We were no longer allowed to have Jewish guests in the hotel. Jews were increasingly isolated from the population by their disappearance and/or arrests, for which we were told they were sent off to "camps"—ostensibly for their "protection" *[This was also the American "public" justification/explanation for interning Japanese-Americans after Pearl Harbor]*. At the time, we didn't know what these camps were. Those Jews remaining in town were required to wear a large yellow Star of David on their clothes, identifying them as Jews.

For many years, two Jewish women from Baden Baden had frequently stayed at our hotel. After this isolation and persecution began, they came to the hotel for fear of being discovered and sent away. We hid them in the attic and cared for them for six weeks undetected, until an employee of ours turned us in. As a result of this, the government then took over the management of the hotel and restaurant; they had previously confiscated it after Kristallnacht.

To place these things into context—the lives of the German people changed in many ways after Hitler took over Germany in 1933. We were constantly watched and totally controlled by the SA Brown Shirts, SS Black Shirts, and Gestapo. It was an uneasy time, and people were afraid to have honest conversations with friends or even family, especially if children were within earshot, for fear of being reported as being unpatriotic and "dangerous" to the regime. Youth training was mandatory for my age group—twelve and thirteen year-old boys and girls. I was not forced to join because of my father's near-blindness, for I was needed to work in the family hotel and restaurant.

I continued schooling in Frankfurt, until I graduated in 1942 after eight years. It was there I learned British English. After graduation I attended a special school in Frankfurt, until an unexploded bomb landed across from the school. My father put a stop to my attending that school because of the apparent dangers.

I saw Hitler on many occasions when he came to Frankfurt. He used to stand up in an open limousine and give the "Heil Hitler" salute to adoring, cheering crowds along the street. In fact, all citizens were required to greet anyone in a German uniform with "Heil Hitler" or suffer consequences. His speeches were very long, sometimes for hours on the radio. In stores and public places, all work stopped while he was talking. He never mentioned God's name in his speeches, and many churches were closed during the Nazi regime.

After the invasion of Russia in 1941, the Germans pulled Russian farm workers, young women as well as young men, from their fields, transported them to Frankfurt on cattle cars, and housed them in our confiscated hotel. (We continued to live in and operate the hotel, for no wages.) These farm workers were illiterate, unwashed, full of lice and fleas, and most had never seen an inside bathroom, toilet, or even a bed to sleep in. Stories abound of how they would put potatoes or other foods into the toilet to wash them. We gave them grapes to eat, and they threw the grapes into the toilet, then hit the flush handle, assuming that would clean the grapes. However, to their surprise, the grapes disappeared.

The government also used these young men and women as laborers to work in the factories in Frankfurt, producing war supplies for the German army.

Bombing of Germany started in 1942 by the British, a year later by the Americans. The British bombed by day; the Americans at night, wave after wave of planes. The first wave dropped explosive bombs; the second wave dropped incendiary bombs

Helga's mother and kitchen staff
at the Hotel Victoria, Giessen

that started burning, then exploding the buildings. The resulting fires did not respond to water; only sand smothered those fires. There was a two-story bunker under the hotel available to the public. It held two hundred people. On one occasion, my dad tried to deal with what appeared to be a dud incendiary bomb that had landed nearby. When he handled it, it exploded and destroyed one eye. The other was already severely impaired, and he was blind for six weeks.

Our hotel was hit once, and we finally had to leave Frankfurt very quickly to avoid being killed in the relentless bombing. We left with just the clothes on our backs and headed approximately fifty miles north of Frankfurt towards the town of Giessen.

After we arrived in Giessen, my entrepreneurial father found a woman who owned a building that was available and helped my father start another restaurant enterprise. The feeling there was that Giessen wouldn't be attacked, but not this time. We barely got out of town and drove away at high speed. One hour later the city was on fire.

After the Giessen hotel and restaurant were bombed out, we went to my Aunt Anna's farm in Weilmunster, which was my father's home town, near Frankfurt. Aunt Anna was married to my father's brother. Mother, Father, and I all lived on the second floor of my aunt's home. (My older brother Heinz had joined the Navy and was stationed on a mine sweeper out on the

North Sea.) More misery awaited us there. We were not allowed to go into the main living quarters of her home and not allowed to use the bathroom in the house. We had to use the outhouse. There was no running water on the second floor where we were living, and we had to haul buckets of water up to the second floor for drinking, cooking, and bathing.

Helga, 1947 Giessan, Germany

Aunt Anna would not sell or supply my family with any food. We only had coupons, which were not enough, and we were starving. She had an ample supply of food for all; she poured milk out to the hogs but would not give us any to drink. She had a vegetable garden and also ample supplies of meat from her chickens, goats, and cattle. We had nothing and had to resort to stealing vegetables from other farmers in order to have something to eat.

One day a German soldier walked into the farm, begging for food. He threw his gun down. He looked like skin and bones. He told us stories of the concentration camps, which we had never heard of, how the inmates used their blood to leave messages for their families. He slept in the barn and was gone by morning. We had a hard time believing what he told us.

Finally, at the end of the war in 1945, American tanks appeared while we were living in Weilmunster. The U.S. Army rolled into the valley from four directions in tanks and occupied the town. We were not afraid of those American tanks. The military authority then posted proclamations that defined the rules and regulations of the occupation forces. For example, curfews from 7 P.M. to 7 A.M. forbade residents to be out after dark or they would be shot. Fraternization was forbidden too, but that rule was ignored, with predictable results!

The mayor of Weilmunster was asked by the U.S. military authorities if anyone could help with interpretation from English into German and vice-versa. I was only seventeen years old but had studied English in school, and that's when I was recruited as an interpreter for the U.S. Army! Most soldiers spoke slang, and I spoke the King's English learned at school. I was the only person there who spoke English, and the American soldiers needed me to translate. My duties involved registering all residents, even collecting weapons, which included knives, live ammunition, hand grenades, rifles, pistols, and machine guns. Germans also had to get new passports and turn in their old ones to the American authorities.

The Military Police supplied me with K rations, which I shared with my mother and father back at Aunt Anna's farm. They had heard about how my aunt treated my family regarding the food situation on her farm. So they developed a plan with me how to raid the farm and how I could help them. They were hungry for home-cooked meals and had found out that our family had run a hotel and restaurant in Giessen and in Frankfurt. So they helped supply us with food, and my family cooked home-style meals for the MPs at the farm. In fact, I was almost shot by the Military Police one night while "legitimately" getting food supplies from the U.S. Army!

My father was very creative and talented and knew many of the villagers in Weilmunster. There were many vineyards in the area. U.S. Army personnel were always looking for drinks other than water, so with my father's help they started a crude wine-making operation in Weilmunster. The MPs also recruited some of the German POWs to collect and clean empty bottles to be used for storing the wine from the distillery.

My first husband Edward L. Kelly was a Military Police sergeant during his assignment in Germany. He was there about four years. We were married in Giessen, West Germany, in March 1949. It took approximately two years for the military government to investigate my background in order to get permission to marry.

On June 9, 1949, Ed and I boarded the *General Thomas Barry* in Bremerhaven for the trip to America. That trip as a war bride took nine days on rough seas. The accommodations for men and women were separate, including married couples. The ship arrived in the port of New York on June 18.

After the war and arrival in America, Ed was employed with the Plumbers and Pipe Fitters Union. His job was involved with the installation of nuclear power plants throughout the country. As a result of Ed's responsibilities, we resided in many states, at least ten in all, including Alaska. These many relocations complicated my getting American citizenship. It took approximately three years, since I had to have individuals from each of my addresses verify my residing at these locations. I had to write to many of these people and request that they vouch for my honesty, integrity, and willingness to become an American citizen. That is why I appreciate being a citizen of the United States of America.

The preceding narrative was compiled from interviews with and written material from Helga. The following essay is something she wrote for her two children Mo and Mike at Christmastime in 1970 in Morris, Illinois. It is revealing in that she describes her honest, spontaneous emotions about her past life as well as her feelings about life in America.

Why Do I Love America

When my children asked me about my education, which I received in Europe during the Second World War and was cut short because of the bombings, it brought to mind the many days and nights we ran for our lives, the horrible feeling of sitting in basements waiting for death, hoping not to be buried alive, drowned, burned, or suffocated.

When the first bombs fell on Frankfurt, and one of those hit the school across the street from my school, my parents decided it was better to die together than to wait for a child perhaps never to come home from school. When the time did come, and we were burned out and lost all but what we had on our bodies, at least we were together. Months of hunger followed. Christmas was spent in the country, and our holiday dinner consisted of bean soup cooked on a pot-bellied stove, for which the wood was cut from bombed-out buildings and hauled by cart by my dad and me. There was no running water, and I had to haul it from a well and carry it upstairs. The rooms were cold, electricity was scarce, and food hard to come by.

The following year we moved back into the city, finding another business for my dad, but our luck ran out again. Five months later and two weeks before Christmas we were bombed out again and back into the same dismal existence until the war ended, and the American soldiers occupied the country. We were hungry no longer. The GIs shared their food with us, and the white bread tasted like cake.

When I came to America in 1949 I could not believe my eyes—what a beautiful country this is. I still marvel at that and have seen much of this lovely land of ours. Yes, I am a proud citizen of the United States of America. It has been good to me—the freedom and ability to travel freely, to make a good living if you are willing to work, the kindness and generosity of the American people and their ready acceptance of foreigners, the education offered for youngsters, and the endless opportunities for everybody.

I hope and pray that the young people of this country take a second look at what they have and THANK GOD for their ancestors who made this country what it is today and will help to keep it, improve it and cherish it, like a mother does her child.

Helga J. Kelly

Helga Kelly-Bach

⊰Win Schendel⊱

Born in 1931, Win grew up in Hannover as an only child. His father was a well-trained and versatile professional— a practicing architect, then a physician.

Win had to join the Hitler Youth when he was eight, because membership was required. Thrice weekly attendance at meetings was also required on Wednesdays, Saturdays, and sometimes on Sunday. Even at that young age, paramilitary training was part of the "curriculum," and the boys wore uniforms. Many former members describe membership as being similar in many respects to Boy Scouts: an emphasis on comradeship, fitness, service, and good citizenship. As the boys got older, politics entered into their training, and they were called on to serve paramilitary duties. On one occasion when Win was about eleven, a friend told Win's mother that she should not send Win to a particular meeting one night. She kept him home and learned later that the boys in attendance were put onto a truck and taken off somewhere to the front for wartime duties. Later, when he was older, Win was caught in a similar situation.

When he was thirteen he was pressed into anti-aircraft service to help defend his community of Bueckeburg, along with other boys his age and

Six-year-old Win, first day of school with congratulatory bouquet.

elderly men. Artillery barrages began as American forces neared. "My mother and I experienced about a hundred raids. We were terrified of the Americans, portrayed as 'headhunters' by propaganda." After the Americans came as occupiers, they realized they had nothing to fear any longer from planes flying over, and that the American GI was "much like us."

He stayed in the *Hitler Jugend*, Youth Group, until the end of the war. The *Jugend* was often required to march before dignitaries on special occasions. One of these might be a funeral procession for someone in authority (found alive after the war in a concentration camp). It was believed that Hitler "deposed," sometimes killed, early supporters who subsequently disagreed with him, because he feared that their dissension might lead to organized resistance, which would in turn lead to deposing him.

At age nine Win met Hitler under unique circumstances. The family was driving through the city of Bayreuth and stopped to make a visit to the grave site of composer Richard Wagner. It turned out to be a memorable encounter, as Hitler and staff members drove up while the family was there. Hitler was a known devotee of Wagner's works. This was not a ceremonial occasion, and there were no other visitors. So Win's mother urged the young lad to approach the Fuhrer, greet him, and shake his hand, which he did properly—"Heil, Mein Fuhrer." Hitler turned to accept the greeting, accidentally stepping on Win's foot, whose shoe came off in the process. Apparently the Fuhrer was unaware of the situation and didn't acknowledge what gave Win a life-long distinction and very special memory to share.

Eventually Win became suspicious about some things he was witnessing and didn't understand, such as friends leaving school unexpectedly, citizens being picked up and disappearing, the burning of synagogues, etc. He added, "Today, if I noticed things like that in America I would do something about it; I would speak up. Trouble was then we were afraid to speak up." His father was not a Nazi sympathizer nor Party member, which automatically raised a red flag about such an individual's loyalty. Young Win innocently remarked to a friend that he was "glad we don't have a flag, because we would have to hang it up." When his friend repeated the remark to his own father, it reached the attention of the Gestapo. Identifying resistance/dissenters through the innocent remarks of children was a give-away to the sentiments expressed within their homes. Win's father's medical office was in the family home, and the Gestapo visited him there more than once. They took his radio and his car, the latter for military use. Sometimes he was taken elsewhere for interrogations. He didn't reveal to his young son what went on during those sessions, but when he returned home, it was evident that he had been "gone over." As a result of his refusal to join the Party-controlled Medical Society, he was ordered into the military. However, that didn't happen; he simply didn't return from one interrogation session, and his fate was unknown.

The Jewish question affected citizens in general. Win's mother had to fill out an extensive genealogy record to verify the family's non-Jewish heritage. The Nazi eagle icon was stamped on that record as verification that there was less than 1/8th Jew in the blood line.

Another of the tactics of control by the regime was to keep very close touch with the whereabouts of German citizens. Every move or change was accompanied by a required stop at the police station.

Experiencing the bombing was naturally traumatic for this innocent young lad. He saw charred bodies in the street and witnessed people dying in the burning streets as they fled their homes during air raids. "I'll never forget the smell of dead people; it's a sweetish smell."

There was great displacement of citizens as a result of the bombing, and on one occasion, when Win and his mother were forced out of their home in Hannover, officials chose a farmhouse

Win and his mother 1947, confirmation into the Lutheran Church, ordinarilly done at the age of 14. But during the Nazi era such church-related activties were prohibited.

outside of town for them and some other refugees. On the day of their arrival it was raining hard, and their furniture and few belongings were unloaded and left outside in the rain. They were housed temporarily in this particular house, its owners unknown to their new "tenants," and likely serving as hosts was an assignment by the authorities.

After being bombed out of Hannover, Win and his mother were later able to resettle in Bueckeburg, west of Hannover. They made the best they could of what accommodations were available. Immediately following the end of the war, for about a year the schools were closed, and there was no order, no police. Win describes how craters left from the bombing were filled with water, and he built a flower and vegetable garden around the perimeter, including some tobacco plants. He also raised angora rabbits in cages.

His father was gone, and he admits that although he loved his mother, he was always more afraid of her even than of his teachers. She had been a teacher, and no doubt retained some of the disciplinary strategies she had applied in the classroom. For example, the rod in both places was a familiar and accepted tool that even young students could expect to result from the most minor misdemeanors; returning late from recess would be one occasion. Both boys and girls could qualify for the rod's application to their hands or to their backsides.

The day Win became a citizen of the United States of America, 1952

Approval by U.S. government for Win to immigrate to the United States.

After the war, Win somehow learned that his father was buried in a graveyard in the town of Gerden, west of and near Hannover. That graveyard is no longer in existence as a burial grounds, and the fate of the human remains it contained is unknown.

In 1952 Win and his mother emigrated to Houston, where she had relatives. It was Win's idea to leave Germany and search for opportunity elsewhere, and his mother was agreeable to accompanying him on the venture. Coming to America took three years of trips to the embassy in Bremen and its bureaucracy to accomplish (including investigation by the FBI). Requirements included a health examination, in Win's case sponsorship by relatives, promise of employment, and always the assurance that applicants didn't have Nazi associations. The pair boarded a freighter, which made several stops along the way and finally reached New Orleans three weeks later. Now retired in Colorado, Win worked as an engineer in Houston and later as an insurance agent and manager in Colorado.

It is clear that Win is a very patriotic American, dedicated to supporting the American way of life, and he considers it a privilege to be an American citizen. He and his mother attended the American Legion's citizenship school weekly for a year, becoming citizens in 1956. Anyone who has seen the instruction volume accompanying that course of study understands the effort and commitment required to pass the course. It is an accomplishment not to be assessed lightly, and Win well understands how important it is for citizens to vote and to vote intelligently. As a result, he is wary and critical of the complacency he has found in America, having experienced the worst of how government can abuse its citizens, as well as the world around them.

Win and his wife Joanne

❧ Mutti's Story ❧

by M.J. Brett

M.J. Brett is an American author who has written the story of a German woman's trek halfway across Europe during WWII with her three young sons. The title of her novel is <u>Mutti's War</u> (Blue Harmony Press, available on Amazon). It is based on the true wartime experiences of Brett's German husband's family, and is recommended reading. Mutti, Regina Woolf, is Ms. Brett's mother-in-law.

Mutti broke Nazi laws to smuggle her children out of East Prussia and Soviet laws to try to get them to the West zone. She had to make choices no one should ever have to make, but this excerpt from the book describes just one of her attempts to deal with three hungry, tired, scared little boys, on their search for her missing husband and the boys' father. The family's wartime saga is dramatic from one end to the other.

Potatoes and Pitchforks

Regina Woolf, a naïve young mother from East Prussia, had to smuggle her three small boys out of Konigsberg in August of 1944 in order to save them from the Russian advance on Germany. Walking the children across Poland, then mainland Germany, then Czechoslovakia, and back to Germany during WWII was not an easy task. She had to defy Nazi laws, close the door of her home and walk away, not knowing if she could ever go back to her old life. In addition, she had no idea where her husband Gustav was after he was drafted into the military.

Mutti's quest to find Gustav, then missing for two years, brings a deep mystery to his high-ranking job in the Wehrmacht.

What she finally discovers tested her heart and soul.

After six weeks on the road, the boys are hungry, exhausted, scared of the strafing planes, and Mutti (short for the formal *Mutter* or Mother) doesn't know how to go on. She must find something to eat for the children, as they have gone without for three days, and the youngest, Franzi, cries constantly from hunger.

The weary family traveled as far as they could by day, taking turns pulling Franzi in the wagon Willi had found broken and had repaired. They'd been gleaning discarded vegetables for their meager evening meal. But the road led uphill, and the hillside farmers seemed to have used all food for themselves. The deformed, dried out, or even rotten potatoes and turnips the boys sometimes found along the way, had disappeared. It had been three days since they had had anything to eat.

They stopped that night in the forest near a village called Nijdek, camping on the banks of a small stream. But Mutti had nothing to boil in her can that night.

She could see how thin her boys had become. There was unmistakable evidence of malnutrition. Her own dress hung loosely on her shapeless body as well, but it was the pain in her children's eyes that forced her decision. Leaving the younger children in Willi's care, Mutti walked to the nearest farmhouse. Although she had never before resorted to begging, her children needed something to eat soon.

Vati Gustav, Willi, Rainer & Mutti, 1938

184

A large wooden farmhouse loomed in the growing darkness. It was attached to the barn in the fashion of the *Sudetten Deutsch*. Mutti could barely make out the ramp slanting up to the barn's second floor where hay was normally stored, so it could be forked down easily to the animals waiting underneath. The animal warmth, in return, helped to heat the adjoining house. She never liked the pungent animal odors in such a farmhouse, but the residents never seemed to notice. This farmstead looked as though it had existed since the Middle Ages, with its thatched roof extending out to cover an outdoor privy and washstand.

"I hate doing this," she thought, nevertheless forcing her feet to march on. She burned with shame.

When Mutti knocked on the door, she heard rustling, footsteps, and a door slamming. She knocked again. A woman her own age opened the door a crack and peered at her. "What do you want?" she asked.

"We've been on the road for over a month, and my children are terribly hungry. Do you have any food at all that I might give them? I've only a little money left, but I'm willing to work for you. I can cook or cut wood."

"We don't want anyone poking around here, and we don't have any food to spare, either." The woman started to push the door shut, but an older man appeared behind her and forced it open wider.

"Where are your children?" he asked. A sly sort of smile played around his lips.

"Waiting for me by the river." Mutti answered, warily. Something was strange about this pair. From the rustling noises at her knock, she suspected they were hiding someone, perhaps an Army deserter.

"Come out to the barn. I can give you a few potatoes if you will pitch some hay. You look healthy, if a bit skinny."

The woman looked at him strangely, extending her hand to his arm as though trying to restrain him. She looked alarmed. "Joachim, we must have enough for the others."

"Hold your tongue, Frau," he ordered, pushing her hand away. "We can find a little extra if she is willing to work."

"Come on, Girl," he said, motioning Mutti to follow him.

The woman stood watching from the doorway for some time before she sighed and closed the door.

Mutti noticed he used the terms "girl" and "frau" as though they were proper names.

Once in the upstairs barn, he kicked aside some hay and pulled up a floorboard. A large tub of potatoes was hidden underneath. He held out three withered potatoes, but as Mutti reached for them, he pulled them back. "You said you'd work. There's the pitchfork." He pointed to the tool leaning in a corner.

Mutti picked up the pitchfork. "Where would you like the hay moved?"

He pointed. "Over there, you pretty little thing." With a smirk on his face, he moved between Mutti and the barn door. "You can have the potatoes when we're through."

The hair on her neck prickled some primitive warning, but she needed those potatoes. She also knew her waiting boys would soon be getting frightened. Determined to hurry, she lifted the hay from one part of the barn floor and heaved it to where the farmer had indicated. Mutti could see no reason why the newly indicated spot was any better than the old one, but it was not her barn. Her muscles strained, since she'd never before pitched hay.

Mutti could feel the man watching her intently. Glancing warily over her shoulder, she saw him edge around toward the door. She kept working, but she could sense his motion. Suddenly, he grabbed her from behind and shoved her into the pile of hay. Instinctively Mutti fought, scratching at his face, kicking and pushing him away while trying to crawl backwards. The man grabbed her legs. She kicked him again and struggled to her feet. He pushed her against the wall, cutting off her escape, and knocked her down again.

Mutti rolled over toward where she had dropped the pitchfork, grabbed it, kicked him again, and managed to swing to her feet in one fluid motion. The man scrambled to a crouched position. Mutti aimed the pitchfork at him.

He laughed. "You won't use that thing on me. I'll tell the authorities you were trying to steal our food, and they'll lock you up. I'll bet you don't even have papers for this part of the country."

"Of course I have papers," Mutti lied, hoping she could bluff him. She wasn't sure she could actually stab someone, and she hoped this vicious man wouldn't force her to find out.

"Come on, my little one," he cajoled, all the time maneuvering her around the floor. "Give me that pitchfork. Lie down on the hay, and I'll make you happy. I'll bet your man has been away for a long time now." He leered at her again. "Or is he already dead?" His voice was revolting, wheedling, suggestive.

She knew he was trying to distract her. Her eyes followed each move he made. The man circled slowly around her, inching closer. Mutti also moved around, trying to keep the pitchfork between them to gain some space. When she had positioned herself close to the door, he lunged toward her again. She could wait no longer. She swung at him hard with the flat side of the pitchfork to knock him off balance, then pushed the points straight at him. He yelped and grabbed his side.

Mutti hurtled out the door as he fell. She might be faster than he was, but she needed those potatoes. She ran down the ramp and hid behind a water barrel, shaded by the overhanging roof.

The man burst from the barn, cursing loudly, and limped in the direction of nearby trees where he obviously believed she had run. She could see him still holding his side. Upon reaching the trees, he called out, "Where are you, Girl!?" When silence was his only answer, he returned to the barn more quietly, as though searching in the dark for some clue.

Mutti was unsure whether to run, which would give away her hiding place, or wait for him to go away. Endless moments ticked by as she crouched with the farm team's harness hanging over her head. Torn between the two actions, another option swayed her decision – those potatoes for her boys. She stayed still.

The man stumbled around rattling implements in the tool-shed and cursing loudly. A lantern appeared at the door of the house, and the woman's voice called out, "What are you two doing out there? Get back in here, Joachim, I need you, NOW!" With a final curse and much muttering under his breath, the man walked toward the house, clumped across the porch and entered, slamming the door.

Mutti couldn't suppress her giggle, as she realized this lout of a man was afraid of his wife. She could hear them screaming at each other. While they argued, she slipped back up the ramp, through the barn door, and picked up her three potatoes. She hesitated, then lifted the floorboard and took three additional good ones. It serves him right, she assured herself.

As Mutti worked her way back downstream, she could barely hear Willi hooting at a nearby owl. The owl kept answering back, and the two sounded almost alike. She smiled, realizing he was trying to distract the younger boys, who were both afraid of the dark.

Rainer and Franzi were up a tree with Willi, waiting with solemn faces. Willi had kept them from following their mother, first by holding them down with force, then by making them climb the tree. Mutti proudly held out her apron in front of them. They squealed with delight at the sight of the potatoes and shimmied down the tree in mere seconds.

For reasons she did not explain to the children, Mutti moved their camp further away from the farm before lighting their little fire and cooking finely chopped potatoes in water from the stream. The boys ate every bit of her potato soup and pronounced it excellent.

Only after she had boiled the can to clean it did Rainer ask, "What did you have to pay for the potatoes, Mutti?"

Mutti smiled. "Oh, nothing much. I just had to do a little work with a pitchfork." This time she did not feel guilty about stretching the truth.

The boys soon fell asleep. Only then did her uncontrollable shaking begin, as always, after danger had passed. What could she have done had the man been stronger or younger? And what would Gustav have

Mutti, Regina Woolf 1944

thought about her stealing the extra three potatoes?

The following is a brief excerpt from Willi's story in SAME WAR DIFFERENT BATTLEFIELDS, cited previously. It describes another touching incident resulting from the sort of wartime situation that impacted children—not as dramatic nor as tragic as many other wartime stories, but an important issue for young Willi (Ulli). "Eric" is the Americanized version of his real name, Ulrich, or "Ulli" to his family. Brett changed all names in Mutti's War, so in the novel, he became "Willi."

Willi's Shoes

I think Vati (Father) had given Mutti (Mom) a lot of money before he left, but soon after the war with the Soviets started, money wouldn't buy anything. There was simply nothing to buy, whether one had money or not. Clothes were recycled between family members, and later even to other families. Prussians had always been too proud to do that before the war. We passed clothes down to the next boy, which Mutti thought quite practical, and it didn't bother us a bit because Mutti would always buy me more clothes. But soon there was nothing to pass down. There was no more to buy, and I had less and less to wear, and with my growth spurt, my shoes no longer fit either. Mutti and Nanny cut down one of my father's business suits to make me a suit for school, but shoes were a problem. Unfortunately, it was winter and snow was on the ground, so Mutti could not be persuaded to allow me to run barefoot. There seemed to be no one who was my size who could pass on their shoes, and certainly none to buy. Finally, Mutti gave me her old gardening shoes to wear to school.

I might have been all right had the other children not noticed. I still remember the feeling of humiliation as Gerte and Hilde pointed their fingers and giggled until the other kids noticed too, and they all made fun of me. "Why, Ulli has on lady shoes," Hilde said, and everyone repeated the phrase in unison, "Ulli has on lady shoes! Ulli has on lady shoes!"

I did the only thing that made sense to me at the time; I ran away. After that, I walked to school, attended all day, avoiding other children of course, and walked home, in the snow, barefoot. I carried Mutti's shoes in my knapsack and put them on just as I got on our street, so she wouldn't see me without them. The truth came out when I became very ill, and Mutti and Nanny tsk-tsked over my blue, blistered, frost-bitten feet and scolded me continually. I cried and said I wouldn't wear lady shoes no matter how much they punished me. Three days of bread and water did nothing to change my mind, so Mutti kept me home from school until we could trade for a pair of worn-out shoes from an older boy who only had a younger sister, so his could not be passed down. The younger sister got Mutti's gardening shoes, and I got the boy's rundown-at-the-heels shoes. But they were far better than wearing my mother's, so I never complained that they hurt my feet.

Willi, 4 and Ranier, 2

⊰ JohannPfeffer ⊱

Johann's memoir describes an out-of-Germany experience of prejudice and discrimination.

I was born in 1934 in Croatia, which was part of Yugoslavia that was separated during Hitler's time, forced back to Yugoslavia in 1945, and is now an independent country (since about 1992). My father was a farmer; he was Austrian but born in Yugoslavia (Austria-Hungary, now Croatia), and my mother was Hungarian. I had six siblings, and I lived in Croatia for eight years until 1942, then in Poland and Germany for a while. During the war, we considered ourselves German citizens.

My father was not a Nazi and was not involved in politics. He did belong to a German Cultural Club, but that was a social group. Nearby Serbia, also part of present Yugoslavia, was staunchly allied with the Russians, and Croatia was pro-German. There was definite animosity between the two populations. My dad was considered an enemy of the Serbs because of his Austrian name, which linked him to the Germans. On one occasion, the Serbian guerillas/partisans came to our farm and wanted to take him. They subsequently let him go after interrogating him. But he often hid in our barn when they were in the neighborhood; he was afraid they would take him again.

After the Germans came into Croatia during the war against Serbia and Russia in October of 1942, they said we must leave Croatia. We were told we were going to Germany, but in fact were taken to Poland. When the Germans occupied Poland in 1939, they took many of the Poles to Germany for slave labor. Their houses were left vacant, and their possessions left behind.

We lived in a Polish village in one of these houses, part of a big refugee camp. There was no store, but all food and cigarettes were provided. My older brother joined the Hitler Youth while we lived there; I was too young.

After five months, the Germans decided that we new "immigrants" should work as farmers and take over a Polish farm, although our former grocer was allowed to sell groceries in Poland. My family acted like they didn't know the German language like some other refugees did, so the Germans sent us to Germany to farm and to learn German. In 1943 we were re-settled on a big farm north of Munich. We were paid for our labor. We got food stamps from the government and had enough to eat, but nothing excessive. A neighbor had a car that ran on charcoal; there was no fuel at the end of the war, and that car had been adapted to operate on charcoal.

Several people worked on this farm, including French POWs. We lived in a big house. It was like a triplex; a Polish family shared the house, and a Munich refugee family stayed upstairs.

There were Serbian prisoners working on a neighboring farm. Neither the Serbs nor our family spoke much German; we all spoke Croatian. The Serb and Croat language is the same, except the alphabet is different. Consequently, when they came over to visit, we could communicate with each other. The manager of the farm reported that my dad associated with Serbs, and he was taken to Munich to the SS headquarters for questioning. He told his story, and they let him go.

Johann, 1951

During and after the war, the German government, then later the American occupiers, provided food stamps. We had enough to eat, because we also had our own garden. We did not suffer like some people in cities and in other parts of the country. The Germans also gave us clothing taken from the Jews and other concentration camp internees; Dachau was five miles away. Jewish labor from the camp was used to build the Autobahn. I visited the camp site on a trip to Germany in 1962 and learned that the gas chambers didn't operate there.

The area near our farm was bombed from 1943-45, because there were munitions factories nearby. We saw huge, six-engine planes protected by smaller, one-engine escorts. The nearest factory was five miles away, but the bombing was frightening. We hid in the basement. Planes went over frequently, and we were told to dive into the nearest ditch if we were outdoors when they flew over. The more maneuverable escorts would fly low over us.

One day in 1945, toward the end of the war, American forces came up the main road to about a half-mile away, but we didn't see any of our troops at that time. There was a German tank hiding nearby, and when the Americans saw it, the shooting started and we hid.

In 1946 we moved to another farm, closer to Munich. By 1955, I was twenty-one and ready to leave Germany. I had completed my education, apprenticed as an

Johann, Korea 1959

electrician for three years, and worked until 1957, when I left for the USA. Jobs were scarce in Germany. I had friends in Denver, and America appealed to me. I applied for immigration, but it took until 1957 before I got a sponsor and was ready to go. The National Catholic Conference in New York City sponsored me, and I headed to the USA to a job with an electrical contractor. However, by the time I arrived he didn't need me and I needed a job.

I did a lot of different things in a lot of different places. I worked as a dishwasher near Philadelphia for a couple months. Next stop was Cleveland, where I connected with a lady I knew in Croatia, a former neighbor. I worked nearly a year there as a helper in a machine shop. Then I was drafted in 1958, although I was not yet an American citizen. I served in the Army for two years, including a year in Korea as an Infantry rifleman. In 1960 I was discharged at Fort Lewis in Washington state and took a bus to Cleveland, stopping briefly to visit Croatian friends in Denver. I lived briefly in Los Angeles, worked as a bus boy in San Francisco, then went to Germany for a year. My parents were still near Munich. Back in San Francisco I worked in control electrical wiring until 1969, when I came to Denver again to settle permanently.

I am presently retired and living in Aurora, a suburb of Denver.

⊰ Ursula Stack ⊱

Ursula's story presents distinctive insights to which we haven't previously been privileged—a description of growing up in wartime Berlin within a Nazi household, where fear of the government was not a concern like some other contributors have reported. However, being "connected" didn't spare the family from the ravages of bombing, food shortages, and the terror of Russian occupation of postwar Berlin.

When Hitler took over in 1933, Ursula's family enthusiastically embraced his message. He promised the German people bread and jobs. He responded positively to the despair Germany experienced as a result of the terms of the Treaty of Versailles which ended World War I. Most importantly, he gave back hope and assurance that things would get better, that Germany would be a great nation once again.

With such promises, it isn't surprising that Ursula's father became a Nazi, joined the S.A. (the dreaded Brown Shirts), and then became a member of the Gestapo. Exactly what he did during the war years wasn't known to the family, although it is known that he spent time in Poland. He turned mean and rough, and when he became abusive toward Ursula's mother, they divorced.

I had a wonderful childhood, the oldest of six kids about two years apart. I was born in 1927, and we lived in Berlin. My dad was an electrician until he started off with Hitler. I remember when I was little, a few times they brought my dad home and he was unconscious. They were fighting the Communists out in the street, and he had gotten hurt.

We had one room that was always locked; it belonged to a friend of my father. There was a two-story-long flag with a swas-

Ursula's sister Irmgard, age five and Ursula age eight

tika on it hanging from the window of that room. I remember from my mom talking about it, but I do remember myself holding on to my mom's apron when the police came to the door to take down the flag. My mom told them, "Sorry, but I can't get in there; it is rented out, and they should take down the Communist flag at the bar across the street if they want this flag down." The flag at our apartment stayed up. All this was before Hitler took control of the government.

My dad later became Gestapo (undercover state police). He wore a Rohm dagger with his uniform. Rohm was a man who got shot. I remember my dad taking me to work with him at his office across the Reichs Kanzlei from Hitler's house, up a beautiful stairway. Halfway up the stairs was a plaque; that was where Rohm was killed.

I was in the *Jung Made* or *BNM* (*Bund Deutscher Madchen*). It was for German girls, like the American Girl Scouts. There was a group from age seven to fourteen, then a senior group until age sixteen, then to a women's group. I stopped at fourteen, because after eight years of schooling you go to work. You learn a trade for three years or go to high school and university. In BDM we had lots of fun. Like here in the U.S. we respected the flag, and we were very proud of it. We had meetings about things that we were going to do, like service projects, learning handiwork, raising money, being courteous and helpful, and so forth.

We went to parades and took part in rallies. We went on streetcars (no autos), and we did lots of walking. And if any high officials came to Berlin, we went out and waited for hours to see them. The police always let us stand in front because we all looked so nice in our uniforms: dark blue wool skirts, white blouses, and a triangular, black scarf rolled up and held by a braided leather knot. We had gold-colored jackets like corduroy, very fitted, with little pockets to hold money. We had always to look neat. I remember seeing Churchill, Chamberlain, and Mussolini. Mussolini was supposed to come at two in the afternoon and didn't get in until midnight. It was raining cats and dogs, and we stood under the Brandenburg Gate to stay dry. How fanatic you get when you are young!

One time I was at a parade when Hitler's car came. Everyone was so excited and kept pushing. The police had a line holding hands to hold the people back, and they let me stand in front of them because of the crowd. And then the people started pushing, and the line broke, and I got pushed forward and fell in front of Hitler's car. They stopped, and the police picked me up. I wasn't hurt, but the funny thing is, I remembered it when I came to Colorado Springs. We went to the Old Town Museum,

A tender photo of four-year-old Ursula with her beloved father Karl Wesner in better times

and here was one of Hitler's cars parked! It made me laugh. It was an older car; he had lots of them. Another time, I presented a bouquet of flowers to the Fuhrer.

I also remember being at the opening for the 1936 Olympics in Berlin. We had to wear our jackets and sit in seats that were marked, so that when we were told to take off our jackets, it spelled out *"Gross Deutschland"* (which means Great Germany) on our white blouses.

In the summer we had trips to the country, taking about two hours to a farmhouse where the farmer would let us stay in the barn, and we would sleep on the hay, washing in the morning with cold water from the outside pump and cooking on a little oil stove. We carried a backpack just like the soldiers did, with a blanket rolled up around it. It was very heavy, so some of the bigger girls carried mine for me, and all I had to carry was my guitar. We would walk around in the woods, sing folk songs, and play the guitar.

In winter we were busy with building toys for needy children. With a jigsaw and blocks of wood and light weight wood, we would make trains, cars, dollhouses, building blocks. We painted and decorated the dollhouses. Every year for three months before Christmas, we did things like that.

During the war years I was working for a salon as a tailor's apprentice. We did just designer originals, but with so much bombing going on, we had to go into ready wear. There was a little basement built out into a bunker, so every night we had to carry all the finished clothes and all the material down into the basement. Every morning we had to carry it all upstairs again to work on it.

I was fourteen when I started to work. You are treated as an adult, and "you will act as an adult." So you grow up fast, but that's not so bad. No time for BDM anymore but still going to the theater and opera and movies. I was an autograph hunter, and some of our customers were movie star wives. My boss used to send me to deliver sometimes. She would say, "No, Ursula, no autographs." When I came back, she would stand there laughing and say, "OK, what did he write down for you?"

My boss was a very elegant lady; I looked up to her. She trained me a lot faster than some of the other apprentices; she had three of them. She taught me more than she had to. She made me learn some office work and paid me more money than the others. It wasn't much, but I tried to do my best.

We had duty twice a month to stay overnight. Each company needed one person each night in case of fire from bombing. We had cubicles in a downstairs room with a cot and blanket and pillow. I was on duty with a men's tailor and a furrier. Instead of sitting and playing cards, they went upstairs to work. I went along, so I also learned from them men's tailoring and to work with fur. I made myself a jacket out of scraps of white rabbit fur, all by hand.

On Saturday we did not work; we had trade school. They taught us all the little tricky things that they thought our bosses didn't have time to teach us. I also went for Red Cross nursing classes for four hours, four times a week from 6-10 P.M., and I barely made it back home before the sirens went off. After that training, during the last two years of the war I worked as a Red Cross nurse.

For entertainment we went to nightclubs to listen to music; there was no dancing allowed during the war, but we had a lot of parties with friends. Everybody's living space was cramped, including our house with six kids and an old lady living with us because we had to rent out one room. Too many people without a place to live. We had a curfew, so when we had parties, we had to stay over, sleep in the bath tub, on the floor, wherever you could find a place to lie down.

But we had a great time playing American music (and dancing privately). When we would go to the theater, we would often end up in a different shelter. Most theaters had big basement shelters for the crowds. Night clubbing you just went for the music and drinks. There was no age limit for drinking. They had beautiful bands but no dancing. We weren't allowed to dance because it was wartime; soldiers were fighting and dying, and such "gaiety" was inappropriate. We used to go to the balconies where they stored extra chairs and tables, and one person was a lookout for police coming and checking, and we would dance there.

We had good times until two years before the war was over, and things started to go bad. We grew up with clean streets and houses, and good food. Hitler was an admirer of Grecian things; he built buildings, beautiful great highways. He sponsored sporting events and built facilities for them, and he felt that everyone should be able to afford to go to the theater.

But he was also a stickler for a pure race; that's when the trouble started for the Jews. I remember my mom getting mad; she lost her lawyer, her doctor, and one of the store owners where she shopped. They were Jewish and were gone. I lost my best friend, Stephanie Hirsch. Her parents sent her to South America to family they had there. Before I knew it, her parents were gone too. After the war I went out to eat, and there was Mr. Hirsch! When I played with his daughter, he was disabled, in a wheel chair. Now after the concentration camp he walked with a cane, but he lost his wife; she didn't make it.

But the war years were tough. Constant alert for bombing. While I was working learning a trade in tailoring I never knew if the next morning the street car would take me to work or if there was enough damage that I would have to walk for two hours to work. Food was rationed, but with a big family, we had plenty. We used to carry our holiday roast and all our butter down to the shelter with us. The last two years we had bombing at 10 A.M.

and at 10 P.M. We were happy when the weather was bad; then the Americans couldn't fly. We never got undressed until after midnight because there was no time to get dressed when the sirens went off. So we went to sleep with our clothes on and suitcases packed. When the siren went off, everyone grabbed a suitcase and off we went to the shelter. The suitcases had our important papers and pictures in them. In the shelter you would sit and knit or read or visit with your neighbors, hoping and praying your home was still there. My mom used to say, "How can anyone make war with a country like America?" I remember my mom sitting like a mother hen with five kids in front of her, huddling over them when we heard the bombs fall.

They always told us that the one that hit, you won't hear. When you hear the sound of all the planes humming coming in for the bombing, it was awesome. Kids were tired in school because they didn't get enough sleep. I remember the one that hit shortly before the war was over. It must have been the last one to destroy anything because most of Berlin was already destroyed. Where I worked was gone, our school was hit, and we were stuck in the shelter. The doors would not open, and the lights were out. I checked that my mom and the kids were OK and went with a candle to some of the other rooms to see that everyone was all right.

The bombing continued for three years. We laughed at the English bombings; they were just phosphor fire bombs. They were very dangerous; you couldn't get them out with water, just with sand. But they were not as damaging as the other bombs. We always said that the Americans still let our house stay when everything around us was bombed out. The back of our apartment building was bombed out by German planes trying to get the Russians out.

When my brother was here visiting, he reminded me of some things, some of which if my mother had known, she wouldn't have let me do many things. My brother reminded me of the woman who slapped me and screamed at me "Sister, how can you be so calm?" (German Red Cross nurses were called "sister.") A lot came back to me when I saw the Oklahoma bombing. I broke out crying, remembering things like standing and waiting for men to dig to get people out of a bombed-out house. We could hear sounds, and when they got closer more debris would fall, and some we could never get to. Another time we got them out, and one girl was stuck under a beam with her arm, and we had to stop the guys from removing the beam because she was under it too long, and we needed a doctor to amputate her arm.

The job I got paid for as a Red Cross employee was on duty at a train station. No trains were going from that part of town except the one to Hitler's house outside of Berlin. I was never on duty when he left there, but Goebbels and Goering went a lot. When trains came in, we had to go over to the train and check wounded soldiers: examine wounds, put on new bandages, take care of boils, or help get them off the train. I used to like to kick officers who were not injured off their seats to make a place for a wounded soldier. We were allowed to do that.

When I was on night duty, I would come home in the morning and lie down to sleep in my uniform. At 10:30 A.M. the sirens went off, and we went to the shelter. Sometimes I had to keep on working after the bombing if I was needed and just had enough time to get home to clean up and put on a clean uniform and go back to work.

Later I was transferred to be a nurse in an ambulance. There was a driver, an intern, and a nurse. The ambulances we had were like those you would see in a WWI movie—a big box on wheels. After the bombing we would go out, both sides of the streets on fire, dust and smoke everywhere, and sometimes just enough space for the ambulance to go through, both sides of the streets with big holes and the smell of gas. After a bombing, the Women's Association would come out and offer sandwiches and hot soup and drinks for the people who were bombed out.

I remember one time I had four people with concussions in our shelter, and I was the only nurse. They were getting sick to their stomach, and I was holding a bucket for them. One of the women came and asked if I wanted a sandwich. I had just come off night duty; I was so hungry I said "Yes." Our Field First came in and said, "WHAT ARE YOU DOING?" I had no other help and was so hungry—what are you to do?

A bombed-out church served as a hospital. When the Russian Army entered Berlin in April of 1945, they were anxious to use the local medical personnel for their own purposes. I removed my Red Cross nurse's uniform to avoid being taken. When troops entered my apartment, I hid under a mattress. Other women were not so lucky. An elderly Red Cross nurse in the building was raped. Others were taken and never seen again.

My family had no relatives outside of Berlin where they could seek refuge during or after the war. As some neighbors in our building fled to the West, even to America, they gave the keys to their basement storage cubicles (which also served as bomb shelter) to other residents in case they didn't come back. The store of potatoes and coal they left behind were very welcome in those bleak postwar times.

After everything settled down, I went to the west side of Berlin (the American zone) to find a job working for a diplomat's family. I could no longer work as a tailor. Somehow I was allergic to the things they used in the material, and I kept breaking out in a rash. So, I became a maid. It was a great job; I learned a lot of American cooking, and they told me they would take me to the States. Mrs. Collins, my employer, had all her household goods shipped out of Berlin just one day before the airlift started, and everything closed up around Berlin. Then they got transferred to Russia, and there was NO NO NO way I was going to Russia. Not even with a diplomat's family. So I put in for a visa to go to the U.S. I could go as a tailor, or a nurse trainee, or maid, or cook.

The second American family I worked for in Berlin had fired their cook and asked me to cook until they hired a new one. They liked my cooking and hired a maid instead, so I stayed as a cook. There were many things I could do.

One thing was sure, in Berlin you didn't know when you woke up if the Russians had taken over again, so you lived it up as you could: dating a GI, going to the club, you had peanuts to eat, cigarettes to smoke, and a clean, good-looking American soldier. We used to be so strict, but with what happened with the Russians, my family—mother, sisters, and I—we had a guardian angel with us that nothing happened to us. But I thought that after being so good all those years with my real nice friends, maybe now a Russian would get me; I hated the idea. My mom said I was just waiting for the Americans to come.

The Russians came in April; I turned eighteen in May. The Americans stopped bombing when the Russians came in. The Americans were on the Elbe River waiting because the Russians were going into Berlin. In our apartment building we had red carpet going up the stairs and in the hallway. The Russians put their horses in there, in the hallway where you first came in on the red carpet, and that carpet went up the four-story building. They took mattresses out of apartments and put them down there and had horses on them.

Since my mother was divorced, we were alone, and that was our luck. My dad was a big shot, and they were looking for him. That is why I never looked for my dad. I was afraid that he would think someone was looking for him. I loved my dad; I was his favorite. The last time I saw him was after the Russians came in. He was standing downstairs, and my mother said, "Your father is down there; you better go see him." He always came by to see if we were OK after the bombings. On this last meeting, he explained that he was a hunted man because of his political affiliations as a Nazi and Gestapo, then he disappeared and was never seen or heard from again.

I met my husband Jerry in a funny way. He came to the house with some friends. I was sick, and a girlfriend of mine and her boyfriend came to see how I was doing. I was really sick; I had brain fever. After all those things going on during the war, finally I folded up. I had a high fever and was in and out of consciousness. Jerry came along with them, and I didn't even know they were there. They told me he wouldn't date anyone; they couldn't get him a date for anything. Then one day the doorbell rang, and my landlady came and said that there was a GI who said he wanted to see how I was doing; he knew I was so sick. I thought it was such a nice thing that a stranger would come to see how I was doing. I was getting better. Then he came on Saturday and asked if he could come by the next weekend. I said OK, and he came by on Wednesday, Saturday, and Sunday.

We weren't allowed to get married until about ten months before we went to the States. The military wouldn't allow it. The reason for the wait was to keep too many GIs from marrying German girls. The Army figured if they were made to wait long enough, they would get discouraged and not get married. From 1945-1948 it was that way. They would ship the bride back to the States and the guy to Korea. We met in 1948 and didn't get married by the church until 1954. Our daughter, born in 1949, was four years old by that time! We actually got married three times: first by a German lawyer, then by the German Civil Court, then by the Catholic Church in Berlin in 1954.

When my daughter was born in 1949, it was airlift time. I nursed her, but my sister in East Berlin lost two babies because there was no milk and her babies died. Jerry could not get food for us either. Once in a while he smuggled oranges or apples out, but their uniforms were so tight they couldn't carry anything out in their pockets. There wasn't much food at the PX, where military families shopped. I had only six diapers, so I was constantly washing, rinsing, boiling, and drying diapers. It was impossible to get blankets and clothes. Jerry waited for months for clothes for the baby to come in. When the airlift finally lifted and they got things in, he bought everything they had.

We were rationed one loaf of bread a week, vegetables were dehydrated, and Canadian flour that was great to make hot cereal, with milk powder. It is amazing what a human being can live on. The airlift was a wonderful thing; it brought in food and coal. In the East sector, my mom and the kids didn't have much.

After my daughter was born, we rented a room with a lady who had a big yard full of vegetables and fruit, and we had all we could eat.

My family loved Jerry. He loved kids, and the kids all came to him. His family was all right with him bringing me home. His mom said, "He loves her and he's happy; she must be all right." German families were generally glad the GIs were there for their daughters instead of the Russians. But they knew you would leave Germany.

We had four months to get ready to get married. Jerry was supposed to leave in January, and the paperwork takes a long time. There were seven of us girls getting married, and we all ended up in Fort Carson, Colorado, at the same time. I didn't have to wait long for my papers because they got clearance from the investigation when I worked for the diplomat's family. I also found out that I had a visa waiting that I would no longer need.

After our wedding they kept Jerry in Germany, saying he was sick and all kinds of excuses so the three of us could travel to the States together. He was supposed to leave in January, but we didn't leave until March. It was quite a trip on that ship. It was nothing like a cruise ship! When we got to the U.S. I was so disappointed not to see the Statue of Liberty. We checked in after we got off the ship, and we left in buses to the train station. As we crossed one of the bridges, I screamed "There She is!" Everyone was so tired, and they all fell to sleep on the bus. My screaming woke them up, but they missed it. But I saw my Lady Liberty, and I was happy. My husband told me he had crossed three different times and had never seen her.

By May we were in Colorado Springs and no apartment to rent. It was hard, but after a few weeks we rented a little cottage and have been Coloradoans since.

My mother told me that when I was four years old, I said to my father, "When I grow up, I'm going to be a secretary." To

Jerry and Ursula, Mother and stepdad, with half sister Gigi

me a secretary meant making a lot of money, " and I'd buy a car and drive to America." Now, where in the world did I get that idea, to go to America? My father said to me the last time when he came to see me, "Don't stay here; go to America. Get out of here." He is the one who put that idea of America into me from little on. Where did he know it from? I never got to find out.

I love the States. Everyone has been so nice to me, Jerry's family and friends, then my landlady in Colorado Springs. I made my citizenship in March, 1956 and for me this is home.

Ursula's story is reprinted here from <u>Same War Different Battlefields</u>. She passed away in 2013.

⤙ Hermine Boyer ⤚

I was born in 1939 in Heiligenstadt in northern Bavaria, a small village of eight hundred people, between Nurnberg and Bamberg. I had two younger siblings—brother Heinrich and sister Roswitha. My father John Raithel had a business degree and worked in the office of the *Reichsarbeitsdienst*. This was a government agency that was concerned with building and maintaining infrastructure such as the Autobahn, streets, bridges, railroads, etc. The word translates roughly as "Work Service" and was similar to the American WPA during the Great Depression of the 1930s. It was a relief agency designed to reduce unemployment, providing employment to Germans affected by the post-WWI Depression and was in effect before the Nazi takeover in 1933. My dad was a member of the Nazi Party, which was a requirement for his employment, and he supported the regime. He even wore a brown uniform on the job.

My mother never joined the party, but she was a Nazi supporter, in fact, more so after the war. She resented the Americans because they had won the war. She wouldn't even allow me to accept candy from the GI occupiers. Later I married one, but that's a different story for later.

My maternal grandfather was also a Nazi sympathizer. He was a self-made, successful entrepreneur who owned a brewery and gasthaus in Heiligenstadt, a construction company, stone quarry, brick factory, farm, and a lot of land and woods. He was the richest man in town, which was accompanied by resentment and jealousy on the part of other local residents. His son, my uncle Karl, would eventually be sole heir to those enterprises.

When Hitler came to power, one of his concerns was getting more space for the growing German population, which he called *lebenstraum*. Addressing the problem directly, one of his policies was to decree that all properties would be passed on to the eldest son, instead of divided among heirs. The reason for this was that through the years, such division, farmlands in particular, between members of large families in a comparatively small country, resulted in farms that were too small to be profitable as businesses nor self-sustaining for the families that owned and operated them.

Consequently, Uncle Karl, who was really the second oldest son, inherited Grandfather's assets. His older brother Fritz was mentally handicapped and unable to function as Grandfather's heir. In fact, he was placed in an institution in Nurnberg at the time we were fleeing Heiligenstadt toward the end of the war. We were told that he died there of pneumonia, but after the war we learned that he indeed had been poisoned. The regime's policy was to eliminate "defectives" from the gene pool to enhance Hitler's desire to create a perfect race of Germans. *[Many met their ending in the death camps, but apparently there were additional means to accomplish that goal, and an explanation of "pneumonia" was one of them.]*

Uncle Karl was trained as an engineer, and he was not only a Party member, he was a member of the SS. His job as *Kreisleiter* was like a County Commissioner. He got his directives from the Politik Bureau in Bayreuth, where he stayed about three years. His job was a political appointment from the Nazi Party. At the end of the war, he knew that as such he would be a hunted man. He fled Heiligenstadt when we did but stayed behind us and separate from us in order to be as inconspicuous as possible. He hid in the woods. Eventually he was arrested, tried, and sent for two years to an American prison facility in Bayreuth. After he was released, since the Americans had appointed a trustee to run his businesses, Karl was effectively idle for some time before he could reassume control over his various businesses.

I was so young during the war, not quite six when it ended, that I was not personally affected nor traumatized by what was going on. My father was away, serving in the Army in Russia. Our village escaped the bombings. In school during the Hitler regime, teachers had to be Party members, which had no impact on me. *[But others have told of blatant indoctrinating strategies including students being led to "squeal" on what was happening at home.]*

In 1945 as the American soldiers approached, our family fled Heiligenstadt, anticipating the American capture of Uncle Karl. We hoped to reach Jessendorf bei Landshut, a village in the Alps where my parents had friends we hoped would give us refuge. We piled onto a tractor-drawn wagon driven by sixteen-year-old Helmut, brother of my aunt Lini. My grandfather was also on the tractor. In the wagon we had Aunt Lini, Aunt Rika (Uncle Karl's wife), and her four children, Aunt Herta and her child, my mother, my brother, sister, and me, Aunt Annie, plus two refugees from East Germany and their three children—a total of seven women and eleven children. We accomplished our mission, and I remember sleeping on the floor in my parents' friends' house. We stayed in Jessendorf for two weeks before returning to Heiligenstadt. Some stayed in private homes; some stayed in the local schoolhouse.

During this time, my dad was in Russia in a POW camp in Siberia. He was captured at Stalingrad in May 1944. He was sent to Siberia to work in the mines, where he dropped from a hundred sixty-five pounds to ninety pounds in just two months. He was often moved between POW camps by train over the next year, working in mines and on farms. My mother didn't know if he were dead or alive. He was released in 1946, about a year and a half after his capture. He did not escape from prison but was transferred to Fursenwalde near Frankfurt by a fifteen-hour train ride. He was told he was released because the Russian Army did not have enough food for its own people and couldn't feed the prisoners any more.

The prisoners were instructed to walk home; there was no other transportation for them. My dad walked back to Hof, some three hundred-fifty kilometers (more than two hundred miles). Hof was where his mother and sisters lived, a hundred kilometers north-east of Heiligenstadt. He ended up in a German Army hospital, probably occupied by the Americans at that time. My mother visited him there because they didn't know if he would survive. We children weren't told about this critical situation.

He did come home, but he was a changed man. I didn't remember much about him before he left for the war because I was so young, but I was aware that he wasn't the same Daddy I had known, and I heard the grownups talk about it. He brought home many demons with him from his wartime experiences and committed suicide in 1952.

After the war, Party member teachers were not allowed to teach, and their replacements were often untrained "educators." My aunt Herta's husband Fritz was a school teacher before the war. He never was a Party member, but his brother-in-law Uncle Karl was Kreisleiter. That served Uncle Fritz well under the regime but was a disadvantage after the war. As a result, many of those former, unemployable teachers were forced to do manual jobs. Since Uncle Fritz was not allowed to teach, he worked in my uncle's quarry, until he was *enthnazifiziert* (deNazified). Ex-Party officials were scorned, not hailed as heroes. They all had to go through the de-Nazification process, and even then they did not always get their positions back.

CARE packages came from the U.S. and were distributed at school, but children of Nazis were excluded. I didn't receive anything. Nor did we receive any postwar "instruction" about the Nazi era and its crimes.

I met my future husband Don through my sister and her husband. Harro, my American brother-in-law, was an assistant on the remote U.S. Air Force radio relay station located atop a hill outside of town. Don was stationed there after completing his technical training in Biloxi, Mississippi.

The first time I met Don was while watching a movie with Roswitha and Harro at the radio relay station. And here was this skinny airman just arrived from the U.S. All these Air Force men lived in town at a local gasthaus, because the site had no housing, and there were only about six or eight stationed there. My town is a very small town, about eight hundred people, so after a short while the airmen were just part of the local scene. They all learned and spoke German and were part of all the festivals and dances we had. Nobody looked at them as Americans until my sister married one and I started dating Don. Then "fraternizing" became a scandal.

My uncle Karl didn't hesitate to remind my mother that we had lost the war because of the Americans. My poor mother was torn. On one side she liked Don and Harro, but she also knew it was true how Germany had lost the war. Uncle Karl did not speak to us for ten years. When I visited home with my two children Barb and Chris, and he saw me in town, he crossed the street in order to avoid us. But time really does heal wounds. Later on, when he spoke to me again, he wanted to know all about my life in the States.

Wartime was much harder for my mother than for me, because during and after the war the family only had each other to make it through. During the war almost all the men were away, and the women had to hold things together. After the war, because of Nazi affiliations they faced persecution from the Germans as well as the Americans. And a good German girl avoided the American GIs. *[Apparently there were plenty of good German girls who ignored that taboo.]*

When I think back to those times, some things become increasingly clear. The men appeared devastated from the war;

the one exception seemed to be my uncle Fritz. He had professional problems as a former teacher, because he had married into our Nazi family. Initially that association had been to his advantage, but after the war he eventually overcame those challenges of being restricted from teaching.

My father was never the same after the war, as I described earlier, committing suicide in 1952. Uncle Karl finally got his business back, but with the help of his younger brother Siegfried, eventually ran it into the ground. Karl's son Alfred took over the business in the late 1970s and has turned it into a highly successful company. Alfred never removed his father's name from the business and never took credit for his accomplishments. In fact, all my cousins and siblings have been successful in whatever they have done.

The women seemed to have become stronger and more independent. The ladies in my family formed a bond of trust (no doubt helped by the wagon trip) and supported each other all their lives. No matter what issues existed between the men of the family, the women were always open, friendly, supportive, and helpful. While Uncle Karl ignored me, his wife Aunt Rika always came to my mother's house and asked about our well-being. My cousins and I have never lost contact to this day.

My mother, having lost her husband and raised three children with little income, was always a charitable person, sharing with friends and strangers alike. She sent all three children through higher education.

I still admire all my aunts, and especially my mom, to this day. They were wonderful people, despite all their wartime-related adversity.

Geburtsregister Nr. _21_ des Jahres 1 _939_

Geburtsschein.

Vor- und Zunamen: *[handwritten]*

Geburtstag und -ort: *[handwritten] 1939 [handwritten]*

Vor- und Zunamen: *[handwritten]*

sowie Stand des Vaters: *[handwritten]*

Vor- und Zunamen der Mutter: *[handwritten]*

[handwritten] (Ort) *[handwritten]* Oktober 1939 (Datum)

Der Standesbeamte:

[signature]

(Unterschrift)

Gebühr _____ RM

Gebühren-Reg. Nr. _____

Gebührenfrei.

Nr. 1932.

Buchdruckerei Emil Mühl, Bayreuth

Hermine's birth certificate. Note swastika
on the center, circular stamp.

⊰ Stephan Q. Lani ⊱

teve was born in 1931 and grew up in Austria near a small village on the Swiss border west of Innsbruck. He was raised by his grandparents and a single mother. His grandparents operated a mountainside gasthaus and farm. Living in the mountains, Steve had to learn to ski at age five in order to get to school! After his mother married in 1940, there were eventually seven children in the family—five boys and two girls. His stepfather was a miner from Yugoslavia and did construction work building railroad tunnels, highways, and air raid shelters, and relocating war-critical facilities underground. POWs were often used for labor on these projects, and Steve's dad was not allowed to discuss these operations at home.

The mountain Steve grew up on in Tschagguns, Austria

After the Anschluss in 1938, which unified Austria with Nazi Germany, life in Austria during the succeeding wartime was accompanied by many of the same conditions and challenges as those experienced by native Germans in Germany. At ten years of age, Steve joined the *Hitler Jugend*, which was mandated by law. He describes it as consisting of meetings, marching, singing, summer camps, and learning some military-related skills such as identification of airplanes, and learning to shoot a rifle, as well as cleaning and assembling it. It was a positive experience for the boys exposed to membership. It stressed discipline, good health habits, community service, camaraderie—goals not unlike those of the Boy Scouts of America. Steve adds that there was very limited juvenile delinquency during the Nazi regime.

Steve left home at age ten and moved to Bregenz, near Lake Constance. There was not a high school in every town. (Grade designations do not correspond to their American counterparts. German *Gymnasium* is equivalent to junior high and was originally attended by boys only, while girls went to the *Lyceum*.) Such a situation required a student boarding while away from home, and good students got free schooling, housing, etc. Steve received these benefits.

Bregenz was a fortified community because of airplane manufacturing factories nearby. Allied bombers flew over regularly.

Steve writes: "During my time going to school in Bregenz, I was exposed to the reality of the war. Bombers would fly overhead almost daily in daytime and at night. This was always a cause for air alert sirens to warn all citizens to seek bomb shelters. Sometimes on the way to or from school, we would hide under trees or bushes during the alerts and observe all the action in the air above. This included exploding aircrafts, anti-aircraft firing, dogfights among fighter planes, and all the fireworks that ensued. Damaged bombers would generally drop their bombs, not on any specific target, adding to more casualties and damage to our area. Needless to say, it was very frightening, and we were lucky to be able to observe this from a distance.

"I also spent many hours in daytime or at night in various bomb shelters with school friends and teachers. While inside the shelters we could hear explosions and nearby bombings outside, hoping we would not be the next target. During night raids, the sky would light up like fireworks from all the action, and fortunately my school and my friends did not suffer any harm.

"Nineteen forty-five brought an end to the hostilities in WWII. Schools and dormitories closed and became shelters for the refugees and military housing for the occupying French Army troops. This interrupted my education and planning what to do next with my life."

Consequently, Steve left school after the eighth grade at age fourteen. Austrian as well as German students commonly left school after the eighth grade if they weren't continuing to the university and often entered apprenticeships to prepare them for vocations in the trades. Steve worked in a distillery for a short time, then in 1946 had the opportunity to start an electrical apprenticeship. He served for three years, a hundred miles from home, and lived in the home of his "boss," with three other apprentices. The boss's wife ran a hotel, and there was a workshop in the basement. A bicycle provided transportation for the apprentices to various venues in all weather. "This trade served me well during all my working years until my retirement."

After the war, the family decided to emigrate to the U.S. with all seven children. Grandfather had died in 1943. With bureaucratic considerations, it took a year to satisfy all require-

U.S.M.S. *General Stuart Heintzelman,* the ship on which Steve's family arrived in America in 1951

Steve in his U.S. uniform, Fort Bliss, Texas, 1955

ments, which included physical examinations, shots, and satisfactory responses to postwar political scrutiny. A blitz language course was offered by the U.S. Army for civilians of various nationalities, in preparation for emigration. Steve became the family spokesman/interpreter, the only one who spoke any English, but he was not yet fluent.

The refugee transport ship was the *General Stuart Heinzelman,* and it arrived in New York on December 22, 1951, after a terrible, stormy Atlantic crossing. In New York, many of the twelve hundred of the ship's refugees were put up at a refugee hotel for three months, while recruiters from employers throughout the U.S. offered job opportunities to the immigrants. Steve noted that some of the situations the new arrivals accepted turned out to be less than what was promised and expected.

Steve went to work for the Newmont Mining Company in Leadville, Colorado. Housing was provided there for five refugee families of different nationalities, and all expenses were deducted from their paychecks. Although he had completed his apprenticeship in Austria, because of his limited English, he had to serve as an electrician's helper in the mine. He literally had to learn the trade all over again.

Steve worked at the mine until 1954, when he was drafted into the U.S. Army. He was not yet a citizen but became one during the two years he spent in the service. He served an additional six years in the Army Reserve.

"At the end of my military service, I married a young lady in Detroit, and we settled in Denver where we met many immigrants from Europe who became our friends. Several German clubs offered us many opportunities to join and enjoy German music and dancing, entertainment, and lasting friendships. I worked for several electrical contractors over many years in the metro area of Denver. During this time, our three children became adults, pursuing their own lives.

"My marriage dissolved in 1986, and I found a new love that gave me a new lease on life. Barbara and I married in 1988, and we have enjoyed many wonderful years together. I retired in 1996 after forty-five years working at my trade. I enjoy every day of retirement and living in this great country called the USA. Thanks to my lovely wife Barbara, my life has been a wonderful journey for the past twenty-five years. Life is good!"

Steve and his wife Barbara vacationing

❧ Maxine Merten ❧

I was born in 1923. I had one younger sister, Christiane, and a brother four years younger, Hubertus, who was cared for by a nanny. He was in the military service during the war, and he survived. My father and his brother managed a large estate called a "domain," which they leased from the State. It was not far from Berlin in an agricultural area. They raised barley, wheat, sugar beets, and several kinds of vegetables. Our family lived on the property. The closest large city was Leipzig, and our village was nearer to Halle. The village at the domain was called Beesenaublingen.

My parents were loving parents, but I was closer to my mother. Father was a strict disciplinarian and a demanding head of the household. He came from an affluent family, and my paternal grandparents lived in Halle.

During my younger years, I went to school for four years to the village school in Beesenaublingen, then by train daily to Bernburg, and later to Halle to a girls' pension with ten other girls. I attended the University of Munich briefly but withdrew because of the frequent bomb attacks.

During summer vacations, we children lived with our other grandfather in Munich. He took us everywhere to see the many artistic and historic treasures of the city. On one occasion, Hitler was scheduled to make an appearance in Munich, and somehow a meeting was scheduled for us kids to meet him personally. These were strictly propaganda occasions, which he exploited at public events held in the plaza. Knowing this was planned for me, I became so nervous I got sick, and the meeting was cancelled.

My father was drafted late in the war. Because agriculture was so important, he had been deferred. Born in 1889, he served in World War I and was an officer in the Reserve, then later served in the WWII Army as a Lt. Colonel in the Russian campaign around Kiev. He was not a supporter of the Nazi regime. He raised questions about the regime, its motives, strategies, etc., a risky position since any negative views were taken as unpatriotic and dangerous and could have serious consequences for the speaker. Among the military, however, who could see how badly the campaign in Russia was going, no doubt such observations when verbalized were assumed confidential. When my father made an off-hand remark, he was overheard by another officer, immediately arrested and imprisoned in Vienna, then transferred to Berlin. I don't know how my mother learned about this, and she tried to get him released, which was only possible by proving that the accused was innocent of being a dangerous enemy of the government. Of course that was a difficult if not impossible challenge, probably by design. He was not a member of the Party, which immediately ran up a red flag about his loyalty. He was executed on orders from Himmler in February 1945.

Uncle Erich, my mother's brother-in-law, had a domain like my father did. He too was arrested close to the end of the war and placed in Buchenwald. He did not survive.

The domain where we lived and the area surrounding it became part of the Russian zone. Forewarned of the Russians' brutal treatment of the inhabitants of the areas they occupied, especially the rampant raping that involved females of all ages, my mother sent my sister and me by chauffeur to Uncle Hans's home, my father's brother, in Bavaria at Wasserburg Castle. Soon after, Russian troops knocked on the door and told my mother to vacate the premises in ten minutes. With my brother, she left and found refuge with her mother in a lovely old mansion called Villa Kobe (the family name). Grandfather was no longer living, but he had been a successful businessman and industrialist. After the war this area was in the American zone. Uncle

Hans was so depressed by the outcome of the war, he later committed suicide.

Other refugees were also taken in at Villa Kobe. At times, there were twenty-five people living there. The Russians didn't bother Villa Kobe. When they ransacked houses elsewhere, they stole and sent looted things back to Russia. What they didn't want they threw out into the street, but made good use of the contents of any wine cellar.

My sister Christiane and I had already left Wasserburg. Right after the war, with no jobs, those Germans who knew English could get employment with the American occupation forces. I did as a telephone operator. Christiane and I left Wasserburg and transferred to Augsburg where I rented a room with a family, and Christiane worked in the same apartment building as a housemaid for an American captain and his wife.

It was not uncommon for the GIs to flirt with telephone operators when they heard the frauleins speaking with a German accent. I met my husband that way. I married Robert in 1949 in Augsburg and came to the U.S., arriving in New York at Christmastime. Holiday lights in the city overwhelmed me and actually sickened me after the deprived conditions of postwar Germany. Our destination was Indianapolis, where my husband was from. I found that Germans who had immigrated to the U.S. before the war were embarrassed by Germany and the Nazis after it became known what their oppressive rule was all about. We in Germany who experienced it didn't know all that was going on at the time and couldn't do anything about it anyway. We were trained to accept without complaint, to be obedient, and loyal.

Christiane didn't fare as well. While preparing a hot bath for her employers, she was badly scalded and spent two painful months in the hospital. Supplies were non-existent, and Robert brought her salves and medications from the American hospital. She passed away from those injuries. It was a terrible loss to me personally.

The accompanying letter was written to me on the occasion of my twenty-first birthday in December 1944. My father knew at the time that he was scheduled to be executed, and the letter is remarkable for the optimism it reveals, making no mention of what lay ahead for him and our family.

[Letter to Maxine which she has translated, addressed by her German name from her father confined in Berlin at the time, awaiting execution. A most sensitive, uplifting message, articulated under the most stressful circumstances, and tragically, near the end of the war.]

My dear Mechtild,   Dec. 22, 1944

To your birthday, which turns you into an adult, I am sending my warmest wishes for blessings and good luck. May the dear Lord protect you further and keep pain and misery from your soul and body. After a happy childhood at home and at school your life goes through a hard time of frenetic battles of our country for present and future.

Also you have experienced difficult things in the last five years: you lost a dear beloved friend (Caffefila), survived heavy bomb attacks in Leipzig and Munich which interrupted your college studies, which you started with great enthusiasm! But don't become fearful and hesitant, stay brave and determined, and don't lose your goal in front of your eyes, that you have planned to reach.

Even if you are not pleased with your present activities try to see the best and learn from the experiences. Always try to find a job which you might enjoy and learn from it. Everyone builds his own happiness.

Today is winter solstice and I hope the year 1945 brings a turn and the end.

On your birthday, a Friday, you will be in Halle with your grandmother. Since the moon is full that night, the "Tommy" will come to congratulate you. *["Tommy" refers to English bombers.]* I wish you all "*waffenschwein.*"* But on Saturday—Sunday you may be in Neubeesen house, and I will be there in my thoughts. Last year in Odessa, this time Berlin, where next year?

With my birthday kiss I am taking you tight in my arms.

Your Vater.

Please greetings to my dear old mother. I thank her for the Christmas package, which arrived first and is so far the only one.

I missed her note with description of content and cigarettes.

Greetings to Schimmel *[the family's housekeeper]*

Maxine explains the term "waffenschwein," a term used to wish good luck in all you do, that you will always be a winner. It literally translates as "weapon, pig," a military slang term used among servicemen.

❖ Karl Finzel ❖

It may not be common knowledge among American readers how much disruption among Eastern European civilian populations occurred as armies criss-crossed their countries, which resulted in their continued displacement and resettlement after the war. Poles and Germans, in particular, were expelled from countries that were not consistent with their ethnic origin. They often found they were not welcome back in their native country because land, food, housing, and other resources were limited by the war's destruction—a situation compounded by the political nature of their involuntary resettlement, imposed on both sets of populations, immigrants as well as natives. Some of the memoirs published here describe this situation, including that of Karl's parents in Luxembourg before and during the war.

Karl Finzel was born in Germany in 1923 and raised in Luxembourg. His father, originally from Dusseldorf, was church organist at a large church in DudeLange, second largest city in Luxembourg. It was a city of steel mills with a population of 17,000, many of whom were Italians. Father's training had been at the Organ Music Conservatory in Aachen, considered the best. Predictably, Karl's exposure to music was on the piano at age fourteen, then on the organ at eighteen. He too became an organist, but his parents disapproved of that choice for his vocation, and he was sent to Dusseldorf to serve as an apprentice in a photo shop. The family lived a comfortable middle class lifestyle in Dudelange. Karl's father owned a music store and also gave music lessons.

Karl describes his education thus; public schools in Luxembourg were really Catholic schools in that very Catholic nation. Teachers were all men and strict by American standards.

Once a week the chaplain came to class to teach catechism. Luxembourg was very French-oriented, and actually three languages were in use; in addition to Luxembourgisch, French and German were common. Some of the population was trilingual, and an educated Luxembourger might even speak four languages. In Karl's school, classes were conducted in German in the morning and in French in the afternoon. German was spoken in his home.

In Luxembourg, Karl's father retained his German heritage and never became a Luxembourg citizen. This was not problematic until after the war. He disapproved of the Nazi ideology and the regime that enforced it. Fortunately, living in Luxembourg did not expose Karl to the indoctrination of youth that was prevalent in Germany, and naturally he was not required to join the *HitlerJugend*.

Germany invaded Luxembourg in 1940 as its campaigns spread across western Europe. Early in the war, young teenagers were not drafted as they were toward the end of the war. At eighteen Karl was drafted, because he was living in Dusseldorf at the time, into the *Arbeitzdiest*, a public labor force that provided three months of paramilitary training for the young recruits. They learned to follow orders and to "do the job right." Their exposure to using armaments was minimal; Karl remembers his troop was taken to the firing range only once, and he fired just one shot. "Perhaps ammunition was too scarce." Later he was used as an anti-aircraft gunner.

His military service began in the Air Force in 1942 at age nineteen. He was stationed in several locations on the continent but saw no combat. His assignments took him to Holland, Normandy (before the Allied invasion), and Naples, while Italy was still part of the Axis and occupied by Germans as well as Italian troops. Allied planes were rarely seen, and those seemed to be reconnaissance missions, checking out the harbor. Karl then went to Palermo for two days and finally to Cap Bone in

Tunisia. At that point he was given leave time and a permit to visit his parents. However, there were no ships or planes available to him, so after waiting in the airport for a week, he didn't go home. He considered that this permission to go home was for propaganda purposes, to show the civilians that this soldier could be spared from action at the front. He has wondered if his absence from the action may have saved his life.

Back at the front with his unit, they were surrounded by British forces. The Germans just raised their hands and surrendered willingly, stressed out, demoralized, and relieved that the war was over for them. However, the younger troops like Karl didn't really understand the implications, since they hadn't experienced the shooting war as the older troops had, especially those who had fought in Russia.

The prisoners were first shipped to England. They were marched to a large open arena like a football stadium, on their way walking to the POW detention camp. Polish guards dressed in British uniforms presented the only bad experience of that situation. They beat the prisoners at random, as Karl puts it, "with hate in their eyes. They screamed and hollered at us, beating us with rifle butts. The British weren't like that; they were like the Americans." After they were in the camp, Karl remembers they ate better than the British population did. He didn't smoke, and with his cigarette allotments he would go to the fence and trade them to the British guards for chocolate, potatoes, and other "treats."

The fighting war was over for Karl, but a new and mostly positive experience awaited him in America. He also has good memories of his time in England. After the war ended and he had emigrated to the U.S., he traveled throughout England on several occasions. Sitting on a train looking at the countryside, it reminded him of the beauty of Germany—its houses, gardens and natural beauty. He wondered, "Why did that crazy Hitler have to make a war against the English? Why all the hate? Why can't we live together?"

The rest of Karl's story is described best in his own words:

"POW passengers were hoping we wouldn't be torpedoed by a German submarine. We were traveling in an Allied ship, and U-boats had been successful sinking convoys. They were operating all over the world, all the way down to South America to Brazil and Argentina, looking for British or American prey. But by this time of the war, the submarine fleet had been decimated, and they weren't quite so effective. We made it, and seeing the Statue of Liberty in New York harbor in the early morning sunlight was the first indication we had of our destination.

Out of New York we were put onto a nice, clean Pullman car, not a cattle train. I had two window seats, and Black waiters to wait on me. It was the first time I had ever seen a Black person. First stop was Camp Carson, Colorado, near Colorado Springs, at the foot of beautiful Pikes Peak in the foothills of the Rocky Mountains.

They separated the officers from the enlisted men and gave them separate barracks. We were separated perhaps so there wasn't a question of obeying two sources of commands. There were Nazi fanatics among us, thinking they would still win the war. Life was good for the prisoners; we even had POW cooks and bakers that we chose ourselves, and meals were a pleasant experience. The Geneva Convention outlined/required that the troops be fed the same rations as their captors.

I think the Americans wanted to maintain a certain military discipline so there would be order. Every morning there was roll call. At seven o'clock we had to be dressed, the whistle would blow, we had to stand in line, and the POWs were counted to make sure we were all there. I had no idea how many of us there were, probably several hundred. Things like that were kept a secret; anyway, I didn't care.

I was interned there about a year. At first, we didn't do anything; then I worked briefly on the railroad, putting rocks under the ties with a big crowbar. Later I worked in the laundry room washing clothes for the troops. We were paid about a dollar a day (when candy bars were five cents), and I saved three hundred dollars, which I was able to take home after I was released; I had a certificate from the U.S. Treasury Dept.

So, off and on we had a job; it kept us occupied and out of mischief. Mine was a slow-moving job, and what we heard all the time was 'Okey dokey—take it easy.' It was the mentality at the time; I think they were afraid they would run out of things for us to do. They wanted to make sure they had work for us. I also worked for Pierre Barque, a Frenchman, the camp photographer, and was able to assist him on occasion. Before the war I had worked as a photographer's apprentice in a shop in Dusseldorf. I helped M. Barque develop films, print pictures, etc. While I worked with him, I couldn't speak English yet, so our dialogue was in French. When I left Camp Carson he gave me a gold ring with a diamond in it. I still have it. He appreciated me so much as a human being, he blessed me and gave me the ring for life. That's how he paid me, as a bonus for my service.

I had the impression that there was no war in the U.S.— no bombings, no shortages of consequence. Through the International Red Cross, prisoners were allowed to write one letter home each month, and I could communicate with my family. Through the Red Cross, my mother received the first letter that notified her I was in Colorado.

I wrote my mom that I would like to learn English, and would she send me some books. Two months later I received my dictionary and other books. Every day I learned forty words, including meanings, punctuation, and spelling. (I still have those books; I've covered their bindings to protect them.) So, I could speak with the guards when I was working, as we always had supervision. Since I could speak French, that also helped me as a POW later in France.

After the end of the war, from Colorado I was sent to Camp Cook at Vandenberg Air Force Base in California, briefly to Salt Lake City, and the last location before repatriation to Luxembourg was Camp Butner in North Carolina. There I worked in the cotton fields with practically all Black people. That was a special experience. We didn't have any exposure to the civil rights situation, and it was before the real movement got underway in the '60s. We didn't know about it in Germany, and while we were POWs we were kept isolated and didn't know about such things. There was no TV, no newspapers or books for us, which we wouldn't have understood in English anyway. We didn't know what was going on. We just knew that Germany had lost the war and that we would be going home. Otherwise, we were happy because we were fed, warm, housed, and had good treatment. We didn't know about the condition of Germany after the bombing destruction—no jobs, no food, etc.

The last place I was taken before I was released was the camp in Bolbec, France. The French were in charge, of course. I didn't speak French fluently, but I was a Luxembourger, and they treated me well and as an equal. They knew I was not a typical German raised under Hitler and fanatic. When I had been in France before being shipped to Naples, one day I had the day off, and I took long walks through the countryside in my uniform, with swastikas on the arms. There was a farmer in his field, and I talked to this man. I asked him for information to get to a certain village. He said, "How come you speak French?" I said that I was raised in Luxembourg. So we got involved in a dialogue. Ten minutes later he stopped what he was doing and took me to his farm. His wife prepared a nice meal, and we had a real cordial discussion. Then I continued back to my unit, and it shows you that when there is no hate, when you speak the same language, when you try to understand each other and respect each other, there is peace. That's what we need to do today in this world, instead of having all these security guards and aggressive organizations; we need more diplomats to compromise and try to avoid war. But Hitler didn't want that.

My parents were no longer in Luxembourg; they had been deported to Germany after the war. My dad had made a big mistake by not applying for Luxembourg citizenship. He worked there as a church organist and was an entrepreneur, a foreigner living in Luxembourg for twenty years or longer. After the war the hate was great in Luxembourg against the Germans. All Germans were considered Nazis. We don't blame the Luxembourg people, but the government dispossessed my parents, took all their property: their home, clothes, car, money. All they were allowed to take was one suitcase of clothes. They were put onto a truck and shipped across the border to a little town, Landstuhl. In the town square they were told to get off the truck, 'The local people will take care of you.' They ended up as refugees in Landstuhl in western Germany near Ramstein and Kaiserslautern. My parents were taken in, had one room above a bakery. The baker supplied them with food, mainly bread. That's where they were when I found them after I came home. They didn't know I was coming. We had been out of touch for a long time and didn't get each other's letters any more. I don't remember how I found them; there must have been some kind of communication, perhaps something like Red Cross or one of the refugee agencies. I moved in with them, sleeping on a cot at the foot of their bed. I was twenty-two years old.

My father and I started a radio repair business through exchanging radio tubes and fixing radios for people who sent in two tubes they could not use in exchange for one they needed. We employed two White Russians, and our business grew and flourished to the point we were able to purchase a motorcycle, then an automobile, then a house. French and American soldiers frequented the store. We also sold radios and records and became quite successful."

Karl had a dream of going to the U.S. where the people had been very kind to him as a young POW. Eventually, in 1954 he emigrated to the U.S., stopping off in Colorado Springs on his way to California, where he hoped to open a photo store. When he returned to Colorado Springs as a civilian immigrant, Pierre Barque helped him get a job in a local photography shop. "I had lost contact with him but I knew where he was living in nearby Black Forest. So I looked him up. I walked in the door, and he recognized me after all these years; it was nine years later. He welcomed me with open arms and said, 'What are you doing here, and where are you going?' I said, 'Well, I'm an immigrant now here in the U.S., going to California, opening up my own photo store.' That's what I intended to do because I had such a store in Germany. I had my darkroom equipment with me. He said, 'Oh, now, don't go to California. This is a nice town; why don't you stay here?' I said, 'I have no job.' He said, 'That's no problem.' He picked up the phone and called Dietz Bros. Photo Shop downtown. My car was all filled with my personal belongings, and I had parked two blocks away. I walked into the store, but Pierre had called first and said, 'I have Karl here. You probably need some help.' Mr. Dietz said, 'Send him down. We'll look him over.' So I met Bill Dietz, had a job interview, and after fifteen minutes he said, 'OK, Karl, I'll hire you.'

"I had no place to live, so when they closed the store for the evening, I drove off on Nevada Street about ten blocks, and there was a sign 'Room for Rent.' I rented one room for $25 a month; I had no furniture—nothing. I shared a primitive bathroom with a person living in the same building."

Karl's father sold his store after a while, and his parents returned to his mother's hometown of Itzehoe, close to Hamburg, where they built a nice home. His mother put in a lovely flower garden and died while sitting on the steps of the house, after suffering a stroke.

Karl is still a very active and distinguished gentleman. He celebrated his ninetieth birthday in 2013 among many friends, family, and admirers. His four-language vocabulary doesn't include the word "retirement."

Postscript

On Christmas Day, 2013, Karl passed away. His wife Doris has written an addition to his memoir, something he was not willing to share during our interviews, but information that adds dimension to his story.

"When Karl was back in Germany in the train with the other POWs, the whole bunch of them was to be turned over to the Russians, to be sent to the Atlas Mountains to work there. The hope that you would get out of there was slim, and Karl, having been working in the orderly room because of his knowledge of three languages, had been able to find his name and the plans for him. But he decided that Karl Finzel had other plans for his future. At the border, in a town called Bebera, he got off the train with his duffel bag and said to the American guard, that he had to use the toilet, which was a small detached hut. The soldier let him go. Once inside the outhouse, Karl climbed up into the rafters and waited until the train left the station. In the confusion, and because the American soldier had forgotten that he was there, he was not missed. Once the train had left, Karl climbed down and told the curious station master that the Americans had released him, and he needed a ticket in order to get home to his parents. Of course, he had no money and no papers, but the man was kind and gave him the ticket.

When Karl finally turned up in the little room above the bakery in Landstuhle where his parents were living, his mother almost had a heart attack. Her boy was home safely! Living above the bakery, albeit in a tiny room where they put up a cot for Karl, they had enough to eat and could start a new life.

Even at age ninety, Karl was afraid that if it were common knowledge that he escaped, he might have to pay the consequences."

Karl Finzel and Doris

⤙ Doris Tavernier Finzel ⤚

I was born in May 1936 in Heidelberg, Germany, the third daughter of my parents Rudolf and Amalie Tavernier. My father was the only son of a small-town Lutheran minister, Johannes Tavernier. My grandfather's forefathers were Huguenots, and my mother came from a staunchly Catholic family in the Black Forest. Her father Johann Winterhalder started and owned a clock factory—Winterhalder Clocks, which later became Hawina and Junghans Clocks.

At the time of the Third Reich, it was of great importance to be totally "Aryan," in other words not to have any Jewish blood in your veins. However, many years later, I learned that my mother's great-grandmother had the first name of Salome. It was unheard of that a non-Jew would be given that name. I am sorry to say that I never knew how my mother felt about this and whether she was scared to death someone would find out, and she as well as her children might be persecuted for that reason. My mother died a suicide at the age of sixty-one; and as I had left Germany when I was nineteen and she was just forty-nine, we never had the kind of in-depth discussions and exchange of ideas and fears and such. I regret this so much and hope that my children will read this memoir and learn from it. One thing my mother told me many years after was about the infamous Kristallnacht—the night when Storm Troopers destroyed synagogues and went to the homes of Jews, and with the butts of their guns, destroyed all the crystal chandeliers as well as removing the people from their homes, never to be seen again. When in my innocence I asked why my mother did nothing about it, her answer was, "I had three small daughters, and the only thing my interference would have accomplished was that I would have been taken away as well." So this fear was everywhere, and the most basic instinct of humans is survival.

My father had intended to become a professional officer, but in 1917, at the age of nineteen, he lost his left leg at Verdun and could not continue his military career. Instead, he went to Heidelberg University and studied law.

As a twenty-eight-year-old lawyer for the city of Neustadt in the Black Forest, he met my mother. One can imagine the uproar in that small town when the Catholic daughter of one of the leading citizens decided to marry the son of a Lutheran minister. But both families agreed to the union, and my grandfather even married the couple in the Church of the Holy Spirit in Heidelberg. The day my dad asked for my mother's hand, he walked from his residence to her father's house wearing a top hat and carrying red roses. Of course everyone who saw him knew instantly where he was going and what he was about to do. When my dad arrived at my grandfather's house, my mother was sitting in the bay window pretending to do needlework. My dad told us this story many times. He was welcomed into the house, and my grandfather told him that he had no objections to the marriage. But he warned him, "Amalie does not like to cook." My dad replied that she would never have to, and he was true to his word. We always had a maid or cook, and on her day off or if my dad were away, we went to the restaurant down the street.

My father was a *"Justizrat und Notar"* in several towns and eventually in Heidelberg for many years. The translation is "Chief Counsel of Justice," a justice advisor like an attorney (there is no such title in America). My father did property deeds and other similar work; it was a government position. As an employee of the government, it was mandatory to be a member of the Nazi Party. A very ingenious way to get people into the Party was for the government to pay the Party dues for everyone, at least at the beginning. I'm not sure of that, but then there was no way to get out.

We lived in lovely flats and always had a live-in maid. My dad was very well-thought-of in our town, and people would stop him on the street to ask his legal advice. The most important advice he always gave them was, "Never sue anyone." And this from an attorney!

World War II started in 1939. I was three years old, so growing up, until I was nine, I knew nothing else than that there was a war going on. Of course, I had no idea what a war was.

The war dragged on. We had ration stamps, but I was too young to realize that this was something out of the ordinary. As time passed, food was getting scarcer and scarcer, but I did not notice. Being a university town with no industry to speak of, Heidelberg was not targeted for bombing by the Allies. But Mannheim, a mere fifteen or so miles away, was bombarded heavily. Every night after we had gone to bed, the sirens would blare, and we had to get up and rush into the bomb shelter, which was a fortified section of the basement in our house. My brother was born in 1944, so we had a baby to carry down there, too. But curious as children are, we would often go to the door and look out at the night sky to see many planes flying westward toward Mannheim. We would see the flak shooting at them, and we could see the bombs dropping. Then the night sky would light up red with all the fires. Mannheim was at least eighty percent or more destroyed.

Our grade school, which I attended for the first two years, was just four blocks from our house. Every now and then we had a drill when we had to put on gas masks and hide under our desks. I found this to be a game, which in a very fun way interrupted sitting still at the desk. Mind you, we had to stand up when the teacher entered the classroom and remain standing until told to sit down. Then we had to sit with our hands on the desk and thumbs underneath. If you misbehaved, the teacher could spank you on the hands with his ruler. Sometimes all the students had to go out into the schoolyard and raise their right hand in salute to Hitler. I remember we sang patriotic songs, and perhaps somebody made a speech. The only thing it meant to me was that my right arm got very tired, and I switched it with my left. Again, this was always a nice interruption of the classroom lessons. I was in this school for the first two years; then the war ended, and we had no school for a whole year.

Then came the time toward the very end when we heard over the radio that Hitler was dead. Mind you, I was only eight years old, and all I knew of this man was that he would scream on the radio, words I never understood. Then came several nights and days we had to spend in the basement as the Allies were advancing. In a last ditch effort to keep them from crossing the rivers, all the bridges were blown up by the Germans. This delayed the river crossing for about five minutes!

I remember one day peeking out the door and seeing American soldiers creeping up the street and hiding behind each house. They saw us children and motioned for us to go back inside. There was some shooting close to the cemetery, and then came tanks and jeeps and other vehicles full of American soldiers. We were all hanging out the windows, and my dad said, "We are so lucky that it is the Americans and not the Russians." How true!

Again, we had been fortunate. Toward the end of the war when so many men had been killed, every male was drafted, even as young as fifteen. My dad, with his disability, was called to be in transport of goods to the fronts. But he became sick and was at home with us when the very end of the war happened.

The American soldiers wanted to take our house, and a young lieutenant came to the door to tell us we had to leave. But my mother, with her charm and her school English, asked him into the living room and offered him a glass of wine. She convinced him to let us stay. This young man, to our horror, put his feet on the coffee table! Unheard of then. But we did not have to move out at that time.

The hotel just down the street was home for many American soldiers, and one of them always stood guard. One soldier in particular, Tom, was so nice and would drop Hershey bars or something else sweet into my brother's baby buggy. I knew a few English words, and he called me "Dorty." I think he had a daughter my age back in the States. The soldiers were not allowed to fraternize with us Germans, but this rule was not strictly enforced. One day Tom gave me to understand to bring him a bottle. I asked my mother, who gave me an empty wine bottle. We had no idea why he wanted this. He went inside the hotel and came back with the bottle filled to the top. I rushed home to give it to my mother, and to her surprise and delight, there was real coffee. We had not had that treat for a long time, and to this day, I wish I had learned the young man's name so I could have thanked him properly.

With so many refugees from the Russians and others being bombed out, there came the time when we would have been forced to take another family into our home, so we moved in with my aunt in Neckargemuend, a suburb of Heidelberg, and lived there for seven years. My two older sisters and my younger brother and I went to school there and in Heidelberg once we reached high school age, which in Germany was the fifth grade. My aunt planted potatoes and tomatoes in her garden; she had an apple tree and an apricot tree, and these were very much needed to supplement our meager food supply.

Until the very end of the war, everyone greeted each other on the street with "Heil Hitler!" As a child, I did not know what that meant but never thought about it either. When going to the neighborhood bakery, butcher shop, or any other public place, upon entering one had to say this also. Then overnight it was totally forbidden to say these words. Instinctively, without being told by anyone, we children never uttered that phrase again. As a matter of fact, history stood still. There was no school for a whole year, and then when school began again and we started learning about history, we began with the Romans and the Spartans, etc., but there was never any mention of Hitler or the Third Reich or WWII. When I graduated in 1955 from high school, we had never had a lesson or history book on that subject. I do not know how it is today.

After the war, the currency was based on the Reichsmark, which became less and less valuable. If you had money, there was nothing to buy with it. For birthdays we got a few marks, and I will never in my life forget the day the currency was changed. This action was called *Waehrungsreform*. For every ten Reichsmarks you got one Deutsche-mark. One day I had money in my purse and nothing in the stores to buy; the next day my wealth had shrunk to nothing, and there were blueberries and everything you could wish for, all out of my reach. I have always loved blueberries, and to be denied them at my young age, when they were obviously available, was not an easy thing for me to comprehend.

The years from 1945 to 1948 when my father was unemployed, as there was no German government, were lean ones for us. My parents sold the piano, and one after the other, most of our Persian rugs and other household goods, in order to be able to feed us. Even with his wooden leg, my father, sometimes joined by one of my sisters, would ride his bike to the small town where he had grown up and where people remembered him and his family, to bring home some flour or eggs or other unobtainable foods for us, which he could turn into delicious meals. His hobby was cooking. My mother never cooked a meal in her life! There were times when we lived for weeks on bean soup fortified with yeast flakes , and when they had it, our parents gave us cod liver oil. Yuck! To this day I cannot stand the smell, let alone the taste of this.

I can only imagine the troubles my dad and my aunt went through to feed us. All I remember of my mother during that time was that I would go into the master bedroom, which my parents shared with my little brother, and while she was still in bed she would comb my hair and braid it for the day. Then it was off to school on the train or the railroad, to return in the early afternoon.

My dad must have been a very tough man. When he lost his leg at Verdun, he was placed on a gurney, and the triage doctors would walk among the wounded and treat the ones they thought could be saved. My father was not among them. He was left overnight to die, but his strong spirit would not accept this fate. He told us that he screamed at the top of his lungs, "You can all go to hell! I am going to live!" He was finally treated the next day after spending what must have been a horrible night in pain. One of the doctors at this field hospital advised Dad to smoke; it would help with his digestion. For almost the rest of his life, he was a chain smoker. In the very, very lean years after the war, when he was out of a job, and we barely had enough to eat to keep us alive, we children looked for cigarette butts in the gutters to bring home. I even learned to roll cigarettes for my father from this stuff.

The winter of 1947 was especially harsh and cold. We lived right on the Neckar River, which flows through Heidelberg and Neckargemuend. That winter the river froze over, which is a rarity, and we would ice skate on it. My aunt's house had the so-called *kachelofen* for heating. This centrally-located tile stove in the foyer was fed wood and heated the main floor adequately—if you had wood. The upstairs rooms had tiny openings to this heater, which served to keep them from freezing. But there was no wood. We barely had enough, despite my dad's efforts to go into the nearby woods and bringing home kindling and any piece of wood that had fallen from the trees. He brought this home in a little wagon. The woods in all of Germany at this time were the neatest you could ever imagine, as everyone was in the same boat. They went to gather anything that was not nailed down. In the kitchen was my aunt's cook stove, which took briquettes or wood to cook our meager meals. The result was that this was the only room in the house that had any heat.

My dad developed a bad infection on his stump and could not use his wooden prosthesis, but he had to sit clad in coat and hat right next to the stove. I remember playing solitaire on the kitchen table, having to take off my right glove every time I wanted to turn a card. At night we three girls shared a hot water bottle to warm the bed. By the time it got to me, it was lukewarm. The sheets would freeze where our breath touched them; so did the water in toilets.

For toilet paper, we would use newspaper torn into pieces. I have always loved reading, and this was my reading "on the throne." I remember reading "De Gaulle," the name of the French president, and thinking it was an abbreviation of the words *"der Gauleiter,"* which meant the "section leader." A section leader was an appointed man in each neighborhood during the Third Reich, who had to patrol the streets at night and make sure that not the least bit of light came through the blackout curtains everyone had to have at their windows.

A few years after the end of the war, the people who had been members of the Nazi Party but had not held important positions in it had to be de-Nazified. It was some kind of process in which the powers that be decided whether the man or woman was of high enough character to be let back into society. I think my dad had to go to friends and ask for their recommendations, and finally he was de-Nazified and rehired for the same position he had held, only at a lower level. However, he soon regained his status, and in 1952, we were able to return to Heidelberg into a new flat.

Among his many duties at that time, my dad also did adoptions for Americans who wanted to take German children who had been orphaned. One such family came to his office one day, and the young man asked my dad how he was doing. "Oh," he replied, "I have already sweated through my first shirt today." And would you believe, some time later there came in the mail a package with several shirts for my dad from the American family.

The Americans started a program in the schools that allowed us to have a hot meal at noon. The ingredients were given to the schools where German women tried to fix something edible from American things like corn and dehydrated sweet potatoes, things we did not know and which they did not like to cook. But hunger is the best cook, and we ate what was given to us.

Doris, 1952

We received packages from American school children. One such package came to my classroom, and we had a lottery, as there was not enough for everyone. I won a set of jacks. Nobody knew what to do with it, so I threw away the pegs and kept the little ball.

A brother of my mother had emigrated to Michigan before the war and was in charge of or working for a clock factory in Zeeland, Michigan. Right after the war had ended, his wife, our Aunt Liesel, would ask her friends and neighbors for outgrown clothes to send to us. I was so fortunate to be just a couple years younger than my cousin in Michigan and got her clothes and the clothes of her friends. I was the best-dressed malnourished girl in my school!

One of my sisters was married by then and was in the U.S.

I graduated from high school in May of 1955, and because my mother told me to, I came to my sister's house in Louisiana shortly thereafter. I had planned for this to be a visit, but three weeks after my arrival I met the man I was to marry.

He had just returned from Korea, where he had been stationed as an officer in the U.S. Army, and had started in the management program at Sears Roebuck. Our daughter was born a year later. My husband was transferred with the company many times in our twenty-six-year marriage. Five years after our daughter Claudia, along came Eric. Both children attended thirteen different schools in twelve years, due to the many promotions their dad received as he climbed the ladder to become store manager for Sears in different states. At that time, this was quite a nice position to have, and we were always able to buy a newer and nicer house when we had to move. I found it exciting, but it was hard for the children to have to leave their new friends behind so many times.

My husband was the consummate workaholic, who had absolutely no time for his family and never took a vacation. I soon realized that my life was not fulfilled, and I went to school to become a licensed practical nurse. When I realized that I could support myself, I filed for divorce and went back to school to get my RN and graduated magna cum laude. I loved my job in the hospital on the cardiac floor, sold the house we had been living in and bought a smaller house, and thought I would never remarry. I was very happy.

When my brother was eighteen, he had the dream of coming to the U.S. and eventually becoming an army officer. He left Germany and came to stay with my sister, who lived in Louisiana then. He enlisted in the Army and was sent to Korea and to Vietnam. He changed his mind about being in the military and left after his required time. He studied law at Denver University and worked in the financial field. He now lives in Palmer Lake, Colorado with his lovely American wife, is retired, and will not ever speak of his experiences in the military.

Every time I had a vacation, I traveled to Colorado Springs where my sister was living, and I fell in love with the mountains and dry climate. I went so far as to look for a job there but found nothing I really liked.

One day, my sister was reading in the local newspaper in the Personal section. A man had written an ad looking for a woman to eventually marry. He described himself as an affectionate, successful businessman, divorced after twenty-six years, who loved to travel, candlelight dinners, the better things in life, etc. He was hoping to meet someone with similar interests in the age range of forty-five to fifty-five. Recent photo to be included. My sister cut out this ad and sent it to me. Upon opening the letter, I thought, "Oh, goodie," thinking she sent me an ad for a nursing job in Colorado Springs. But when I read the ad it just spoke to me, and I sat down and wrote a short letter to this stranger, describing myself and my life, and included a picture of myself standing among my tulips and daffodils. I was just fifty then and put the letter into the mail, not expecting much. The fact that I was born and raised in Germany and the flowers around my feet in the photograph made a great impact on the gentleman who had placed the ad. He too was born in Germany, raised in Luxembourg, and was a consummate gardener. He had received over one hundred replies to his ad and had met several of the women who had answered it.

To my surprise, a couple days later, there came a phone call from an obviously very German man. This was the man who had written the ad. I was so excited by the fact that he was a German, who had grown up in Luxembourg and was now living in Colorado Springs. We spoke on the phone for a long time and seemed to really hit it off. At my sister's urging I flew to Colorado Springs over New Year's 1987. Karl was invited to her home. He showed up with two bunches of roses—one for my sister and one for me. As he entered the house and saw me, he took a step backward and said, "But you are even more beautiful than your picture." Who wouldn't like that!? We had a fun time together, and three days later, I went back to Tulsa where I was living and working and put my house on the market.

Every week there came in the mail an airline ticket, and I would go to work on Friday with my suitcase packed, drive to the airport, fly to Colorado Springs and then back home again on Sunday evening. Come May, I quit my job and moved in with Karl. We were married in September of 1988, twenty-five years ago, and still live in Colorado Springs.

⊰ Dr. Hans Holzaphel ⊱

Dr. Hans passed away unexpectedly in California in late 2013, before we finished his story. Consequently, certain questions go unanswered, as he has no family, and there are gaps for which we would like more details. But his is a unique story as is, and readers will learn yet another aspect of the German WWII experience.

I was born in 1932 in Mainz, Germany. My father, Dr. Wilhelm Holzapfel, was a highly intellectual, decent man who grew up in Gross-Urnstadt, Germany, son of a long-time family there—ten generations dating back to the seventeenth century. I have a copy of the family tree.

I adored my grandpa, August Holzapfel. He had vineyards and honeybees and produced commercial quantities of Riesling wine and honey. He also had several orchards. He was a highly respected citizen and spoiled me on my visits and vacations in that small rural community. He was a patriotic German but negative to noncommittal about the Hitler regime.

My mother Ruth was the eldest of four daughters born to Willie Wolff in Idar-Oberstein. Grandpa Willie was a very jolly, affluent diamond merchant, a non-practicing Jew. I was told that in the 1920s, he had a chauffeured Mercedes and hunting preserve. He served in the German Army in WWI.

Then came 1933, Nazis in power, and things got bad. I was a little kid, and my parents wisely did not confide in me. My father was brilliant, got his Ph.D. at twenty-six and aspired to be an educator. He was also involved in nuclear physics and space exploration and had corresponded with Einstein in the 1920s. He understood the theory of relativity. In 1933-34, he refused to join the NSDAP (Nazi Party) and was dismissed from school service. As a result, we lived in relative poverty. Grandpa Holzapfel saved us with proceeds from his agricultural enterprises.

By 1938, I entered elementary school in Darmstadt. My father had "retooled" to theoretical physics and found a job in industry. Nazi gangs were terrorizing Jewish citizens (Kristallnacht, etc.). Grandpa Willie lost his home and business, and with his wife, escaped to Antwerp, Belgium, where he had business connections. I got to visit him there in my summer vacation and had a good time. Little did I know of the impending horrors.

At his peak, Hitler was an evil leader but charismatic speaker, whom many German citizens foolishly admired. The Gestapo (trenchcoats), SS (black uniforms), and SA (brown shirts) ruled and enforced the "law." Resistance was not visible and was ineffective. When the Hitler Youth was formed, it involved indoctrination and training in military as well as sports.

Meanwhile, Willie's second daughter Hilde married a Jewish man and emigrated to the U.S. Willie's two youngest daughters were in a prep school in England.

In September 1939, Germany invaded Poland and in 1940, much of Eastern Europe. France, too, was defeated soon after. Concentration camps existed but were not advertised. My mother counted ten Jewish relatives of a prosperous older generation who were "relocated" and perished.

Grandpa Willie and his wife Elvira left Antwerp, travelled south through western France just ahead of the Wehrmacht, and made their way to Lisbon in neutral Portugal. In 1941 and '42, we received letters from the Portuguese Consulate that the folks were okay.

In 1941, we moved to Nuremberg, where my dad had found

a job. I went to school there and remember a very severe winter. Food was scarce, my parents were stressed, and there was nocturnal aerial activity by the British Royal Air Force.

In 1942, we relocated in Wetzler, best known for Leitz Optical Ltd., manufacturer of the Leica camera. My father got a hush-hush job in a small firm there. It appears they were working on gyroscopes to use in missile guidance systems. Papa was solid, fearless, and wise! He was sent to Peenemunde (where he knew Wernher von Braun), where the Germans were testing missiles, shooting them into the Baltic Sea.

The air raids by the U.S. and RAF were brutal and scary. We lived in Wetzlar and later in tiny Allendorf, where my pop headed a think tank. Mercifully, U.S. troops liberated us about the end of April 1945. They were good guys, especially with the kids, dispensing candy, soap, cosmetics, and cigarettes. The frauleins liked those big, good-looking GIs, who were generous with nylons and perfume. The U.S. military government 1945-49 was fair and efficient.

[Dr. Hans wrote out a complete family history, which is irrelevant here, but there are some incidents of general interest worth repeating. Several family members came to the U.S. after the war and had successful lives here.]

From cousins Peter and Andrea Herz, the children of my mother's youngest sister, it appears that the youngest daughters of Grandpa Willie,—Inge and Hanna, left England when WWII was looming. They reunited in Antwerp with their parents Willie and Elvira Wolff and made the overland trip south with them ahead of the German Army into western France. The party was stopped at the Spanish checkpoint by an SS officer. His father happened to be an old friend of Willie's, and the officer waved them through. In addition, they had obtained phony passports to El Salvador, which helped their escape. They travelled toward West Africa by boat and were intercepted again, by a German

U-boat. The passports worked, and they never landed in Africa but went transatlantic instead to America.

There are two possible outcomes, which I can't verify, as all are deceased. According to one version, a boatload of Jewish refugees landed in New York City, where they were refused entry (anti-Semitism) and diverted to the Caribbean. Turned away at Santo Domingo, they finally settled in Havana. *[This situation is reminiscent of the pre-war episode of the St. Louis, which eventually was forced to return to Europe because the Western Hemisphere, including the U.S., refused them entry, ostensibly because they didn't have correct papers; Jews were denied citizenship in Germany. Many of the passengers ended up back in Germany in the gas chambers. See Dr. Rudolph Jacobson, Same War Different Battlefields.]*

Willie had run out of diamonds, but thanks to a wealthy New York relative, Richard Goldschmidt, they acquired entry into the U.S. Inge and Hanna were able to get jobs from 1942-45. The aging Wolffs lived with second daughter Hilde in Alabama, while Inge and Hanna went to New York City and found jobs and husbands.

My mother Ruth came to the U.S. in 1947, where she stayed with an ex-classmate and her Jewish M.D. husband. *[Dr. Hans doesn't tell us what happened to his father.]* She took basic jobs, and in May 1949 was able to arrange for me to come to the U.S. I worked and studied, earned a BS from RPI. (now Rensselaer Polytechnic Institute) at Troy, New York in 1953, and in 1957 earned my M.D. at Albany, NY Medical College. From there, I entered hospital training in Santa Barbara, CA, and practiced medicine in the Los Angeles area. I retired in 1985. My claim to fame: I never got sued!

Dr. Hans Holzaphel

◄ Ilse Charleston ►

I was born in Milwaukee in 1931. My parents had met in Germany and married in Milwaukee. When I was four years old, my parents decided to return to Germany to Berlin, due to the Depression in the U.S.; also my mother was rather homesick. When the war with Poland started in 1939 and ended soon after, everybody hoped this would be the end of any wars. My father was upset about this war, as he had been drafted and served in WWI. Since I was a young child, I really did not understand the real meaning of war, but I would later.

Life went on as normal, but then in 1940 Hitler declared war on France, Belgium, and the Netherlands, and when this was over, Germany still was confronted with England, because they had declared war on Germany in 1939 when Germany attacked Poland.

On August 26, 1940, we experienced our first air attack on Berlin by the British, and slowly the real war started with all its ugliness. There were more air attacks, and eventually with America's entry into the war, more Allied attacks

Ilse on the left, her mother, and a school chum, 1938

on Berlin and many other German cities. This meant we had to spend much time in the basement and consequently did not get much sleep.

My father was evacuated with his company to the eastern part of Germany. My mother remained in Berlin, and our school was closed. I stayed with my aunt in Silesia (now Polish territory) from late 1941 to early 1942. Later, the air attacks on Berlin were not as frequent, and our schools reopened. So I returned to Berlin, but in 1943 the air attacks increased.

When I returned from summer vacation in August, we were informed that all the schools were closed, and our school was to be evacuated to Gumbinnen in East Prussia. It is now Russian territory. My parents were upset because it was located close to the Russian border where the fighting was going on. I was able to get permission to stay with my grandmother in Stolp, in Pomerania on the Baltic Sea, now Polish Territory. I stayed there with her until late fall of 1944, then returned to Berlin.

The war on the Eastern front was getting closer to Germany. There were daily bombardments, but life went on. All the theaters, concert halls, movie theaters, and even some restaurants were closed in Berlin. My school was destroyed, so we had classes at a different school. Everything was rationed since 1939, and as time went on there was not much food available in the stores.

My mother continued to work at Siemens. Siemens and Halske Co. was/is a large company known world-wide. It produces electrical products such as telephones, electric trains, microscopes, and x-ray equipment.

At Christmastime 1944 my father was able to come to Berlin, and we were able to spend a few days as a family.

My confirmation was on March 4, 1945. On our way to the church, the siren started. We decided to continue to go to church, and our pastor performed the service, even with bombardments going on. Thank you, Pastor Bode.

On April 23 heavy bombardments finally destroyed our apartment building, and the fire spread rapidly from building to building. We had to leave the basement with the most important possessions we were able to carry. Eventually we had to remain on the street, where street fighting was going on. The Russian Army was in Berlin. We each put a white handkerchief on our arm to indicate that we were civilians, and they should not shoot at us.

We finally found a place to stay; we were three families in one apartment. No water or electricity was available due to the destruction of those facilities in the bombing.

On May 8, 1945, Germany capitulated, and the war was over. The Russians took over Berlin, and they started to do a lot of looting, raping, and stripping of watches, jewelry, and anything of value. *"Uri, Uri!"* was their catchword. *"Uhr"* in German meant "watch" in English. So when they came up to you and pointed to your wrist, they said *"Uri!"* meaning "Give me your watch." If you did not comply, they would pull the watch from your wrist.

Regarding raping—there were times my mother and I were threatened, but we were lucky and not "selected." However, it was that constant state of fear that was exhausting and stressful. During that time, you had to expect it when the soldiers came up to you and said, *"Frau, komm . . . ."* You either complied or if you refused and tried to run away, they would shoot you. One of my aunts was killed by a Russian officer because she ran away.

Since there was no water available, we had to stand in line to get it from old, hand-operated water pumps that had been built on the streets in the 1800s for horses to drink from. Electricity was not available until later June and July and restricted to only two or three hours a day. We were also very hungry.

In July, other Allies came to Berlin and realized they had to feed the people. My mother and I received a ration card for 1000 calories per day called the "Hunger Card", one version of five such cards, which in the beginning gave us dried peas and a little bread, but only for a while. That was not a good diet for our digestive system. Hardly any food was available except on the black market at high prices. Since the copy of the card

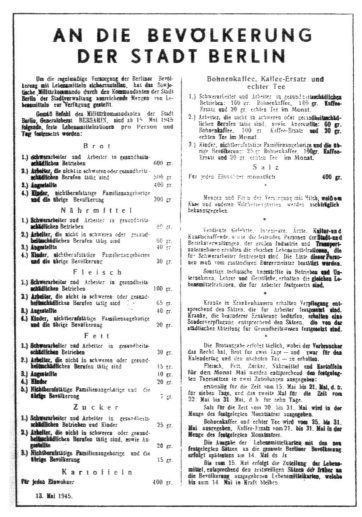

The Allies had a duty to feed the vanquished Germans. This notice of May 13, 1945, sets out the rations for Berlin. Four ration cards were issued according to the recipient's usefulness to society. Workers received twice as much as children. Later, two more categories were invented, including the sixth hunger card. Needless to say, very little of this largesse was really available.

printed here is in German, I'll explain: Workers received twice as much as children. This card was for children and non-working family members and/or non-working people in general. The consequence of this was that my mother and I eventually developed typhus, even though we had been vaccinated against it. We recovered but many people died.

Ilse with her mother and father, 1952/53

The summer of 1945 was very hot, and the Russians had us remove the dead bodies that were all over and clear up the rubble, all under their supervision. Bricks were recycled for rebuilding. Seeing the destruction, I was amazed that we survived.

Berlin was then divided into four sections among the four Allied powers. We were in the Russian sector. Germany was also divided into four zones. The Russians put us on Moscow time; the difference was about three or four hours, and the adjustment was not easy. Then all our savings accounts were closed, and we were never able to withdraw any of our savings; they were lost. Luckily we had withdrawn some money before the end of the war.

My father came home. Because all the railroads were destroyed, he had to walk from the Sudetenland to Berlin. We found a different apartment, and in September schools were reopened. Our school had been partially damaged during the bombing, and as winter arrived, students as well as teachers had to sit in their coats and blankets because there was no heat. The broken-out windows were covered with newspaper. But we managed to learn.

I graduated from high school and business college and started to work, besides going to night school for special courses. In 1946/47, theaters, concert halls, and movies (mostly Russian propaganda movies) started to open. People were hungry for some entertainment.

I wanted to return to the U.S., but on June 17, 1953, there was an uprising in the Russian sector of Berlin and in the Russian zone against the Communist government there. Too many people were trying to leave, especially the young ones, and the authorities tried to prevent this. It put me in a spot because I worked in West Berlin but lived in East Berlin. My ration card was taken away, and it was recommended that I get a job in East Berlin.

Then friends of my parents in Milwaukee offered to sponsor me to come to Milwaukee. It was not an easy decision to leave my family behind. Due to the

Ilsa with her husband, 1960

fact that I had dual citizenship—German and U.S.—I was able to enter as a U.S. citizen. The American consulate in Berlin was very helpful at that time.

When I arrived in Milwaukee in 1954, I had to find a job and living quarters within a week so I could repay for my trip as soon as possible. I stayed only a few days at the home of my sponsors. I arrived on Tuesday and started to work on Saturday. My only choice was to work as a housekeeper. Then, with the help of a friend, I was offered a job at St. Joseph's Hospital and started to work in the dietitian's office as a secretary. Later, I worked in medical records, pathology, and the research laboratory as a technician. I also worked for one year in Chicago at the University of Illinois as a medical secretary.

In the meantime, through friends, I had met a wonderful someone, an American, and we decided to get married. So I returned to Milwaukee and started to work at the Medical College of Wisconsin. Luckily a German orthopedic surgeon had been looking for a bilingual secretary in German and English. This was a great opportunity for me. Unfortunately he left after a few years, but I stayed in the department for another twenty-nine years as administrative assistant to the department chairman.

None of my family came to the U.S. after the war. My parents were getting older and had started to rebuild their lives. They remained in the Russian sector of Berlin, hoping that Germany would eventually be reunited.

I had hoped to return to Germany in five years, but the Cold War lingered on for another forty-five years and complicated many things in my life. Due to the Berlin Wall that had been built in 1960, I was unable to see my parents. My mother died in 1963, but in 1971 I was able to have my father visit Milwaukee for four weeks. At that time, the East German government gave seniors permission to visit relatives in West Germany or West Berlin for four weeks. Since my father was retired, he applied for a pass. Through the American Consulate in West Berlin, I was able to get a four-week visa for him to visit us in Milwaukee.

As to my reception in the U.S.—generally good. People were nice and also helpful. Of course, I met some people who showed anti-German feelings, but that was expected, and you learn to live with that. I am thankful to the people who helped me through the years of my career, especially my husband, who was my protector in so many ways. Sadly, he died of cancer in 2007. I now live comfortably in a nice condominium in Franklin, Wisconsin.

Ilse

Sabine Spierling

My father Werner called Hitler the "murderer of my youth." And with good reason.

When WWII began in 1939, Werner was twenty-five years old. At the urging of friends, relatives, fellow citizens in the village where his family had lived for generations, and ultimately Hitler himself, Werner felt forced to join the military to fulfill his obligations as a German citizen. Before the war, Werner's favorite hobby had been to fly a non-motorized glider airplane over the fields near his home. As a result, when confronted with the inescapable duty of military service, he felt it was his destiny to join the Luftwaffe. However, unlike a number of those around him, he never saw the war effort as a great and noble calling, and his heart was never in his military service. His only goal was to withstand and survive the war and return safely to those he loved. Indeed, he was a reserved and introverted man, who deeply distrusted Hitler from the start. He never believed the propaganda that became omnipresent and central to many Germans' belief that the war effort was a righteous endeavor.

Werner's reservations about Hitler's Third Reich stood in stark contrast to the enthusiasm my mother Adele felt for the war effort. At the beginning of the war, she was at the impressionable age of nineteen; she came to wholeheartedly believe a significant amount of the Third Reich's propaganda. Adele was the daughter of a member of the *Junker* landed nobility in East Prussia. She described her life before the war as boring and isolating. Adele's mother had passed away when Adele was a child, and her father was less attentive to the social development of his four daughters. Until Hitler came to power, there

275

were social ranks to be observed. Because she was from a family that had a relatively high rank in the pre-war social order, she was not allowed to play with the children of the workers on her farm, and the next neighbor of the "right" class was miles away.

Once Hitler came to power, he ordered the various social classes to intermingle socially as part of his vision that German citizens were a single, unified "*Volk*," or people. The National Socialist Party organized numerous weekend parties in every village—parties that involved elaborate decorations, music, food, and dancing. Adele recalled those parties with great fondness and recalled as well the sense of common purpose that was pervasive in her village at the time. Landowners were also encouraged to invite German military personnel stationed in their area to their homes for family dinners. Adele's father felt obligated to invite soldiers to his home, and Adele enjoyed flirting and dancing with the officers, who were so handsome in their uniforms.

Werner and Adele in their twenties

In order to provide Werner with the necessary training on motor-propelled aircraft, the Luftwaffe dispatched him to East Prussia, where he learned to fly a courier airplane (*Fiesler-Storch*). The courier airplane was able to fly very slowly, and Werner's typical route caused him to pass over the farm/estate owned by Adele's father. It was a beautiful piece of land with a lake, where Adele and her sisters often bathed when the weather was fine. Since Werner's route took him over the same location every day, after a short period of time, he and the girls began waving at each other. The young ladies became curious about the pilot's identity, and one of Adele's sisters decided to place stones on the driveway of their home near the lake that spelled out, "Throw down your name, rank, and address." My father responded by writing his name, rank, and location on a piece of paper in a tin chocolate box, weighted it with a stone, and threw it out the window of his airplane. Through this connection, he eventually met my mother, the daughter of the estate owner. They fell in love and got married.

In February 1944 Werner was shot down over England near Ashford, Kent, in his airplane, a DO217M (*Dornier*), and was able to parachute out of his burning plane. He landed at night on a field of a British farmer, who escorted him to his house. He woke up his wife, who bandaged my father's injured hand, offered him tea, and gave him an apple to eat. Then they reported him to the local police station, where he was interrogated. But to my father's surprise, they already knew his airplane type, the bombs he carried, and even the airport from which the Germans used to fly their bombing raids. After a few months in a Scottish POW camp, all the captured German soldiers were shipped to the USA on the famous old *Queen Elizabeth* that was converted from a luxury passenger ship to transporting cargo and POWs.

Most Germans knew by the end of 1944 that the war could not be won, and servicemen considered themselves lucky to be captured by the Allies. To be caught on the Eastern front meant torture, starvation, or internment in Siberia's concentration camps. In that respect, my mother was lucky—being shot down in Britain saved her husband's life. Her sisters did not fare that well; their husbands all died on the Eastern front, and for the rest of their lives, for that generation there were few men left.

During this entire time, my mother did not know if her

husband were dead or alive. She had her own tragedies to deal with. She and her father had to flee from the advancing Russian front in a carriage with four horses. They made it to Berlin and eventually she ended up with my father's family in the West, in northern Germany. Then she got a letter from Wisconsin and learned about her husband's survival.

In the meantime, in the U.S., my father had to work on big farms with other German POWs. He was transported to Wisconsin to work on a farm in, ironically, Rhinelander. Although they had to work hard, Mother was envious that he was fed three meals a day, and she was happy that he was treated fairly well. One day the POWs complained that they had not enough meat in their diet. To their astonishment, the farmer went to his house and came back with rifles that he distributed among the prisoners, telling them to go hunting in the vast forests of Wisconsin. The Germans did as they were told, shot some deer and rabbits and returned back to their camp, happy to supplement their food for months to come. Nobody escaped or even thought of doing so.

Their hope was to be returned to their homeland soon, and survival in the wilderness was just too risky. My father returned back to his native country in 1946, where he started to rebuild his life.

I came to Colorado to live and work here. I raised my family here and became a U.S. citizen. Because of my accent, people are often encouraged to tell me their WWII stories, which is a constant subject in my family in Germany, even though it all happened long ago. For example, I once met an American who told me that he was a guard at an Italian POW camp in New Jersey. The prisoners there also had to work on neighboring farms. After some time, the Americans permitted them to go to New York City for the weekend, ordering them to return on Monday for work. To everyone's surprise, the Italians found aunts and uncles and distant relatives in the city; they stayed with them and could not be found to be returned to their camp. The Americans had no choice but to close the camp!

In conclusion, being a POW in America was not a bad way to fight the war.

Werner and Adele in their sixties

⋆ Rosemarie ⋆

[Who prefers not to include her last name]

I was born in 1931 and raised in Landsberg/Warthe-East Mark Brandenberg in what was then Germany, now Polish territory. It is thirty kilometers east of the Oder River, and two hundred kilometers east of Berlin. My parents provided a comfortable, middleclass lifestyle for my two younger brothers and me. My father was a well-known waterwell builder for large farms in our province. My mother, a bookkeeper, helped in his office along with two more employees. One of my grand-fathers was a master gardener, whose property bordered my parents. So he took care of our large garden too, which provided all our vegetables and fruits. From him I inherited my love for gardening. We three children had to help him with watering and weeding, which was not exactly our favorite pastime then!

In 1937 I started school, the first four years in elementary school. After that, parents have a choice for their children to either continue elementary school until age fourteen and end it there, or after four years go to middle school until age sixteen, or high school to age eighteen. My parents sent me to high school, and they had to pay for that.

When the war in Poland broke out in 1939, most younger male teachers were drafted. After that our teachers were mainly female or older male teachers. I remember well one of the older males came to class in a brown SA uniform, and of all subjects, taught religion! Most teachers were members of the Nazi Party, and after the war, these teachers were not allowed to teach because of those Nazi associations. Their replacements were old, poorly trained, emergency, "fill-in" personnel.

Our father was also drafted at this time. That conflict ended soon after, and he returned home after two weeks. He was not called up again until mid-January 1945, when every able-bodied male fifteen to sixty-years old was required to serve in response to Germany's desperate military situation. My father was previously exempted because his expertise and experience at well building was needed in the civilian sector.

Very often the sirens went off at night, and as a precaution, the family went to the basement of our apartment house at the time. Landsberg did not offer military targets and was not bombed, but bombers flew close on their way to other destinations. Eight other families lived in the apartments too. Toward the end of the war, we took in additional families—refugees from the East who were fleeing the Russians.

My most horrific and dramatic memories begin from the 30th of January 1945, as the front came closer, and Russian troops are involved. My father had just been drafted again two weeks earlier and appeared suddenly one night at our home, woke us up, and said, "You have to leave now! The Russians are getting close!" We looked out the window and saw the night skyline RED; villages around us were burning. While we were getting ready, my father went over to my aunt's house to get her and her three boys out too. Her husband, my mother's brother, had died in the war with Poland. My father hurriedly took us to the main train station with barely a suitcase. Many trains were fully loaded and had already left. He put us on the only train that was still there, said "Goodbye" to all of us, and left. We never saw him again. On that night we lost everything—our home, possessions, and we later learned, our father and grandparents as well.

On our way to the railway station, we had to cross the bridge that went over the Warthe River. We saw many German soldiers ready to blow up the bridge so the Russians would not be able to enter the downtown of Landsberg, but the Russians made it anyway, without the bridge.

Russian troops tried to stop our trainful of refugees, but accompanying German soldiers were able to fight them off. The resulting obstructions meant that the train only went twenty-five miles that first day. Some refugees froze to death while fleeing by horse and wagon and were just left lying on the road.

Later we made it to Potsdam, where we were put up with strangers for ten days. Eventually we made it to Eisleben (Martin Luther's birthplace) where the sister of my aunt took us in. For some months, three families, which included nine children, lived in one tiny apartment; some were quartered in the attic. I remember well that some refugees were treated like dirt by the locals. There seemed to be an apparent resentment over their arrival on the scene.

Finally, a family took in my mother and us three children. The four of us had one tiny room that had only room for one bed, a table, and two chairs. My mother and I slept in one bed, my brothers on the floor. There was no stove for us to do the cooking, but a school nearby had a soup kitchen where many of the refugees could go to have a warm meal (mostly potato or bean soup), and we were grateful for that. Needless to say, we were all malnourished.

Early April 1945 the Americans conquered Eisleben. Some brave citizens went out with large white sheets toward the American troops to hand the city over to them. Not one shot was fired. At that moment all kinds of people started plundering stores for food and clothing. Anarchy set in until the military took over and brought back order.

On May 8, 1945, the war was finally over. Russian troops had taken Berlin, but the city was then divided into four sectors for Americans, French, English, and Russians. Since the Russians gave up three-quarters of Berlin, the Americans gave them part of Germany they had occupied, and Eisleben was in it. Suddenly the Russians moved into that town overnight; we couldn't believe it! We were shocked, and Communism set in. We had to do, think, and say what they told us.

Later, schools opened again, but our new teachers were not adequate at all for quite a while, and in addition, we had to learn the Russian language. Whole classes were brought to movie theaters where we were shown the atrocities the Nazis had done in concentration camps. We had absolutely no idea they existed, and we were all shocked in disbelief.

One afternoon in the summer of 1945, I was in line and about to enter a movie theater when I was recognized and approached by an older girl I didn't know, but who wanted to share some shocking news. She asked my name to make sure I was who she thought I was. She told me right out that my father was dead. Up until then, we had never heard anything about him. I went right home and brought my mother back to the theater. What the young lady described was shocking to be sure. In February 1945, this girl with some other people in Landsberg, found the bodies of my father and grandparents in our garden, where the Nazis buried them. My mother asked her for her address, as this girl was a witness my mother needed for a death certificate.

Even as young as I was, I had great concern for my mother, left with nothing, but sole responsibility for her three children. And it was just the beginning of her ordeal. How did she deal with all this?! With maturity and the perspective of a mother myself, it is a hard question to answer.

From there on, our lives went downhill for quite some time. We knew that we never could go "home" again. (Our part of Germany was given to Poland, along with everything that was left behind.) Since our father and grandparents were dead, there was just a bleak future ahead of us, and to make matters worse, food was scarce. Every day we went *"stoppeln,"* which means finding potatoes, grains, etc. on the fields that had already been harvested. Those fields were not close by but four to seven kilometers away. We got up early in the morning to make the one- to two-hour walk one way and back every evening, carrying our "harvests" on our backs. On those fields we met many hungry people all doing the same thing.

Sometimes I went through the neighborhood asking for and collecting potato peelings for our rabbits. Of course, we didn't have any rabbits. We scrubbed the peelings so our mother could make us potato soup.

By that time, we had a small living space that was given to us by a nice elderly lady who owned her own house. She gave us two rooms, a small kitchen, and an "outhouse" across the courtyard.

Everyone got ration cards, and with them one was able to buy a specific amount of food each month, which kept one barely alive. My mother seldom dared to send my brothers to the bakery for a loaf of bread, because on the way home they had already eaten half of it; they were always so hungry.

By the age of sixteen, I had to quit high school since there was no money to pay for it. At this time my mother received the most minimum payment from the state (called *wohlfahrt*) for her and us three children, until she was finally able to find a job. City College, a community college in Eisenben, gave me the opportunity to attend without having to pay, and so I trained to become a teacher of home economics. Slowly our lives got better.

Finally, in 1950 I found a job in a home for children, a kind of spa where children could heal after having tuberculosis. This home was located in the small village of Trautenstein in the Harz Mountains, close to the border of East/West Germany. We lived there rather isolated from the rest of the world. All employees there, mostly young women plus two elderly nurses, were politically a solid anti-Communist unit. This went on until 1954, when we were infiltrated by a nineteen-year-old young man, who reported us to the authorities. They came to investigate the situation. But before they were able to make any arrests, we were all gone. By this time all the children had already left for home, as each group only stayed for six weeks at a time.

After that I found a job in East Berlin as a housekeeper, where I stayed for about a year. A childhood friend of mine who lived in West Berlin found me a job there, again as a housekeeper At this time, the wall around Berlin was not yet built, so I was lucky to be able to still escape to the West. However, I could not get a permanent residence there, since West Berlin had too many escapees from the East and was overcrowded. In the meantime, one of the elderly nurses from Trautenstein, who had made it to West Germany, found me a job there in another home for children, which I happily accepted.

In April of 1956 I flew from Berlin to Hamburg. Since I was now on the "black list" in East Germany, I was no longer able to travel the roads through East Germany. Berlin was like an island in the middle of Communist East Germany. Now I had the feeling that I was finally FREE! No more watching so very carefully what I was saying or doing. My new job was great as a housemother for fourteen- to sixteen-year-old girls who could not get along at their parents' home or were very immature. I taught them cooking, sewing, and housekeeping.

In 1960 I was offered a job in England for a year and a half, and in November of 1961 I emigrated to Toronto, Canada, where I met and married my husband—also German. In 1964 we got our visas for the USA and lived in Santa Monica, California, for fourteen years. There our son was born, and in 1978 we made our final move to Colorado, where we feel completely at home.

⊰ Ellen Feist Smith ⊱

A few of the survivors included in this collection missed the extreme drama experienced by many of the other contributors. Consequently, they reflect a degree of almost "normalcy" that accompanied the lives of some individuals and segments of the wartime population. For example, farmers generally missed the bombing of the cities and had access to more food, although the government made severe demands on their products by means of quotas. (For buying a pig from a neighboring farmer, Eric Muetlein's mother received a jail sentence of three months.)

E llen Feist, a city girl, was born in Heidelberg in 1931 and moved to Stuttgart when young. Her father was a successful fabric merchant. She had Jewish friends who disappeared, which was common, especially after Jewish children were expelled from public schools. Many parents didn't talk about the political situation, at least in front of little ears, as children were queried by some teachers, neighbors, and "friends" looking to ingratiate themselves for turning in those "hostile" or "dangerous to the Regime." An extra loaf of bread no doubt made that an appealing reward. However, Ellen's father was safely an enthusiastic Nazi sympathizer. "We ALL were at that time." He was not medically fit for military service, which was therefore disappointing to him and the family. Mother Feist had three brothers serving in Russia, one of whom didn't return.

Ellen's school in Stuttgart was closed, and the government took over the building. Children had to attend a different school, inconveniently farther away. At elementary school age, Ellen joined the *Jungmadel*, the German youth group for girls. "We all wanted to! And I once saw Hitler in a parade, riding in an open Mercedes standing up waving."

When Ellen was thirteen, her father took her to the Black Forest to the farm of friends, where she remained safe during the war years, until she was seventeen. It was a large and prosperous working farm, but the menfolk were away in military service, and the women were left to operate the farm. Three sons were off at war; one was killed. There were three girls in the family, plus their grandfather, all of whom worked. "We ate five times a day because we worked so hard!"

Ellen found it difficult to adjust from her city life. She missed her family, of course, which included an older sister. There was no Hitler Youth activity; in fact, there was hostility toward Hitler and the regime. She was able to continue going to school, but the school was a considerable distance from the farm, and she had to walk. She was expected to work on the farm after school. Hay was the principal crop, and there were fifteen cows to milk, eggs to gather, and pigs and chickens to look after.

Freiberg was the main city of the Black Forest area, and although the city was heavily bombarded, the cathedral avoided damage. Church attendance was expected twice on Sunday except during harvest-time. Between church, school, and farm-work, it was a demanding routine that left Ellen with little free time.

After the war Ellen returned home, attended business school, and worked part-time at a local grocery store. She married a GI from Michigan, and in 1956 they came to the U.S. He was re-assigned to Camp (now Fort) Carson in Colorado Springs, where Ellen still resides.

Ellen, 2013

❧ Eric Muetlein ❧

The account printed here is an excerpt of Eric's extensive memoir entitled "The Skinny Kid." This was a daunting task for me because every incident was so fascinating and revealing. The memoir was begun on a typewriter in the late 1940s from scraps of notes he was able to keep throughout the war. He has revised and enlarged it several times since. This story simply overwhelmed me, and I suspect it will have the same impact on other readers. His command of English is impressive, and despite everything he experienced, there is often humor.

Eric has written his own Introduction, although there was only room in this volume for a condensation.

Introduction

This is the story of a seventeen-year-old German boy who went to war in 1944. . . . It portrays a world that has gone mad. A world filled with rage, cruelty, deception, and only rare moments of compassion. . . . And while the description of war scenes may sometimes appear repetitive, it is because war has no other purpose but that of men killing each other, and there is little variation to the methods used to accomplish that.

Although the story represents a mere snippet of my long life, no other period in my life has had a similar impact. During those three years, I experienced the lowest extremes of animal existence. It was offset in part only by the exhilaration I felt when as a prisoner of war I came to the U.S. I discovered a land where people have everything they need, even during wartime, and are free to go to a picnic on Sundays instead of picking potato beetles in the fields as dictated by their government. People who, even though I was an enemy, treated me as another human being. That is more than I can say for my native country of Germany, which instead of welcoming me home as a returning soldier, degraded and abused me.

My paternal grandfather, Leonard Muthlein, was Head Forester and Gamekeeper for the king of Wuerttemberg in the late nineteenth century. Grandpa Leonard and his wife Berta fathered a daughter and ten sons. Ottmar, the youngest, became my father. From him I learned that Grandpa Leonard was a strict disciplinarian who believed in collective punishment. Returning from the woods at the end of the day, if he found Grandma Berta unhappy, he asked no questions. He simply retrieved his stick, backed his ten boys into a corner, and whacked away.

Unable to cope with the stern and harsh regime of Grandpa Leonard, some of the sons left the family early. Uncle Max packed up and left for America, settling in California.

Uncle Emil and his wife Frieda operated their own beauty shop and cosmetics store in Pforzheim. They died in the cellar of their home there in a British bombing raid in February of 1945, which destroyed the city and killed between 18,000 and 20,000 residents—one third of the population of the city. The burning house collapsed on top of the cellar, blocking their exit. The intense heat dehydrated and shrank them to the size of children. When my father found them in the cellar, Aunt Frieda still grasped the suitcase they had taken with them into the shelter. He took their remains in a wheelbarrow to the cemetery and buried them.

My parents were "gypsies," never staying in a place longer than three or four years. They lived in Pforzheim for a while in the 1920s and worked with Emil and Frieda in their beauty shop. In 1927 they were living in Stuttgart, where I was born.

They then operated their own beauty shop in another town, an enterprise that went bad, and by 1933 they ended up in Pforzheim again, working with Uncle Emil. Nineteen thirty-three was also the year Hitler came to power, and I began school at age six in Pforzheim. One of my friends there was Jewish, which really didn't mean anything to me, until one day he did not show up in school and was never heard from again. My parents tried to explain to me what happened, but it didn't make much sense then.

Uncle Max who went to California

At that young age, the regime change did not register, although I became aware of some changes to our personal lives. By 1936 we lived in a large house outside a small farm town. Autobahn construction took place nearby. As we had extra rooms, we were ordered to house and feed a number of the itinerant construction workers, about ten or twelve of them. They were a rough lot, getting drunk, staying up late, being loud, and sometimes one would attempt to bring a girl "home"with him.

My father took a job as a bookkeeper with the construction company, and because he had to travel on his job, he was gone a lot. Then he became manager of a gravel pit, which involved some shady dealings that my mother threatened to expose to the authorities. This would have had serious consequences and did eventually cost him his job.

In 1937 I became ten years old and was required to join the *Jungvolk*, a government-controlled organization. Uniforms had to be worn at the meetings, which mostly consisted of hikes in the country, singing of patriotic songs, and political indoctrination. Sometimes we marched in a parade.

Eric in 1941, age 14 at his parents' resort lodge *Berghaus* in the Black Forest

At fourteen, a boy had to become a member of the *HitlerJugend*. It was a more serious organization; they put us to work doing chores. There was pre-military training, with shooting contests and war games. Political indoctrination was more intense. The next step, at seventeen, was either joining the National Socialist German Workers Party or the SA, although the choice was voluntary. I didn't have to be concerned with it, since there was a war going on, and seventeen was the age for military service. And that was not voluntary.

Nor were our parents spared from government dictatorship. For instance, a mailing would arrive announcing a mandatory meeting, sometimes about required participation in some activity, adding that the card should be presented to the policeman at the door. A government agency even dictated to you when and where to go on vacation. And there were more serious issues, such as joking in public about the regime, which was punishable by a jail sentence. Then there was the red sticker affixed to every dwelling stating that listening to a foreign radio station carried the death penalty. At night, people listened outside your windows trying to determine what kind of station you had tuned in.

My father and his friends would lock themselves in a room and talk politics. Privately he called himself a "proletarian," and only much later I learned of his opposition to the Nazi regime and his frustration about not being able to act.

There was fear across the country. People whispered about the *Arbeits Lager* (work camps) and who had been taken away to one of those. These were really concentration camps, and so-called "undesirables" were put to work there—not only Jews but hard-core criminals, religious fanatics, homosexuals, nomadic folks such as gypsies, and the physically and mentally impaired.

In 1939 the war began. Hitler considered himself a military genius. After successes in Poland, England, France, etc. he made the mistake of attacking Russia in the fall of 1941, with winter coming on. I remember my parents saying, "Now we are going to lose the war." Of course all that was "grownup stuff," while the indoctrination of us kids continued in school and in our youth organizations, where teachers told us that we were invincible and would win the war.

In 1941 I graduated from eighth grade; I was fourteen. My parents had recently leased and moved into a resort lodge, the Berghaus, in the Black Forest. It was in a beautiful setting where I could hike, fish, ski, and have a wonderful, carefree, outdoor life. Having graduated, it was time to make a career choice. I had artistic talent but I also liked electronics. I made a radio that got me into trouble. However, I knew that to become an electronics engineer required a five-year education, and there wasn't time left to realize that dream because I knew I would be going into military service at seventeen.

Then I became interested in chemistry, bought a chemistry set, and also got into trouble because of minor explosions, smelly gases, etc.—none of which was appreciated by my parents or the guesthouse occupants. Fortunately, a chemist who worked at DEGUSSA, a large chemical company, vacationed with us and learned of my ambitions. He arranged for me to enter a two-year training program with his company, starting as a lab technician. I also attended a vocational school with courses in several other disciplines, as well as shop classes. I was able to go home on weekends to the Berghaus. When I left home at fifteen, I was determined to be a chemist some day.

In 1943 there was trouble at the Berghaus that forced my parents to close their operation and move again. Despite wartime shortages and rationing, my mother ignored regulations and bought a pig from a neighboring farmer. It was a success on the Berghaus menu but was reported to the authorities, which prompted a visit from the Gestapo. Mother was tried and sentenced to three months in prison for "a crime against the German war economy."

Eric age 15

At sixteen, in addition to my schooling I became a gunner on an anti-aircraft cannon. I had no ambition for that, but it was mandatory. So I reported to the Flak Battery station for duty from seven in the evening to seven in the morning. Our trainer was an Air Force sergeant who stayed with us in a roof-top bunkhouse.

I did very well in a contest held for young people that involved every category and level of Junior Laboratory Technician. I advanced to

county, state, and national levels and placed ninth nationally. Naturally DEGUSSA was impressed and hinted that I had a great future ahead, that they could get me exempted from military service and assist me to advance my education. However, there was the suggestion that such a course of action might have political effects, like required membership in the Nazi Party. I declined the offer, and as I approached age seven-

Eric at an outing with friends, 1941

teen, did a mandatory three-month stint in the *Arbeitsdienst*, a pre-military service involving labor as well as military-type training. My team built a runway capable of accommodating a new type of fighter plane called a "jet," which required a much longer runway than conventional propeller-driven planes.

Soon after I turned seventeen, I had to make the decision to either volunteer for military service, in which case I could choose the branch of service or be drafted, mostly likely into the Infantry and on to the Russian Front.

We had heard stories told by soldiers on leave from the Eastern front. To be taken prisoner by the Russians, particularly by troops from Mongolia or Siberia, amounted in many cases to a death sentence. Prisoners were stripped of warm clothes, gloves and boots, then made to stand in the snow for hours while the Russians got drunk. Every so often one of the Mongols would emerge from their tent, wielding a saber, pick out a prisoner and chop him down, then return to the party for more vodka. I simply had to stay out of the Infantry. Someone suggested I become a paratrooper, explaining that none were deployed on the Eastern front.

Training got underway in the typical German military fashion, disciplined and brutal. When we did our pushups, the drill sergeant let us go for twenty, then yelled, "In the German Army, we count when we do pushups!" We started over, calling out the numbers. He let us do another twenty and then barked, "In the German Army, we start counting at ZERO!"

In the field, he would make us cross a creek on a greased log. Most of us lost our balance and slipped off right away. Others, appearing that they might make it across, were allowed about halfway, then he yelled, "Machine gun fire from the right! Hit the ground!" The ground in this case was the water of the creek.

To accustom us to the degree of force with which one hit the ground during a parachute jump, they made us take a run to the edge of a fifteen-foot-deep gravel pit and jump down into it, and after the impact, rolling forward over either the left or right shoulder.

Then there was the Tin Donkey, which was a twin-engine airplane with wings removed and wheels blocked. We would lie on the ground behind the Tin Donkey, feet pointed toward it and the open chutes strung out behind our heads. Then they fired up the engines, generating a tremendous prop wash which caused our chutes to balloon out and drag us on our backs. That exercise was supposed to simulate a landing in a strong wind. The trick was turning your body so the legs faced in the direction of travel and letting the chute pull you upright.

A few old Junkers 52 planes and Italian Savoy planes were used for practice jumps, since German planes were needed for the war effort. However, because fuel was scarce, most of the jumps were made not out of airplanes but from the baskets of balloons tethered to the ground by steel cables.

By far, the toughest part of our training was on the ground. We spent endless hours tearing across potato fields to the sound of a whistle. One blow of the whistle and we hit the dirt. Two blows and we got up and took off running again. When they wanted us totally frustrated, they made us wear gas masks during these drills, knowing that our breath fogged up the lenses and rendered us virtually blind.

We practiced on the firing range until we could hit a flare-lit target at night, visible for only fifteen seconds, from four hundred meters. We practiced setting up an 80-mm mortar over and over again until we could get the base plate, bipod, and barrel off our backs, onto the ground, assembled and ready to fire in less than twenty-five seconds.

After a month, I was transferred to the paratrooper school in Wittstock near Berlin, to finish my training there and become a member of the 3rd Platoon, Company 12, Thirteenth Regiment of the Fifth German Paratrooper Division. As we had expected, we deployed to the Western front to do what we had trained to do.

By the fall of 1944, American forces have driven east through and into Luxembourg, where they now are in a holding mode. Our Fifth Paratrooper Division, poised along the border of Germany and Luxembourg, is part of the stage for a counter-attack, an offensive that became known as the "Battle of the Bulge," named for the frontline bulge formed when German forces in their drive toward Antwerp by-passed and surrounded the heavily defended Belgian town of Bastogne. It was a bloody battle fought in the middle of winter in the hills of Luxembourg and the Ardennes Forest of Belgium, a month-long battle to which Germany committed 250,000 men and 1000 new tanks. The offensive ultimately failed to reach its objective, after costing 125,000 German and 81,000 American casualties.

Signs of preparation are everywhere. Nobody needs to tell us that something big is in the making or to explain the low and slow-flying aircraft to drown out the engine noise of hundreds of German Tiger and Panzer tanks being moved into position under the cover of darkness. The weather is mild so far, no snow has fallen yet, and cattle and horses graze peacefully in the fields.

That peace comes to an abrupt end before dawn on December 16, filling the night with deafening noise and flashes of light along an eighty-mile front. The tanks start rolling; then it is our time. None in our squad is older than eighteen, except the squad leader, a corporal. Moving out in front, he is followed by Karl, Kurt, Foerster, then me, and Sepp, our smallest and youngest squad member, from Bavaria. We head for the Our River.

Our first objective is the German village of Roth an der Our. The Americans, taken by surprise by the bombardment, have left the village, blowing up the bridge after crossing the Our River into Luxembourg and forcing German engineers to construct a pontoon bridge. After encountering artillery and mortar fire, our platoon is assembled at the bridge, minus four men we lost in the village.

Next we look ahead to the village of Fouhren. Our orders are to take the town before the end of the day. It is a small village of a few houses and a small church. We are under fire that is coming from a machine gun emplacement on the roof or in the tower of Fouhren's church. It is not a wise decision by the American crew; if the situation calls for a quick pullback, a rooftop is the last place you want to be.

After lobbing a few shells into the town, we launch our attack. Our leader master sergeant Dreese is determined to take these fellows out, and soon a white flag is hoisted from the church. We take seven American prisoners; the rest of the enemy has vacated, and we occupy the village without further resistance. It is late in the afternoon; we have reached our objective, and we hope we can stay and rest. However, our leader Dreese would never allow us to stay in a town overnight unless there was no alternative. Even with winter approaching, we spent the hours of darkness in two-man foxholes, away from town. My partner is Sepp. We leave Fouhren and return to the woods, where we dig. I had found an American blanket, which I share with Sepp after cutting it in half. We cover the foxhole with pine branches and a tarp and stay there the rest of the day, cold and hungry, falling asleep when it gets dark.

The next account in Eric's diary consists of a detailed description of the Battle of the Bulge in December of 1944. Space is a consideration here, and I regret that that valuable account had to be severely abbreviated, because it makes fascinating though horrific reading. I have chosen a few unique incidents, but they hardly give a total picture of the suffering from cold, hunger, noise, bedlam, death and injury of buddies, destruction, and chronic lack of sleep—those grim conditions of combat endured by troops on both sides of the conflict. The winter of 1944-45 was the coldest in one hundred years in Europe, and the endless nights spent in foxholes only added to the troops' misery. In addition, Sergeant Dreese was particularly difficult to accept as their leader and fellow team member rather than an adversary in their midst.

Vianden, Luxembourg, December 17

Early morning sees us setting up a temporary position at the bottom of a ravine along the highway. We dig shallow one-man foxholes among the briars and trees. Suddenly an artillery barrage tears into the ravine. We are barely finished when Dreese yells from the safety of his foxhole.

"First and second squads! Set up mortars facing the highway!"

That was utter madness. We leave our foxholes and crouch by our weapons, without a target to shoot at, exposed to the shells whistling in through the trees and exploding around us and splattering large chunks of mud against tree trunks. We scream at the sergeant to call us back to the cover of our foxholes, which he does after realizing that he may lose half of his platoon in the next few minutes. Slipping and sliding on the wet ground, I dash through the brush and take a flying dive at my foxhole, only to land on the back of somebody who didn't make it to his own shelter and found mine to be handy. In the sloppily-dug, two-foot-deep hole, there isn't room for both of us, which causes my butt to be exposed to the stuff flying about. I swear at the intruder, but he won't budge until there is a lull in the shelling.

Then there comes another single explosion from the bushes nearby. Somebody shouts, "Schindler is dead!" which brings the sergeant out of his hole as if shot from a cannon. Seventeen-year-old Schindler was his favorite. Fast on his legs, he was the "runner," the liaison between platoon and company command post. Schindler has not died from enemy fire, however. Reconstruction of events shows that he had pulled his handkerchief from his pocket, probably to blow his nose. Many of us carry hand grenades in one or both pockets of our jumpsuit jackets. As it turned out, Schindler's handkerchief must have gotten caught on a grenade pin and pulled it. Four seconds later, the exploding grenade ended his life. Dreese has us bury him there in the gorge under a cross fashioned from tree branches. After that, he reports the casualty to Company HQ. When he returns an hour later, he orders, "First and second squad follow me!"

It is dark when the company commander shows up for a brief ceremony over Schindler's grave. He says a few appropriate words, after which six of us fire a three-round salvo and the platoon sings the song *"Gute Kamerad."* It is supposed to make us feel better, which it doesn't, just sadder.

After the captain leaves, we bed down for a few hours of sleep until midnight, before moving out. The night is quiet, a shell exploding in the distance every once in a while. After an hour we come to a town in flames, most likely set on fire by the artillery shells we heard during the march. Screams come from burning barns as horses and cattle perish. Chickens flutter around, and a few pigs run in the streets. A half dozen bodies, both Germans and Americans, are scattered about. We pass through the town quickly, leave the highway and push across fields, where we come to rest in a clearing at daybreak.

Sepp and I haven't eaten in days; for some of the others it has been even longer. Schindler's replacement, Sauter, emerges from the woods carrying a few eggs and a half bottle of wine he found in a nearby farmhouse. It is not enough for all of us. Sergeant Dreese has wandered off some place, giving one of us the courage to say, "Hey, let's eat our emergency rations!" Each man carries two bags of hard crackers, which we call dog biscuits, and two small cans of processed pork, to be eaten in an emergency only. I had already eaten one of the two crackers, knowing that there was a penalty for eating those rations at any time other than in an emergency. I kept it a secret, even from Sepp.

We look at each other, wondering who would have the nerve to go first. It is Karl, who breaks the ice saying, "As far as I'm concerned, when my stomach grumbles the way it does now, it's a damn emergency. The hell with it! I'm going to eat!" Several others, including me, follow suit, chowing down the whole works.

A while later we are on the move again, through the woods, across fields, and past the shelled ruin of a farmhouse. Dead cattle and horses are scattered in the pasture, killed by artillery fire, their bodies frozen stiff in grotesque positions. I feel pity for these animals, almost as if I bore the blame for their demise.

We move on and descend into the village of Brandenbourg, still in Luxembourg. So far, the German Army has not managed even once to bring up food supplies. We forage in farmhouses and grocery stores. A woman has a fire going in the kitchen stove in one of the houses. She invites us to warm ourselves and lets us make a batch of cocoa with the stuff we have pilfered from a store. She watches us for a while, then shakes her head and says, "What a shame that young boys like you have to fight in the war. Why, you are only children! You belong at home with your mothers!" She heats more water for us to clean up, although nobody bothers to shave.

After eating a jar of canned cherries, I fill my mess kit with marmalade; then she says, "The food you have eaten is not enough for young boys on the march. I'll put on another pot of water and boil some potatoes."

However, the call to move out comes before she is done. Lacking suitable totes for food supplies, we empty the grenade bags and fill them with apples and ham. The grenades get stuffed into our pockets in spite of what has happened to Schindler.

More action continues and we find ourselves back in the village of Brandenbourg. At nightfall our squad beds down in a barn among the cattle and horses.

Someone shakes me awake at four A.M. It is my turn to stand guard at one of the outposts, a pile of rocks at the town's perimeter. In contrast to the warm barn, the night is cold and foggy, and I am miserable for the next three hours. At daylight, we move out. While stopping for a short rest, we are met with a surprise. Some weasel among us must have blown the whistle to Sergeant Dreese about our eating the emergency rations. He assembles the platoon and snaps: "Emergency rations inspection! Place them on the ground before you!" Twelve of us have nothing to display. As punishment, we have to carry the mortar components in addition to our firearms and regular gear. Dreese even loads us up with some of the other men's weapons. Then he moves ahead, sits on a milestone and grins as he watches us stagger past him under our backbreaking loads. The other guys offer to relieve us but he refuses. We push along the highway as a heavy fog settles in. When two American fighter planes come out of the fog and swoop over us, we take cover. Convinced that our mobility has been compromised, Dreese relieves the penalty detail and puts the mortar gear back on a cart.

[After several more days of combat. . .]

Down to perhaps 150 from our original strength of 204, we reach the Belgian town of Tintange and find it vacant, then on to Warnach, where we encounter resistance. . . . Fighting house-to-house is bad at any time, but you don't want to do it at night, with fires providing the only light. Nevertheless, it is over quickly, and Warnach is ours. To re-cap—on December 23, 1944, the town was American-occupied. After we stormed it at 3 A.M. on the twenty-fourth, we drove the Americans out in a half-to-one-hour of house-to-house fighting. We subsequently held the town until the Americans re-grouped, returned within an hour and encircled Warnach, in effect trapping us. All this took place in pitch dark. The American account describes that counterattack, which ended later on December 24 with only a handful of us breaking out and the rest killed or captured, as the American account describes. I happen to have been one of our shrunken platoon of perhaps two dozen guys, plus half an MG-squad from the 2nd platoon led by Dreese, that managed to break through into the open under cover of darkness at about 6:30 A.M. Under cover in the woods, we listened to the fighting in town lasting for most of the day and finally die down by mid-afternoon. So actually there was no conflict; the Americans had it first; we took it temporarily, and the Americans took it back—all on Christmas Eve.

The American account of the Warnach battle on December 24, 1944, has this to say:

"When the battle ended, the Americans had killed one hundred thirty-five Germans and taken an equal number of prisoners. . . . The little village cost the Americans sixty-eight officers and men, dead and wounded."

[What follows is excerpts from Eric's diary to a startling conclusion of the combat portion of his memoir. Imagine if you will, that American forces are experiencing the same conditions and challenges.]

On Christmas Eve at midnight Sepp and I have our turn of two hours guard duty. Christmas Day finds us rising before dawn. We move out quietly, heading back through the woods toward Tintange, which we hope is still unoccupied. The snow is very deep in some places, even in the woods. Reaching Tintange at daybreak, we slip into town, nervously hugging the house walls, finger on the trigger. But it is a ghost town.

At mid-morning the seven machine gunners from the 2nd platoon arrive, led by Sergeant Kohler. A gentle guy and not your typical sergeant-type, he owns a bakery shop at home and has a wife and three kids. They are a ragged-looking outfit: tired, dirty, their uniforms torn, no doubt hungry, ammo boxes gone, ammunition belts hanging around their necks, and with only one machine gun left. They have no knowledge of the rest of the company, speculating that they got trapped in Warnach yesterday.

At noon we are about to cook some hot food, but the town has come under heavy artillery bombardment. Fires break out everywhere. Watching a farm cart across the street being thrown up into the air and landing on a roof, we decide it is time to vacate Tintange and head south across the Belgian border into Luxembourg, accompanied by Allied Mustang fighter planes hunting in pairs and forcing us into single file with 300 feet distance between men. It is disheartening to see that the Americans have so much equipment and fuel that they can afford to have an airplane dive out of the sky and go after a single man.

At three o'clock in the afternoon we are back in Harlange across the border into Luxembourg, where we find milk, flour, and lard. Soon a dish of pancakes is dished up, and I am in the process of cooking up a pot of strawberry pudding. Before we can eat, the order comes to move out, so I take the pot with me and step into formation. Dreese stares at me, dumbfounded, but then decides to let it go. After all, it is Christmas Day, and perhaps he thinks an allowance is in order. During the march we pass the pot around, and everybody takes a sip.

At the edge of town we come upon a German supply truck parked at the side of the road, loaded with Infantry men and loaves of bread. Each man grabs a loaf in passing, and then Harlange is behind us. We head north for the Belgian border and Bastogne once again. In a patch of woods we pick up two Infantry men from a supply convoy that had been shot to pieces. Their joining us brings our force to forty-seven.

Late afternoon we make it into Honville, a small Belgian farm village about five miles south of Bastogne. Near the entrance, in the middle of the road is an American truck that had been flipped wheels up by a direct hit, with its load of cigarettes strewn over the pavement. It gives the smokers a rare chance to fill their pockets with American cigarettes.

At midnight, it is my turn to stand guard. Large artillery shells are coming in overhead with a whooshing sound, smashing into Honville about every five minutes. I hate doing guard duty at night. You may picture a soldier, his senses sharp and fully alert to pick up strange sounds, protecting his comrades from surprises while they sleep. A battle-hardened veteran may fit that description, but with me it wasn't like that at all. Standing in the snow underneath a tree in the middle of the night, staring at the stars now and then; if they are out, two hours seems like eternity. Soon thoughts of home and of all the things for which you have no time to think about in the heat of battle creep up on you. As much as you may try, you can't shut them out of your mind. After a while your thoughts drift back to the present, and only sadness remains.

DEATH SENTENCE

After two hours the corporal shows up with my relief and posts the new guard. As I head for my foxhole, he stops me.

"The sergeant wants you to go into town and get a blanket full of bread for the platoon. A supply truck got through not long ago."

He knows I am angry when I say, "I just pulled two hours of sentry duty. Why can't he pick somebody who has slept all night and is rested? I'm not going!"

Failing in trying to make me change my mind, he disappears, but is back a minute later, telling me that the master sergeant wants to see me. We walk over to where Dreese is standing waiting for me, Luger drawn. I admit that I had refused to carry out the order, whereupon he pokes the pistol in my back and orders me to walk into town ahead of him. Turning to the corporal he says, "I want you along as a witness."

It is a stumbling, awkward trip at this dark hour, made more difficult by the sporadic shelling ahead. I pray that the safety isn't off on that Luger.

At the far end of Honville, Dreese disappears into the cellar of a house which happens to be the battalion command post. After a few minutes he waves us down the steps. Major Franke, the battalion commander, sits on the cellar floor, leaning against the wall with a blanket wrapped around his shoulders. The rest of the officers are sleeping. Of course the major has been sleeping too, until Dreese interrupted his dreams. He is visibly agitated over getting aroused at three in the morning because a soldier didn't do what he was supposed to do.

I stand at attention in front of him. Remaining sitting, he glares at me and snaps, "Is it true that you refused to carry out an order given by master sergeant Dreese?"

"*Jawohl*, Herr Major!" I answer.

"Do you know what the penalty is for refusing to carry out an order given by a superior officer in combat?" he questions.

Again I answer, "*Jawohl*, Herr Major!"

No inquiry about my reasons for the refusal. Never mind that it was not an act of cowardice or that Dreese was not actually an officer, nor had he himself given me the order but conveyed it through the corporal. In the major's Prussian mind I had violated military code and was going to pay for it.

It is an unreal scene: candles flickering, a radioman in a back corner working his receiver, the speaker beeping and squealing as he works the dials.

"Well, what is the penalty?" barks the major.

"Death, Herr Major!" I reply.

Then he asks me if I have a shovel.

"*Jawohl*, Herr Major!"

At that moment I know what is going to be said next.

"You will return to the post, get your shovel, and dig your grave."

"*Jawohl*, Herr Major."

Turning to Dreese, he says, "Assemble a firing squad. When he is done digging, shoot him." Dreese informs him that he has twenty-one riflemen out on patrol and is unable to assemble a firing squad, the rest of his men being armed with submachine guns. In the German Army you go by the book, and if the book says that a firing squad is made up of riflemen, then you can't shoot the man with submachine guns. That would be tantamount to having a bunch of Chicago gangsters shoot me. This must have been the major's reasoning when he asks, "When do you expect the patrol back?"

"Hopefully by daybreak," replies the master sergeant.

Franke's final words: "Good! Shoot him after they return. Dismissed!"

The patrol has not returned by ten the next morning. The shelling of the village has become heavier. Several houses and barns are in flames, and a cloud of black smoke is drifting over the hilltop; we are glad to be out in the open.

Sepp and I are having a breakfast of honey when a machine gun burst saws through the tree limbs over our heads, followed by rifle fire from the forest. Pine needles and shredded branches rain down. Bullets ricochet off the granite rocks. Some of our guys fall, either dead or wounded. Dreese yells, "Second squad! Man the mortar!" We think he has panicked and lost his mind; the distance to the target is much too close for mortar fire. Realizing his mistake, he yells at us to forget the mortar, to fire our small arms at will and use grenades. But the fir trees and granite rock formations surrounding our position not only provide cover for us, but also shield the attackers from our view. Americans coming up the hill directly in front of us are out of sight, as we are out of theirs. The really bad stuff is thrown at us from the forest on our left, so we blast the tree line with everything we have. I see one of our wounded men roll into his foxhole, pulling a bed sheet over it.

Meanwhile, two Sherman tanks lumber up the highway on our right, headed for the village, and cutting us off to our rear. Our situation has quickly become critical. With tanks between us and the village, enemy infantry attacking up the hill in front, and fire from the woods on our left, we are trapped. Dreese, having ordered us again to assemble the mortar, changed his mind again and ordered it dismantled, and then the coward dashes across the foot path and disappears into the trees, leaving us under the command of 2nd Platoon leader Sergeant Kohler.

The Americans are closer up the slope now, close enough for us to hear them call out commands. We lob our last grenades down the hill, while the corporal makes a quick assessment of our numbers, counting ten still alive, including the wounded man in the foxhole under the bed sheet. At this point Kohler decides to gamble a break-out with our small group. Our only chance is in climbing up the bank and crossing the footpath to reach the cover of the pine trees on the other side. Even though that will only take a few seconds for each man, it means exposure to the fire coming from the forest.

Risking it anyway, Kohler throws the mortar barrel over his shoulder and crawls up the bank. I follow him crouching low and dragging the bipod. The moment Kohler stands up to cross the paths, a round hits him in the back of the head, just below the rim of his helmet. He slumps forward, dropping the barrel. I let go of the bipod and roll back down the embankment. Just then a grenade explodes nearby, and a fragment hits me over the right eye, followed by another that scrapes my leg. The wound above my eye bleeds profusely.

It is then that Americans step in sight from behind trees and rocks, weapons pointed, and yell at us to surrender. One of them fires a burst through the bed sheet which covered the foxhole with the wounded man in it. The corporal drops his gun and raises his hands, urging us to do the same. We follow suit: Kurt, Sepp, Sauter, and me. The war is over for the five survivors of the 3rd Platoon.

Prisoner of War

Our captors made us discard helmets, ski masks, gloves, and jump suit jackets, then marched us five abreast into Honville ahead of them, using us as a human shield. In town we were lined up against a house wall, and I thought for a moment that now they were going to kill us, although had they been in the mood for that, they could have done it quite justifiably back by our foxholes. Instead, they ordered us to empty our pockets of all contents, and then frisked us, even checking our boots for knives. Finally they herded us into a barn, where we had to sit on the floor with our hands clasped behind our heads. Four riflemen in the loft and two by the door guarded us. A tank was parked outside near the barn door. During the day more prisoners were brought in, among them master sergeant Dreese and Major Franke. Later they moved them to a separate location, probably because of their rank, or for interrogation, or both.

One of the prisoners had a stomach wound and kept begging for water. He died in the afternoon. During the night they kept us awake and sitting up with flickering beams of flashlights, yelling when one of us could no longer keep his hands behind his head and relaxed his arms, or fell asleep.

Shortly after three A.M., trucks pulled up outside the barn. With our hands still clasped behind our heads, they made us crawl on our knees to the trucks and then climb aboard. The drivers headed northwest with headlights turned off. Wearing only the skimpy clothing with which they had left us and without food in our bodies, the cold was unbearable during the half hour trip. When we arrived at an assembly area and had dismounted from the trucks, we were frisked again. There were hundreds of prisoners, among them some of the men who had gone on patrol two nights ago.

At 4:30 A.M. the trip continued to another assembly area where we met units from our Thirteenth and Fourteenth Regiments, also a few guys from the Twelfth.

After a brief interrogation by German-speaking Americans, we headed out again. Once it was daylight we had an opportunity to see the vast quantities of American war materiel stacked up along the route: guns, tanks, trucks, jeeps, ammunition, fuel, and food. We shook our heads in disbelief, realizing now that we would never win this battle, that the struggle, suffering, and dying that had taken place and was yet to come, were in vain.

The trucks stopped in front of a stone building on the out-skirts of a city, and we were herded upstairs into an attic, which was already packed with so many prisoners that everybody had to stand. It was not difficult to conclude from the stink in that place that there was no toilet. Most of us had gone without food or drink for a day or two, plagued by hunger and particularly by thirst. Hours passed. Every so often somebody passed out.

Sometime in the afternoon we boarded trucks and headed out again, by nightfall reaching a prisoner camp, where we were separated according to rank. There still was no food or drink. Almost forty-eight hours had passed since I had that last meal of bread and honey in the foxhole on the morning of December 26.

In the morning we shipped out once more, one hundred men to a truck. Somebody mentioned that we had crossed the French border. It wasn't necessary to tell us; the French popu-lation let us know that we were in their country by pelting us with rocks and making gestures of cutting throats as we passed through their villages on the way to Stenais.

POW Camp Stenais, France

In Stenais we dismounted and marched through the city on the way to the camp. It consisted of a few stone buildings for the administration and row after row of six-man tents. For the next three or four hours we simply stood around, becoming more miserable with cold and hunger. Finally they called us into the office building in small groups, where we were registered and given ID papers. Upon leaving the building, American soldiers frisked us again, tearing the uniform jackets off us, looking through the pockets, then throwing the jackets back at us, handing everybody an empty tin can, and indicating that we were done by giving everybody a swift kick.

Just before dark, three days since my last meal, a truck carrying hot food arrived. We lined up with our tin cans and one by one received a ladle of thick noodle soup and a hunk of bread. The food tasted absolutely great, even though we had to slurp the soup out of the cans for lack of spoons. When we had finished eating, we were permitted to enter the tents which, not surprisingly, had no flooring, so we sat or lay on the ground. God, was it ever cold! Somebody found some cardboard and built a fire in our tent. It lasted only a few minutes, smoked a lot and didn't really warm us, but just looking at the flames made us feel better.

After spending the night sleeping on bare ground, we awoke frozen stiff. The day started with a head count and another short interrogation by German-speaking American officers. One of their questions was: "If we send you home in a prisoner exchange, will you come back and fight again?" Depending on the reply, you were directed to one of two groups. I found myself with the smaller "Yes" group of about three hundred. After our names had been recorded and the larger "No" bunch had departed, an officer gave us a political lecture, ending it with the threat:

"Tomorrow we'll put you on a train and ship you off to Russia. They will be more than happy to re-educate you using very special methods, believe me." We felt like telling him "Oh yeah? Is that the opinion you have of your Russian allies?" Nobody said a word, though.

This episode was of little consequence to me at the time, but shortly it would become another of those crossroads where my life would have taken a different turn had I answered "No" to the prisoner exchange question.

It was December 29 around noon; they put us in formation four abreast, numbering about 1800 prisoners. Under heavy guard to protect us from the French, we trotted in double-time through the city to a waiting freight train at a railroad terminal about a mile away. There the guards would open a boxcar, count off about sixty prisoners, shove them inside, then slide the door shut and bolt it, repeating the procedure until all of us were boarded.

Inside our boxcar we tried to get oriented in near darkness, milling around and stumbling over cardboard boxes on the floor until somebody lit a match. The boxes were food. We realized that we needed a leader for the group and appointed an old master sergeant, who asked us to do a head count, which came to fifty-nine. Then he made us place the food cartons in the center of the floor and ordered us to each find a permanent spot and settle down. We found that the only way to get that done was by sitting or lying on the floor in rows, twenty-nine along one side of the car and thirty along the other, feet pointing against feet.

Using the wax-coated cardboard from the food boxes and wood from the food crates, we built a fire. Smoke filled the boxcar; we coughed and choked until we kicked a couple of sideboards out for ventilation. This also let some daylight into the boxcar.

The master sergeant and two helpers he had recruited took an inventory of our food supplies and made a list. There were loaves of bread, cans of corned beef hash, boxes of graham crackers, cans of peanut butter, and chocolate bars. Doing the math he calculated that each man had the following rations available: one-fifth of a loaf of bread, two and a half pounds corned beef hash, twelve graham crackers, two to three ounces of peanut butter, and three chocolate bars. After starving for three days that sounded rather good, except we had no idea how long the trip was going to last and how we needed to ration our food. To try to settle the issue we took a vote, deciding to distribute all of the bread, all of the corned beef hash, and one chocolate bar per man. That immediately created a number of other problems: how to open the cans? divide a loaf of bread into five portions without a knife? how to divide the corned beef hash? how does each man get his candy bar and not have somebody else grab it as the chocolate is being passed around in the smoke-filled semi-darkness? Then somebody found a sharp piece of steel with which to pry open the cans. We grouped into trios, and each trio was given a can of hash to be divided among them. For lack of a knife the bread was torn into pieces, resulting in loud complaints by those who thought they were getting shortchanged.

Within minutes all the bread was eaten. The chocolate bars were handed around, eaten also and the wrappers used to fuel the fire. In time it got a little warmer in the car, and the group settled down, everybody staying in their assigned places and using their boots for pillows.

After dark the train jerked a few times and then started rolling. Sleeping was difficult since the fire was out and it had gotten cold again. The rattling and pounding of the train only compounded the problem. I woke up during the night when something banged against my head. It turned out to be a pair of boots the man next to me had hung on a nail above me. I yanked them off and flung them into the dark, only to have the recipient of the flying boots say some very unkind words. Then it became quiet again, except for a lot of snoring.

I had another rude awakening when somebody stepped on my shins. Others woke up and complained about that also, but hey—the fellow had to piddle. The open crack on one side of the door had been assigned as a urinal. Using it was another story entirely. This fellow tried to balance himself in the rocking boxcar and aim through the crack at the same time. Well, he succeeded in urinating on the man sleeping closest to the door, resulting in a loud argument. In an effort to get as far away from the door as possible, the men sleeping on that side of the car had to squeeze together that much tighter.

Later that night, somebody had a bowel movement near the door, which caused some fellows to light matches to see what was going on. When one of them learned that the guy had unloaded onto his boots, another scuffle ensued. The master sergeant was simply unable to keep the peace. Not that it really mattered; the December cold seeping through the cracks in the floor and into our bodies kept most of us awake anyway.

In the morning, once fully awake I realized that I was incredibly thirsty but there was nothing to drink among our food supplies. Everybody complained. During a stop we pulled another loose board from the car's wall to get some fresh air, when we noticed that water from melting snow dripped from the roof. We fashioned a trough from a strip of tin can and poked it through the opening to catch the water, a drop at a time. It took five minutes to collect a swallow of water, and catching the drops only worked when the train was stopped. Tempers flared again and the master sergeant handed out the last chocolate bar in an effort to keep us quiet. Eating it only added to the thirst. The stink from crap piling up by the door added to the misery. We enlarged the hole in the wall by pulling additional boards loose, only to have Frenchmen throw rocks through the opening at the next stop.

ΠEW YEAR'S EVE 1944

In the morning during a stop, the door bolts were pulled back and the door slid open. "Water!" yelled one of the guards but did not permit us to leave the car. Within minutes a fifteen gallon tub filled with milky-looking water was lifted inside. Any semblance of order disintegrated at that point, as all fifty-nine men tried to get to the water at once. The lucky ones who reached the tub scooped the water with their hands, sucking and slurping like thirsty animals, while about two dozen of us, me included, didn't get a drop to drink.

"Finished!" the guard yelled. The container was removed, the door slid shut, and the bolts were pounded in place. Soon the train rolled again, arriving at its final destination that evening. Doors slid open; we jumped out, got into formation and marched off under heavy guard. Ships' foghorns sounded in the distance, indicating that this was a seaport. And indeed it was; signs on some of the buildings told us that we were in Cherbourg on the English Channel. Considering the intense fighting that had taken place here during the invasion six months earlier, we were surprised to see very little damage. It seemed that much of it had been repaired, which stood to reason since Cherbourg obviously served as a vital supply port for the American forces.

Once we were past the airport of Querqueville at the outskirts of the city, it was open country. Still plagued by thirst, some of us drank water from the ditch along the road and had to be forced back into formation at gun point by our guards. After a seven mile hike and a final climb up a steep road we arrived at our destination, perched on a cliff above the English Channel: POW Camp Ten, Cherbourg, France.

The camp was divided into twenty-five smaller camps called sections. Our initial home was Section One. It held ninety-eight numbered tents without light or heat, each to be occupied by fifty prisoners sitting or lying on bare ground. Shallow ditches dug around the tents collected rainwater.

I was assigned to tent number sixty-two, and after getting settled, we new arrivals didn't lose any time hunting for water to drink. There was a water tower from which a large pipe ran to the center of the camp, and from there to faucets dispensing ice cold, strongly chlorinated water. We sucked it down greedily anyway, at last able to slake our thirst.

Later that evening we were issued a blanket per head. This was followed by supper consisting of four ounces of bread, five graham crackers, and a tablespoon of lard. After eating it we drank more of the terrible water. The meal left us hungry, but since this was a transient camp we hoped to get moved to another section, where the stay would be extended and the food better.

The tents were too small for fifty men, calling for a sleeping arrangement of twenty-five on each side, tightly bunched like sardines in a can, with our feet pointing to the center aisle. The blankets did a fine job of soaking up the dampness from the ground and transferring it to our bodies. Eventually, we managed to build a fire using empty cracker boxes, letters from home, even photos, and letting the warmth carry us into dreamland and the New Year.

There was no breakfast on this first day of 1945. Instead, our blankets were confiscated and we received a thorough dusting with DDT, in case any of us were infested with lice. The GI administering the white powder stuck the nozzle of the pump down the back of your neck and pushed the plunger. He repeated that with both sleeves and then down the inside of our pants.

After this ceremony they called a long list of names, among them the 250 or so who had failed to pass the interrogation in Stenais when answering "yes" to the prisoner exchange question. Sepp and the rest of my outfit were not included in this group, and we were separated when we transferred to Section Three. That section already held a population of 2000 sergeants, who claimed to be the preferred tenants. This came as no surprise, since German sergeants always boasted that they were the backbone of the German Army, a definition with which we agreed wholeheartedly, but with the qualification that they were the "elongated backbone."

We new arrivals were issued two blankets each and told to disperse among the sergeants, who apparently had been here for some time, judging from the ovens and gasoline lamps they had fashioned from bacon cans. Most of them owned three or four blankets and slept on pallets made from wooden boards placed on the ground. Not having that luxury, sleeping on the cold, hard, and bumpy ground was a nightmare for us. Space was so tight we had to sleep on our sides. If you wanted to turn over you had to wake up your neighbors on each side and make them turn also. Blood circulation was cut off and limbs went to sleep. To go to the latrine during the night, one had to step over the feet sticking out into the center aisle.

The unfamiliar surroundings made it difficult finding our way at night among the maze of tents, and in ankle-high mud. Upon returning to the tent, you found that the sleepers had moved together and that your space was gone. For the first few nights that was accepted, not that many had to make trips to the latrine at night.

The trouble started when the effects of eating uncooked food and drinking bad water, in addition to sleeping on damp ground, exacted a toll in the form of severe diarrhea. Some thought that it was dysentery. Whatever it was, it caused the bowel muscles to quit functioning and often was accompanied by kidney and bladder problems as well. Almost all the newcomers and a couple hundred sergeants had it, and we called it *"die scheisserei" [which in elegant English translates as "the shits"]*. The night was filled with moans, groans, and the terrible sounds of men ejecting blood and slime. With every passing day, my own condition worsened.

Water was not always available for washing after the kitchen helpers had filled their garbage cans early in the morning. If any water was left, we took our pants off and washed them, without soap, of course, on long wooden tables put up outside near the water tower. Then we hung them on a clothesline to dry, which in January weather usually took much of the day. Actually, they never dried completely. Also, you wouldn't dare return to the tent while your pants hung on the line, flapping in the ever-present wind, for fear they might not be there when you returned. Therefore, having used our underwear for toilet paper, we wrapped ourselves in blankets and waited by the clothesline. Most of the time we put the still-damp pants back on, which only aggravated our ailment. Another problem was that without soap, we never got entirely rid of the smell, and because of that nobody wanted to be next to you in the tent. The sickness made us outcasts.

Finally, after realizing that they had an epidemic at their hands, camp administrators erected a hospital tent in the wettest and windiest corner of the camp. It had a capacity of twenty, and I was fortunate to be among the first group to be admitted. There weren't any sleeping cots, but at least we had a dry wooden floor to sleep on. There was no medication in this "hospital."

At this location, high above the ocean, a gusty wind is an almost constant presence. It was no surprise then, that a week later during a stormy night the hospital tent collapsed. We got out just in time before the gale-force wind picked up the canvas and blew it over the barbed wire fence in the general direction of the English Channel. So I grabbed my blankets and returned to tent number sixty-two.

The food was without variety: coffee, graham crackers and orange marmalade for breakfast, a pint and a half of bean soup for lunch. Supper consisted of a quarter pound of bread, and a quarter pound of fish, canned meat, or salt pork. Once in a while, during a water shortage or when firewood ran out, they skipped the noon soup. Kitchen helpers were a gang of carpenters, blacksmiths, artists, and God knows who else, but you wouldn't have found one cook among them. But then they didn't have to cook, anyway. They filled the garbage cans with water; put them on open fires, and when the water boiled, added beans, stirring with broom handles. Voila! bean soup!

Rumors had it that we were allocated more and much better food, but that the German kitchen helpers, interpreters, and camp police were in cahoots with the American administration in helping themselves to the good stuff, hoarding what wasn't eaten, and when they had a truckload together, selling it on the black market in Cherbourg.

One day our lunch was diced beets, unheated and gummy. As hungry as we were, most of us threw the stuff into the garbage. The administration reacted to it by issuing no food at all for three days. In plain sight of us, food supplies were brought out of storage, loaded on trucks, and hauled away. There was cocoa, sugar, and milk powder on those trucks. The rumors about the black market weren't rumors after all.

On top of our list of items needed for survival was the empty tin can. We made stoves out of bacon cans and stove pipes out of pint or quart cans nested together. Dishes, kerosene lamps and lamp shades, knives, and spoons were fashioned from tin cans. The center aisles of tents were paved with bottom-up cans, and a few lucky ones had their sleeping places paved like that.

On January 2, 1945, the first snow of the season fell in the Cherbourg area. The next day we were moved to the former Section One, where we joined 2000 other prisoners for a cage population of 4000. Every day at ten in the morning, a call came over the PA system: "Attention, attention! Cage seventeen, everybody out for head count!" We got up, put our boots on and assembled in the square, grouping by company, and each company dividing into subgroups according to tent number. Once we were in formation, an American officer accompanied by an interpreter and a staff of German clerks started the tally.

The American was a mean son-of-a-bitch. It was not unusual that somebody was missing due to *die scheisserei,* in which case he started the count all over again. Sometimes he was so upset he left us standing in the rain or snow for as long as two hours, depending on his mood, before returning to do the tally over. If in the meantime only one man had left the formation, he repeated the procedure. Then, if he wanted to show us that he in fact was the boss, he did another head count in the afternoon. When he had finished the count, he made us wait until he had gone to his office to verify the numbers. So we stood, some days for hours, in the rags that used to be our uniforms, bareheaded, without socks, in boots that were falling apart, freezing, shivering, and cussing.

One of the adjacent cages was a transient camp. Inhabitants only stayed a few days, and as a rule they still had personal items in their possession, such as rings and wrist watches. They also had tobacco products, something that was unavailable in our permanent quarters. The smokers among us were so desperate that they would give anything, even a wristwatch or a wedding ring, for a few cigarettes. On the other hand, the food in the transient camps was typically less and of lower quality than what we had. Thus a need arose for bartering along the fence, using established exchange values. The administration didn't want us to go near the fences, instructing the guards in the towers surrounding the camp to shoot anyone who was seen at the fence. Consequently, swapping was done only at night, and that was risky because the fences were randomly swept by search lights.

I was the only one in our tent who had the nerve to do it. Although I did not smoke at the time, I always looked for a package of tobacco, because it made about fifty cigarettes, and the fellow who put up the food to trade for it would share it with the rest of the smokers. One night I was handed the customary five or six graham crackers and a portion of orange marmalade, with the request to get a pack of tobacco at the fence. Crawling on the ground along the barbed wire, I went "psst, psst" until I heard the answering "psst" from the other side. I whispered that I was looking for tobacco and the guy said he had a can of Prince Albert to trade. I reached through the wire and felt it. Feeling that it still had the cellophane wrapper and considering it authentic, I showed him the food and we made the swap. Back at the tent the new owner of the Prince Albert happily removed the wrapper from the can and opened it. It was bad news. Instead of tobacco the container was filled with grass and mud. Naturally the angry man pointed out that I owed him either a breakfast ration or a package of real tobacco.

One day in early February there was a PA call for all SS troops, paratroopers, and Navy personnel to register with the camp administration. Many of us were leery, but I went and registered. A week later the registrants were ordered to assemble with all of their belongings.

[Another brief re-assignment followed.]

One evening the German camp chief produced a list of names which he called an "embarkation list." Among the names were the prisoners who had given the "yes" answer during the interrogation in Stenais. "What's embarkation?" someone asked. It was explained, and guess what?!—we were going to America! It was too good to be true! But he repeated it, and no man can imagine our excitement. We danced, jumped, screamed, and shook hands. Out of this hellhole at last!

The next morning we moved out on foot to a rail depot in Cherbourg, where we boarded a freight train. Unfortunately, a layer of thick, stinking, crude petroleum oil covered the floor of our boxcar. Unable to sit or lie on the floor, we sat on our bags, which, along with the blanket inside, soaked up the oil and stank for months thereafter. The only memorable part of the trip was the inevitable rock bombardment of our cars by the French whenever the train stopped.

We stayed briefly at another camp at Bolbec, where accommodations, mud, and food were bad and brought on another onslaught of *die scheisserei*. On February 18, 1945, we departed Bolbec for the port of LeHavre, where a gray troop transport ship, the *Sea Tiger*, was docked. We no longer needed convincing! We boarded and were moved into our quarters below deck.

The following day we arrived in Plymouth, England, where the ship took on American wounded and GIs returning home. We were allowed to go on deck and watched a British coastal battery fire at a target out in the Channel, reminding us that we were still at war. During the next two days they assembled a convoy of two dozen ships, and we left England heading west with an escort of three destroyers and a cruiser.

The trip passed not unpleasantly, although I was sick part of the time; the sea was rough. We were kept busy with chores, and time passed with singing, reading, playing cards, eating, and sleeping. Food was without question the best feature on board. We were expected to eat as much as we wanted, since leftovers were thrown overboard.

On March 5 after seventeen days at sea, our ship separated from the convoy and changed course. Then seagulls appeared, an indication that we were getting close to land and our destination. Toward evening the ship entered New York harbor, and we were allowed on deck briefly to watch dancing girls and a jazz band aboard an excursion boat giving the returning American soldiers a heroes' welcome. We envied them. Unfortunately, fog prevented us from seeing the Statue of Liberty. We packed our belongings in preparation for disembarkation, wondering what this country held in store for us.

We docked, went ashore, and for the first time looked at the American scene: skyscrapers, cars, people, hustle and bustle everywhere. As if we were on another planet! We boarded a train, settling into each car with blue upholstered seats! As the train rolled south through the city and suburbs, we were provided with another brand-new sight—city slums.

POW Camp Fort Eustis, Virginia

Unfortunately, Fort Eustis was only a transient location for us, but bears description. Entering the compound at 4 A.M. we noted with pleasure that there were barracks instead of tents. We couldn't believe our eyes at breakfast: large tables decked out in white tablecloths, dishes, and silverware, and the food was good. After breakfast we transferred to two-story barracks which had heat, washrooms, toilets, and electric lights. The beds had mattresses, pillows, sheets, and quilted blankets. This was another day to remember; for almost a year I had slept in foxholes, barns, stables, haylofts, on dirt floors, wood floors, in sleeping bags and tents, in snow, rain, and mud.

We were outfitted with new clothes: two changes of pants and shirts, three changes of underwear, coveralls, topcoat, raincoat, socks, work gloves, two pairs of shoes, hats and caps, towels, and toiletry articles. Of course, clothes were army issue, but at least no one had worn the stuff before.

An interesting note was that at breakfast every morning, the German camp commander greeted us with the raised arm and a clear and unmistakable "Heil Hitler!" He explained that we were expected to use the official German military salute when encountering American officers. Following the assassination attempt on Hitler by German officers on July 20, 1944, Hitler ordered the military salute changed from the classical 'fingertips on forehead' to the Nazi salute, thus American officers were saluted with the raised arm, but not "Heil Hitler!" It was a silent salute and used until the war ended in May.

March 12 was moving day again. I was among two hundred-fifty prisoners leaving Fort Eustis on trucks traveling south, ferrying us from Newport News to Norfolk. While we waited for the ferry, we had our second, close-up impression of Americans going about their daily routine. Another truck ride took us to our new home at Camp Ashby, between Norfolk and Virginia Beach. It was already inhabited by fifteen hundred POWs, all with the same question: "How are things at home?"

Camp Ashby, Virginia

In addition to three kitchens, there were three PX's, a recreation building for theater, movies, and religious services, a school, library, athletic and soccer fields. They had organized a camp orchestra and a small company of actors and entertainers. Every week we saw two movies, and twice a month a cabaret show was put on by our own group. Sundays we had a choice of Catholic or Protestant services, later a concert or ping pong in the rec room, which also featured a radio and record player. The camp school offered courses in various technical subjects, foreign languages, and shorthand. The library was open daily, and that was where one would most likely find me during my free time. Once a month we were allowed to write home.

Food was excellent and plentiful. On Sundays, the birthday boys of the previous week were invited to the kitchen for coffee and cake—which brings to mind another memorable event; I became eighteen soon after my arrival at camp.

Everyone except officers was required to work. Pickup was made by respective employers, who delivered the prisoners back to camp after work. Most of us were assigned to fertilizer plants, which we called "poison mills." I was assigned to a fertilizer mill detail, but since we newcomers were not in the best physical condition, our performance was far below standard, so they put us on something easier. Invalids or handicapped POWs did easier work in a canning factory, and there was a penalty detail shoveling "animal waste" in a glue factory. The workday lasted from eight to ten hours Monday through Friday, and four hours on Saturday, for which we were paid eighty cents a day. In addition, the German government kicked in another ten cents. That daily wage was paid monthly in the form of coupons, since we were not allowed to have actual U.S. currency in our possession. The coupons were used for purchases from the PX; what was left at the end of the month was deposited in a savings account in the individual's name at Chase Manhattan Bank.

On April 12, 1945, our guard announced that President Roosevelt had died and asked us to stop working and pay our respects by maintaining two minutes of silence. He should have known that we had no reason to respect or mourn Roosevelt. So we appeased him by quietly leaning on our shovels for two minutes.

After three weeks it was presumed that we were now strong enough to make fertilizer. I was assigned to Royster Guano Co. in Norfolk, where I worked for three months. It was a tough assignment; we unloaded railcars loaded with stuff that stank, made you cough, choke, sneeze, and your eyes water. We worked side by side with Blacks, who appeared to be amused that we didn't grow horns as it was shown in their newspaper cartoons. We in turn found it equally amusing that Americans considered us Germans racists, as we learned firsthand about Jim Crow.

On May 7 we learned that we were the losers, and that from now on a different wind was going to blow. Immediately, items such as fresh meat, fresh milk, Coca Cola, and beer were struck from the list of regular food items, (even though we had been paying for the Coke and beer). Cigarettes were no longer available, and there were substantial reductions in such things as fruit, fresh vegetables, butter, sausage, etc. Thanks to the German Red Cross for occasional shipments of chocolate, canned goods, rye bread, even games. We were no longer allowed to write home. Existing rules and regulations were tightened and new ones added. Unpleasant events took place in the aftermath of us losing the war, such as guards getting ugly with work details, and clothes that were not marked properly with the letters PW were confiscated. Violation of a rule by one prisoner resulted in the collective punishment of the entire work detail.

In July, three hundred of us were moved to POW Camp Leesburg, also in Virginia. Another tent city, it was a farm camp set up for summer occupation, and details were assigned for farm work. Subsequently more facilities were added—a recreation room, mess hall, PX tent, and we were shown movies outdoors, seated on barrels, boxes, whatever was available. When a farmer donated a meadow to be used as a soccer field, a sports program was started, and we expended much of our energy playing soccer on Sunday afternoons. Soccer being a relatively unknown sport in the U.S. at that time, our games drew quite a few spectators from the nearby towns and farms.

I was assigned to a large farm, Llangollen Farm, four towns away in Upperville, Virginia, a huge spread at the foot of the Blue Ridge Mountains, owned by a wealthy young divorcee who had been married to a Hollywood actor and was the farm's absentee owner; she visited from time to time. The manor house dated from 1770.

From July to October I worked on several different farms. During that time I also learned how to swear in English, ride horses, clean out silos, do farming chores of all kinds, and raise hell, among other things. Working outdoors and eating well had put me in excellent physical shape. I developed good muscle tone and put meat on my body; the 150-pound skinny kid had grown into a 180-pound man.

Fall 1945 came, and it was five months after the war in Europe had ended. We were reminded that Camp Leesburg was just a summer camp, and we likely wouldn't be there for the winter. Then Schirrman showed up. The story we heard was that Schirrman was a German who had come to the U.S. before the war and enlisted in the American Army. He was a special interrogator. It was said that on occasion he would extract information from a prisoner by placing a wet towel roll around the man's neck and twisting it until he heard what he wanted to hear. His job was to determine whether or not as a group we were ideologically ready to be repatriated—in other words, find out how much of the Nazi brainwashing remained.

We were given a medical exam, which included undressing and lining up. We had to say "Aaah" and raise our arms over our head. The examination amounted to shining a flashlight into each armpit, looking for the ID number which SS troops had tattooed under one arm. SS men were separated and transferred to another camp. However, they found none among us.

On November 15 it was official; Schirrman's report had classified us as politically repaired and ready to return to our homeland. We expected to be home for Christmas!

First there was a nine-day stint at a lumber camp in the mountains in Maryland, and in the meantime I caught a bad cold, as we headed for New York and the trip home. At five o'clock in the morning I stood outside waiting for my name to be called, one of a thousand. Suffering from a cold, it was a miserable experience. Ferried to the pier, American reporters and newspaper folks who were also going to make the trip across the Atlantic were waiting. The rusty old tub, a Liberty ship named the *William Cushing*, would be our host. Provisions for ten days had been taken on board, so we assumed our destination would be Bremerhaven.

On November 29 the ship lifted anchor and was towed out

of the harbor. As I looked at the reflections of the city lights in the water and the illuminated Statue of Liberty, a little sadness crept into my heart, as if this land of so many kind people and wide open spaces, my home for almost a year, had claimed a piece of me.

After fourteen days at sea it came as a shock to learn that due to an overload of German ports, our destination was going to be LeHavre, a French port. Reaction was strong; needless to say, at this point we regarded everything French with a most cynical attitude. Upon arriving, we noticed piles of rubble everywhere, probably the same ones we saw when we left there in February. Frenchmen were loafing on the street corners, hands in their pockets, and the ever-present cigarette dangling from their lips. German prisoners were working everywhere, without guards. Since the war had ended seven months previously, the French must have thought that the absence of guards gave the prisoners more of the appearance of civilian status. We also noticed that the French were not as belligerent as they were a year ago, yet they carried about them an air of arrogance, even though the Americans had won the victory for them. Their greater tolerance for Germans may have arisen from the realization that their land was still occupied, only by a different force.

We boarded trains, rumbled past Paris, and stopped in Compiegne, where the armistice ending WWI was signed on November 11, 1918. Hitler insisted that France sign their surrender at the same location in June 1940. Leaving our bags at the depot we formed a column and marched ten miles through the forest of Compiegne. Hours passed. Every so often one of the older prisoners, finding the going hard, would sit by the roadside to rest, only to be cursed by the guards and prodded with rifle butts into moving on. A few collapsed and were put onto a truck trailing the column. Another ten-mile hike brought us to Camp Attichy, a desolate hole of a POW camp.

We were moved into Cage Twelve, where we spent the

rest of the day and night without food or drink. A couple days later we were permitted to pick up our bags, which had been thrown into the mud in a fenced enclosure. We found that our bags had been raided and some of the valuable contents stolen. Now we knew why our baggage was left at the Compiegne terminal instead of accompanying us on a truck. It gave the French an opportunity to rifle through the bags and take what they wanted. They even robbed a guy's accordion, which he bought in the U.S. for $395. To add insult to injury, they made us empty our bags and put what was left on the ground for inspection. German camp clerks then confiscated most of the items the French thieves had not taken. It was simple, in-your-face robbery, this time not by the French but by Germans. No doubt the loot was later sold to the French.

Camp Attichy was a sprawling compound with a population of 100,000 POWs. Rows and rows of tents stretched as far as the eye could see. They were erected over shallow, rectangular pits dug in the ground. These pits were filled with rotted, foul-smelling straw which served as bedding. We were expected to keep the premises clean and orderly, even though there was only a single water faucet in the tent, which was turned on for one hour each day. After chores, a tent inspection was made at eight o'clock. That usually lasted three hours during which time we were ordered outside in rain or snow; most of the time it was one or the other. And the food was lousy as well.

Our day guards were Polish, and Austrians guarded us at night. Austrians! These were the same people who had fought side by side with us during the war, then claimed to have served against their will when we lost.

If you violated a rule you earned a visit to the bird cage—a 10 X 10-foot square area enclosed with barbed wire. The poor devils stood there all day like storks, with one leg pulled up. When the foot they were standing on got cold, they switched.

"Stripers" were SS officers and soldiers, marked with a white stripe on their backs. They were held in a separate area of the camp, since they were not allowed to associate or even talk with the rest of us. In addition to being practically starved, they were forced to perform the dirtiest and most humiliating chores. It is no surprise that a number of them committed suicide. We failed to comprehend what was happening here—Germans treating their countrymen like animals and liking it. Germans robbing us of our few personal belongings, for which we had paid with money earned in the U.S. And all of this taking place on French soil. Yet the French had nothing to do with it, nor was it an American issue. No, it was a German disgrace.

Christmas 1945 arrived. I truly would have preferred the Christmas Eve of 1944 in the Belgian forest, with only a sliver of bread and a little jelled split pea soup to eat. At least then I was among good men who did bear whatever was handed to them, good or bad, instead of the Communist cowards who ruled Camp Attichy.

More bureaucracy awaited us. We were called to another medical exam, which classified us according to our ability to work and the occupied zone of our residence. The most fit were retained in France to be used as slave labor. The British discharged their POWs regularly. Those that lived in the Russian-occupied zone were not anxious to return there and frequently gave their "home" address as that of a friend who lived in the American or British zone (but not in the French zone). This happened to Fritz, one of my tent mates from Leesburg. He hailed from the Russian-occupied province of Brandenburg and gave the address of a friend who lived in Worms, located in the French zone. A year later, in the fall of 1946 he sent me a postcard from a camp in northern France. A year and a half after the end of the war he was doing forced labor in a coal mine in Pas de Calais.

On December 29 we were told that those living in American

zones East and West were going to be shipped out with the next transport leaving for Germany. Two thousand of us boarded yet another freight train waiting a thirty-minute hike away. Mid-afternoon we stopped at the German border in the Saar Valley. Women and children greeted us. We held up cardboard signs we had prepared, sang, hollered, and in general carried on like idiots. We were home! Toward evening as the train rattled on through the German countryside, we heard church bells ring in the New Year. During almost a year in the U.S. I never once heard a church bell ring. Many of us broke down and bawled.

Our lot of two thousand finally arrived at POW Camp Heilbronn, past Heidelberg. Another two thousand POWS already occupied the camp, waiting to be discharged. Discharged POWs were required to leave the city within twenty-four hours. My thoughts were "No kidding, just let me out of here, and see how long I am going to stick around. If need be, I'll walk home!" For three days I stood outside in the cold every morning, anxiously waiting for my name to come up. Then on January 6, with one thousand POWs left in the camp, we were informed that we had been selected for labor details and should get ready to transfer to another camp. This started a riot. Men who had been wounded in battle stormed the administration building, tore off their clothes, and showed their scars.

On January 11, for the umpteenth time we packed our bags and boarded Army trucks, making the trip back through the Neckar Valley past Heidelberg, arriving in the evening at the town of Giessen, near Frankfurt. We were unloaded at the former airport, and standing in near-darkness were divided into groups according to skills. This was one time when I didn't volunteer for anything, deciding that this time they can do with me whatever they pleased. Which is exactly what they did. About fifty of us "unskilled" peons, were marched off to the mess hall to be fed, then assigned to various barracks.

After a few days I was assigned to an outside work detail near the airport. The former field had been converted into a supply depot. There was row after row of canvas-covered stacks of chocolate, canned fruits, meat, cigarettes, etc. They wouldn't let us go near the stuff though and put us to work repairing bombed-out buildings, away from the depot.

ABC Camp where I was assigned housed about eight hundred POWs, although we were no longer identified as such. They made us remove the PW markings from our clothes, replacing them with the single, stenciled word 'UTILE' across the back. It meant "practical" or "useful," and I suppose this was intended to make us look like civilian workers and get our captors out of the quandary of having to explain why they were still holding prisoners eight months after the war had ended. However, this was not a bad place; food was good and plentiful, there was a library, shoe repair shop, and a tailor. Loudspeakers provided musical entertainment after work. But I didn't like the work at all. German supervisors were a pushy and mean bunch of sniveling ass-kissers. Because of the supply depot nearby, we were frisked thoroughly before returning to camp after work. The penalty for possession of so much as one American cigarette was severe—a good beating at the provost marshal's office, a shaved head, and three days in the guard house. The reward for catching us stealing was forty cigarettes for the Polish guards, twenty for Germans.

We U.S.-educated boys were too smart for them, anyway. Surviving in the mud camps of France and spending almost a year in the U.S., besides making two trips across the Atlantic, we had learned every trick there was to learn. We had our own lookouts on the rooftops, signaling the guards' locations, and when it was safe we rolled into action stealing valuable supplies. It wasn't that we were hungry; it was the challenge of stealing from under the noses of the black-frocked morons who were promised a bounty for catching us.

The Polish guards had a particularly difficult time with us, probably because they were still scared to death of us in spite of their guns. We had one incident where one of them caught a POW stealing cigarettes. He proceeded to walk him to the provost marshal's office at gun point, when the German made a grab for the rifle. They wrestled on the street when a second Pole ran up to help his buddy, pointed his gun at the POW, fired, and instead shot the other guard in the stomach. After that the Poles shot at everything that moved near the supplies. When we threatened to go on strike, the Americans decided to take the guns away from the Poles and give them nightsticks, but the Poles wouldn't have any part of that and stayed armed with guns.

I received mail from home on February 14, 1946, the first since becoming a POW. Two days later I had a visit from my parents, who had to bribe a German security guard and the Polish guard at the gate to see me for five minutes in the woods outside the camp. We had not seen each other since August 1944. They both cried, and it broke my heart seeing how much they had been battered by the war years. They were able to come back again the next day, which was a Sunday. For the first time, family members were permitted to visit in a special visitors' building, for a few specified hours. My parents had stayed in town overnight so they could visit with me a second time.

The next visitors' day was March 3. This time my two sisters had come to see me but couldn't get in until one o'clock because we were doing a penalty drill for "lack of discipline on the way to work." About two hundred visitors waited outside the fence that day, watching us do that drill all morning.

We were moved once more in March, and there was talk again about pending discharge. According to rumor, May was to be the month, although we also believed that the Americans circulated the rumors to reduce the number of escapes. They threatened to ship you off to a coal mine in France if you were caught. Although it may have been an empty threat, it nevertheless served as an effective deterrent for a lot of guys.

But not for me.

The Escape

My nineteenth birthday in March 1946 was also my last day behind barbed wire. Two former POWs who had signed up as civilian workers were visiting in the camp, entering through the front gate after presenting their ID cards to the Polish guard. These were not picture IDs. One of them let me borrow his ID, and his friend and I walked out through the rear gate, me using the borrowed ID and the friend using his own ID. Then we sauntered off into the woods. I handed him back the other man's ID, and he returned through the front gate as a visitor.

In my pocket were fake discharge papers which my parents had bought from a man who had himself discharged by entering a discharge camp and filling out the required forms, using someone else's name and personal information. He then collected the discharge paper and sold it to the party who had ordered it. The going rate for the document, which carried authentic personal data except for the signature, was between four hundred and five hundred marks. Doing this repeatedly, a guy earned himself a fair amount of pocket change.

Within an hour I was on a train headed for Nurnberg and Neuendettelsau, where about two hundred GIs of an American Signal Corps unit were stationed. My younger sister's GI boyfriend had arranged for her to be employed there, and she talked the sergeant into getting me a job in one of the kitchens, managing the two food storerooms. The fox was now in charge of the henhouse.

When someone learned that I could play the accordion, they found one for me, and from then on I sat on the club stage every evening playing their favorite tunes and watching them and their girlfriends dance. They enjoyed the new entertainment, and I drank all the beer, gin, and whiskey I wanted. I gladly accepted money, candy bars, cigarettes and soap. When the unit transferred in May, they asked me to come with them, but I decided that the longer I stayed with them, the greater were the chances of somebody discovering that I was an escaped POW. It was time to go home.

I was home in Starnberg, Bavaria, on June 1, but I did not enjoy my newly-won freedom. Restless and bored out of my mind, I spent time by the lake, days and sometimes nights, fishing or just puttering around. Decent jobs were not to be had, and sometimes I longed for the days back in Virginia.

But it wasn't just me. The war had left its mark on my family also. Life in postwar Germany was a day-to-day struggle for survival. Food was severely rationed. I don't remember the exact numbers, but it was something like one liter of milk per person per month, one egg a week. That was if you could find it. People stood in line to buy what little merchandise was available. The stores closed after selling out, and the rest of the people in line went home empty-handed. Only farmers had enough to eat, so our family members made train trips into the countryside about once a week. Since money was grossly inflated and virtually worthless, people traded the farmers anything from jewelry to bedding for food, hoping not to get caught by the train cops who randomly searched through bags and luggage. This type of trading was considered a black market activity, punishable by fines or jail. Yet hunger makes people take risks; didn't I know that too well.

Eventually the stress disrupted many families and destroyed long-time relationships. Our family was no exception. We had frequent arguments, disagreeing about anything and everything. The break came on July 14, 1946, when I walked out the door after a particularly violent confrontation with my mother, during which she tore the discharge paper, my sole ID, into shreds.

Determined not to return, I departed, although I had no idea where I would go. I had little money and only the clothes I wore, a razor, and a toothbrush.

At the marina I rented a rowboat, drifting about on the lake for a few hours and contemplating my situation. Having made my decision, I rowed back and walked downtown to the office of the local Military Police and surrendered as an escaped prisoner of war.

Starnberg Jail

Two MPs and a German clerk staffed the office. They asked me a number of questions: from which camp had I escaped, when, and how. Then they looked through a list of names of escaped POWS. Not finding my name, they informed me that my story would have to be checked out by the CIC, and they were going to hold me in the local jail until tomorrow when a CIC officer would be available to interrogate me.

No one contacted me during the next two weeks, and now it was July 28. A Polish inmate named Zelasny and I made plans to break out of jail this day. It was Sunday, with only one jail guard on duty.

[Eric describes a failed attempt to escape during which the guard is overpowered, Zelasny is killed, and Eric is badly beaten. Confined in a small, one-man cell with four other inmates, Eric spent the next four days and nights with his wrists chained, assigned to a four-foot-square space on the floor and not permitted to use a chair or bunk.]

It wasn't until the story appeared in the local newspaper that my family learned of my whereabouts and contacted the local American military administration. As a POW, I was under their jurisdiction, so they sent a sergeant to the jail to meet with me. That sergeant was a square-shooter; he took me to a gravel pit and had me shovel rocks onto a truck. At break-time we went to the villa where he stayed; he broke out a couple beers and we talked about the good old USA.

A German-speaking CIC officer came to see me in early August. He apologized, explaining that the CIC had not been informed of my arrest until the previous day. He informed me that the penalty for escape by a POW was thirty days in the guardhouse, after which I would be sent to a discharge camp and officially released. Concerning the attempted jailbreak, that was a matter for the German authorities, as I was no longer under the protection of the Geneva Convention as a prisoner of war. The German Criminal Code book stated ". . .a prisoner of war in a German jail or prison becomes subject to German law." The article had not taken into account the unlikely scenario of a German soldier held by another government as a prisoner of war being incarcerated in a German jail. "It probably never happened before," he admitted.

Appearing before a judge on September 4, 1946, I was sentenced to one year in prison and sent to Bavaria State Penitentiary, labeled as a "dangerous man" and put in with the heavies. Life there was more than grim. Hunger and cold were the hardest to bear, even harder than the loss of freedom. In December they finally turned on the heat in the cells and also bunched us up to four men in a one-man cell, thus

1948 - The Skinny Kid in the Bavarian Mountains

reducing their heating cost by heating fewer cells. We were allowed one book a week, and once a month we were taken to basement showers in groups of ten. Shaves and haircuts were infrequent as well. Occasionally there was an attempted or successful suicide. Lack of water was a continuous issue. Sometimes they picked a cell at random, threw the door open and entered, led by a police dog followed by guards with rubber hoses. Then the beatings began.

The appeal my lawyer had filed was successful, and the appeal trial was scheduled for November 19. In the courtroom, the proceedings were presided over by a chief judge and two assistants, one of whom appeared to be asleep. In their chambers the judges deliberated and pronounced the verdict: petty mutiny, with a sentence of eight months in jail less three months already served, leaving me with five months remaining—the date of my release to be April 19, 1947.

On January 17, 1947, I was called to the prison office and informed that I had been granted parole and was going to be released on January 20.

The prison gates swung open, and I stepped out into the snow-covered street, wearing only the thin clothes I had on when I arrived here last summer. The bitter cold tore at me, reminding me of that winter in Belgium where this journey began so long ago. But I was not alone then, as I was on this day. There was no one to meet the skinny kid as he left prison. Yes, I had gotten skinny again during these past six months of starvation. Strangest and saddest of all, there was no one there from my family. So I walked to the corner and waited for the streetcar.

Aftermath

I returned to the family in Starnberg, only to see it disintegrate in the ensuing two years. Sister Annelore became pregnant by her GI boyfriend, and I became temporary guardian of Baby Frances until the parents married and moved to the U.S. Sister Magdalene also had a child by her GI boyfriend, who already had a family and shipped back to the U.S. by himself. Thus I became temporary legal guardian of Baby Linda until her mother married and also moved to the U.S. My parents divorced in 1950, and my father moved to Stuttgart.

Soon after my release from prison, I found a job as a lab technician with the local chemical company. There I was able to advance my knowledge and proficiency to new levels. Then I moved to Stuttgart and joined my father and took a job as plant chemist in a well-known company. My dad passed away in 1953. I had succeeding employments in the chemical industry and became a successful and well-paid professional.

However, I found myself struggling trying to assimilate into life in post-war Germany. After exposure to the American way of life, I rejected such things as class distinction and some of the pointless dress formalities of German life. I advertised in trade journals for a situation abroad and received offers from as far away as Brazil, Peru, and Indonesia. Then I received a letter from my sister Annalore in the U.S., who reminded me that I had been in the U.S., knew the country, and "why not come here?" She and her GI husband lived in Hinsdale, Illinois. They offered to sponsor me. My application for emigration was accepted, and after a year-long wait I was on my way to Chicago in December 1956. I lived with them for a while until I moved to an apartment in Joliet, Illinois.

My brother-in-law Paul had also been a POW in America, and he and Magdalene came to Wisconsin sponsored by a farmer.

The living arrangement was minimal, and after they paid him off to compensate him for the expense he incurred providing their transportation to the U.S., they moved to Beaver Dam, Wisconsin, where Paul started a successful metal-working business. I eventually joined them there where I presently reside with my wife Claudette. I became a U.S. citizen in 1975.

Initially I had regrets about immigrating, even though the American people were friendly, with few exceptions. I had been told that it would take at least three months to assimilate, and that was true. I missed my German car, my apartment, my girlfriends, the food, weekend trips to Switzerland and Austria; you name it. It actually got so bad after a month that I considered returning to Germany. Then suddenly, all that was gone, and I fitted into the American society.

Postscript

Eric's brother-in-law Paul, who married his sister Magdalene, makes an interesting addendum to this account of Eric's. Paul was in the German Navy, served on a mine sweeper off the coast of France and put into the ground fight after his ship was sunk. He was taken prisoner in the fighting around Brest and spent time in the U.S. South picking cotton.

Paul has since passed on, but Eric shares one of his war stories. "Paul was patrolling the Brest streets alone one night when he spotted an American a block away. The GI had seen him also, and the two began stalking each other. Paul came to a corner, and when he peeked around it, the American stared him in the face. Their weapons were pointed at each other. As if by a secret signal, both warriors slowly turned and walked the other way."

Eric today

⊰ Epilogue ⊱

The following episode describes a tragic and not uncommon wartime situation that needs to be recognized and discussed in this context of how innocent lives are affected by war. Although I have no first-person recording, I myself witnessed this situation.

Where there are men and women together, despite rules to the contrary, pregnancies will result. Military presence is no different, and participants can be home forces as well as the occupiers—individuals away from the constraints of home. Fraternization between occupation forces and civilians was forbidden in postwar Germany, but couldn't be enforced effectively, and with predictable consequences.

In 1951 I was in Germany as a tourist. I stayed briefly with former college classmates who were billeted in a private German home in Mannheim, where the U.S. had a base. (The husband of the couple was an American serviceman.) There were two children in this German family. One was a boy of twelve; the other was six year-old Karl Heinz.

Karl Heinz had the distinct markings of a neglected child. He was thin, pale, red-eyed, had a runny nose, and was withdrawn except for regular misbehavior. He slept on a pile of straw on the kitchen floor. The parents paid no attention to him except to say, "Karl Heinz makes everything kaput!" and they punished him severely for his misdeeds.

A few months previously, the doorbell rang, and when Frau L. answered it, a young woman stood there with five year-old Karl Heinz. He came from an orphanage in Denmark, where his Russian mother had deposited him after the war. The story was that his father (Frau L.'s husband during the war and at the present time) was a pilot in the German Air Force, taken prisoner by the Russians, and became involved with this Russian woman. Karl Heinz was the result of their liaison. It took a while to locate the father after the war, and indeed it was a surprise to Frau L. to suddenly and unexpectedly find the family expanded by one little boy, fathered by her husband.

Poor little Karl Heinz paid a terrible price for his daddy's dalliance. The older boy was jealous and bullied and abused his young half-brother to the point where my friends moved out of the home in silent protest. It is incomprehensible how the father could have stood by and let his own child be so mistreated. I have wondered and worried all these years about whatever happened to Karl Heinz, keeping in mind that there were many more innocents like him who paid for the misdeeds of their parents.

Author Jean Messinger was born and raised in Beaver Dam, Wisconsin, graduated from Lawrence College in Appleton, Wisconsin, and has lived in Colorado since 1952. Colorado Springs was home to Jean and her husband for nearly forty years. After teaching school for several years, at age fifty, she earned a master's degree in art and architectural history from Denver University.

She considers herself doubly blessed to live in Colorado near her large extended family, which includes seven grandchildren.